T0183963

Lecture Notes in Computer Science 9593

Commenced Publication in 1973
Founding and Former Series Editors:
Gerhard Goos, Juris Hartmanis, and Jan van Leeuwen

More information about this series at http://www.springer.com/series/7408

Arie Gurfinkel · Sanjit A. Seshia (Eds.)

Verified Software: Theories, Tools, and Experiments

7th International Conference, VSTTE 2015
San Francisco, CA, USA, July 18–19, 2015
Revised Selected Papers

 Springer

Editors
Arie Gurfinkel
Software Engineering Institute
Carnegie Mellon University
Pittsburgh, PA
USA

Sanjit A. Seshia
Department of Electrical Engineering
and Computer Science
University of California
Berkeley
USA

ISSN 0302-9743 ISSN 1611-3349 (electronic)
Lecture Notes in Computer Science
ISBN 978-3-319-29612-8 ISBN 978-3-319-29613-5 (eBook)
DOI 10.1007/978-3-319-29613-5

Library of Congress Control Number: 2016930277

LNCS Sublibrary: SL2 – Programming and Software Engineering

Printed on acid-free paper

This Springer imprint is published by SpringerNature
The registered company is Springer International Publishing AG Switzerland

Preface

This volume contains the papers presented at the 7th International Conference on Verified Software: Theories, Tool and Experiments (VSTTE), which was held in San Francisco, California, USA, during July 18–19, 2015, co-located with the 27th International Conference on Computer-Aided Verification. The final version of the papers was prepared by the authors after the event took place, which permitted them to take feedback received at the meeting into account.

VSTTE originated from the Verified Software Initiative (VSI), which is an international initiative directed at the scientific challenges of large-scale software verification. The inaugural VSTTE conference was held at ETH Zurich in October 2005, and was followed by VSTTE 2008 in Toronto, VSTTE 2010 in Edinburgh, VSTTE 2012 in Philadelphia, VSTTE 2013 in Menlo Park, and VSTTE 2015 in Vienna. The goal of the VSTTE conference is to advance the state of the art through the interaction of theory development, tool evolution, and experimental validation.

The call for papers for VSTTE 2015 solicited submissions describing large-scale verification efforts that involve collaboration, theory unification, tool integration, and formalized domain knowledge. We were especially interested in papers describing novel experiments and case studies evaluating verification techniques and technologies. We welcomed papers describing education, requirements modeling, specification languages, specification/verification, formal calculi, software design methods, automatic code generation, refinement methodologies, compositional analysis, verification tools (e.g., static analysis, dynamic analysis, model checking, theorem proving), tool integration, benchmarks, challenge problems, and integrated verification environments.

There were 25 submissions. Each submission was reviewed by at least three members of the Program Committee. The committee decided to accept 12 papers. The program also included two invited talks, given by Chris Hawblitzel (Microsoft Research) and Lee Pike (Galois Inc.), and a panel on "Software Verification Competitions: Lessons Learned and Challenges Ahead."

We would like to thank the invited speakers, the panel members, and all submitting authors for their contribution to the program. We thank Natarjan Shankar for the help with the organization, our publicity chair, Daniel Bundala, our general chair, Martin Schaef, and the CAV workshop chair, Dirk Beyer. Finally, we thank the external reviewers and the Program Committee for their reviews and their help in selecting the papers that appear in this volume.

December 2015

Arie Gurfinkel
Sanjit A. Seshia

Organization

Program Committee

Elvira Albert	Complutense University of Madrid, Spain
Nikolaj Bjorner	Microsoft Research, USA
Bor-Yuh Evan Chang	University of Colorado at Boulder, USA
Ernie Cohen	Amazon, USA
Vijay D'Silva	University of California, Berkeley, USA
Jyotirmoy Deshmukh	Toyota Technical Center, USA
Jinsong Dong	National University of Singapore, Singapore
Vijay Ganesh	University of Waterloo, Canada
Alex Groce	Oregon State University, USA
Arie Gurfinkel	Software Engineering Institute, Carnegie Mellon University, USA
William Harris	University of Wisconsin-Madison, USA
Chris Hawblitzel	Microsoft Research, USA
Bart Jacobs	Katholieke Universiteit Leuven, Belgium
Susmit Jha	Strategic CAD Lab, Intel, USA
Rajeev Joshi	Laboratory for Reliable Software, Jet Propulsion Laboratory, USA
Vladimir Klebanov	Karlsruhe Institute of Technology, Germany
Akash Lal	Microsoft Research, India
Ruzica Piskac	Yale University, USA
Zvonimir Rakamaric	University of Utah, USA
Kristin Yvonne Rozier	NASA Ames Research Center, USA
Martin Schäf	SRI International, USA
Sanjit Seshia	UC Berkeley, USA
Natarajan Shankar	SRI International, USA
Nishant Sinha	IBM Research Labs, India
Carsten Sinz	Karlsruhe Institute of Technology (KIT), Germany
Alexander J. Summers	ETH Zurich, Switzerland
Zach Tatlock	University of Washington, USA
Sergey Tverdyshev	SYSGO AG, Germany
Arnaud Venet	Google, USA
Karen Yorav	IBM Haifa Research Lab, Israel

Additional Reviewers

Arechiga, Nikos
Bai, Guangdong
Berezish, Murphy
Din, Crystal Chang
Fremont, Daniel J.
Liu, Yan
Nejati, Saeed

Prabhu, Vinayak
Rabe, Markus N.
Román-Díez, Guillermo
Santolucito, Mark
Schwerhoff, Malte
Shurek, Gil

Contents

A Proof-Sensitive Approach
for Small Propositional Interpolants

Leonardo Alt[(✉)], Grigory Fedyukovich,
Antti E.J. Hyvärinen, and Natasha Sharygina

Formal Verification Lab, USI, Lugano, Switzerland
leonardoaltt@gmail.com

Abstract. The labeled interpolation system (LIS) is a framework for Craig interpolation widely used in propositional-satisfiability-based model checking. Most LIS-based algorithms construct the interpolant from a proof of unsatisfiability and a fixed labeling determined by which part of the propositional formula is being over-approximated. While this results in interpolants with fixed strength, it limits the possibility of generating interpolants of small size. This is problematic since the interpolant size is a determining factor in achieving good overa performance in model checking. This paper analyses theoretically how labeling functions can be used to construct small interpolants. In addition to developing the new labeling mechanism guaranteeing small interpolants, we also present its versions managing the strength of the interpolants. We implement the labeling functions in our tool PeRIPLO and study the behavior of the resulting algorithms experimentally by integrating the tool to a variety of model checking applications. Our results suggest that the new proof-sensitive interpolation algorithm performs consistently better than any of the standard interpolation algorithms based on LIS.

1 Introduction

In SAT-based model checking, a widely used workflow for obtaining an interpolant for a propositional formula A is to compute a proof of unsatisfiability for the formula $\phi = A \wedge B$, use a variety of standard techniques for compressing the proof (see, e.g., [17]), construct the interpolant from the compressed proof, and finally simplify the interpolant [4]. The *labeled interpolation system* (LIS) [9] is a commonly used, flexible framework for computing the interpolant from a given proof that generalizes several interpolation algorithms parameterized by a *labeling function*. Given a labeling function and a proof, LIS uniquely determines the interpolant. However, the LIS framework allows significant flexibility in constructing interpolants from a proof through the choice of the labeling function.

Arguably, the suitability of an interpolant depends ultimately on the application [17], but there is a wide consensus that small interpolants lead to better overall performance in model checking [3,17,21]. However, generating small interpolants for a given partitioning is a non-trivial task. This paper presents, to the best of our knowledge, the first thorough, rigorous analysis on how labeling

© Springer International Publishing Switzerland 2016
A. Gurfinkel and S.A. Seshia (Eds.): VSTTE 2015, LNCS 9593, pp. 1–18, 2016.
DOI: 10.1007/978-3-319-29613-5_1

in the LIS framework affects the size of the interpolant. The analysis is backed up by experimentation showing also the practical significance of the result. We believe that the results reported here will help the community working on interpolation in designing interpolation algorithms that work well independent of the application. Based on the analysis we present the *proof-sensitive interpolation algorithm* PS that produces small interpolants by adapting itself to the proof of unsatisfiability. We prove under reasonable assumptions that the resulting interpolant is always smaller than those generated by any other LIS-based algorithms, including the widely used algorithms M_s (McMillan [13]), P (Pudlák [16]), and M_w (dual to M_s [9]).

In some applications it is important to give guarantees on the logical strength of the interpolants. Since the LIS framework allows us to argue about the resulting interpolants by their logical strength [9], we know that for a fixed problem $A \wedge B$ and a fixed proof of unsatisfiability, an interpolant constructed with M_s implies one constructed with P which in turn implies one constructed with M_w. While PS is designed to control the interpolant size, we additionally define two variants controlling the interpolant strength: the strong and the weak proof-sensitive algorithms computing, respectively, interpolants that imply the ones constructed by P and that are implied by the ones constructed by P.

We implemented the new algorithms in the PERIPLO interpolation framework [17] and confirm the practical significance of the algorithms with an experimentation. The results show that when using PS, both the sizes of the interpolants and the run times when used in a model-checking framework compare favorably to those obtained with M_s, P, and M_w, resulting occasionally in significant reductions.

1.1   Related Work

Interpolants can be compacted through applying transformations to the resolution refutation. For example, [17,18] compare the effect of such compaction on the interpolation algorithms M_s, P, and M_w in connection with function-summarization-based model checking [10,20]. A similar approach is studied in [9] combined with an analysis on the strength of the resulting interpolant. Different size-based reductions are further discussed in [4,11]. While often successful, these approaches might produce a considerable overhead in large problems. Our approach is more light-weight and uses directly the flexibility of LIS to perform the compression. An interesting analysis similar to ours, presented in [3], concentrates on the effect of identifying subsumptions in the resolution proofs. A significant reduction in the size of the interpolant can be obtained by considering only CNF-shaped interpolants [21]. However, the strength of these interpolants is not as easily controllable as in the LIS interpolants, making the technique harder to apply in certain model checking approaches. A light-weight interpolant compaction can be performed by specializing through simplifying the interpolant with a truth assignment [12].

In many verification approaches using counter-examples for refinement it is possible to abstract an interpolant obtained from a refuted counter-example.

For instance, [2,19] present a framework for generalizing interpolants based on templates. A related approach for generalizing interpolants in unbounded model-checking through abstraction is presented in [5] using incremental SAT solving. While this direction is orthogonal to ours, we believe that the ideas presented here and addressing the interpolation back-end would be useful in connection with the generalization phase.

Linear-sized interpolants can be derived also from resolution refutations computed by SMT solvers, for instance in the combined theory of linear inequalities and equalities with uninterpreted functions [14] and linear rational arithmetic [1]. These approaches have an interesting connection to ours since they also contain a propositional part. It is also possible to produce interpolants without a proof [7]. However, this method gives no control over the relative interpolant strength and reduces in the worst case to enumerating all models of a SAT instance. Finally, conceptually similar to our work, there is a renewed interest in interpolation techniques used in connection with modern ways of organizing the high-level model-checking algorithm [6,15].

2 Preliminaries

Given a finite set of propositional variables, a *literal* is a variable p or its negation $\neg p$. A *clause* is a finite set of literals and a formula ϕ in *conjunctive normal form* (CNF) is a set of clauses. We also refer to a clause as the disjunction of its literals and a CNF formula as the conjunction of its clauses. A variable p occurs in the clause C, denoted by the pair (p, C), if either $p \in C$ or $\neg p \in C$. The set $var(\phi)$ consists of the variables that occur in the clauses of ϕ. We assume that double negations are removed, i.e., $\neg\neg p$ is rewritten as p. A *truth assignment* σ assigns a Boolean value to each variable p. A clause C is satisfied if $p \in C$ and $\sigma(p)$ is true, or $\neg p \in C$ and $\sigma(p)$ is false. The propositional satisfiability problem (SAT) is the problem of determining whether there is a truth assignment satisfying each clause of a CNF formula ϕ. The special constants $\top$ and $\bot$ denote the empty conjunction and the empty disjunction. The former is satisfied by all truth assignments and the latter is satisfied by none. A formula ϕ *implies* a formula ϕ', denoted $\phi \rightarrow \phi'$, if every truth assignment satisfying ϕ satisfies ϕ'. The *size* of a propositional formula is the number of logical connectives it contains. For instance the unsatisfiable CNF formula

$$\phi = (x_1 \vee x_2) \wedge (\neg x_2 \vee x_4) \wedge (\neg x_2 \vee \neg x_3 \vee \neg x_4) \wedge (x_1 \vee x_3) \wedge (\neg x_1) \quad (1)$$

of size 14 consists of 4 variables and 5 clauses. The occurrences of the variable x_4 are $(x_4, \neg x_2 \vee x_4)$ and $(x_4, \neg x_2 \vee \neg x_3 \vee \neg x_4)$.

For two clauses C^+, C^- such that $p \in C^+$, $\neg p \in C^-$, and for no other variable q both $q \in C^- \cup C^+$ and $\neg q \in C^- \cup C^+$, a *resolution step* is a triple C^+, C^-, $(C^+ \cup C^-) \setminus \{p, \neg p\}$. The first two clauses are called the *antecedents*, the latter is the *resolvent* and p is the *pivot* of the resolution step. A *resolution refutation* R of an unsatisfiable formula ϕ is a directed acyclic graph where the nodes are clauses and the edges are directed from the antecedents to the resolvent. The nodes of a refutation R with no incoming edge are the clauses of ϕ, and the rest of the clauses are resolvents derived with a resolution step. The unique node with no outgoing edges is the empty clause. The *source clauses* of a refutation R are the clauses of ϕ from which there is a path to the empty clause.

Given an unsatisfiable formula $A \wedge B$, a *Craig interpolant* I for A is a formula such that $A \to I$, $I \wedge B$ is unsatisfiable and $var(I) \subseteq var(A) \cap var(B)$. An interpolant can be seen as an over-approximation of A that is still unsatisfiable when conjoined with B. In the rest of the paper we assume that A and B only consist of the source clauses of R.

The *labeled interpolation system* [9] (LIS) is a framework that, given propositional formulas A, B, a refutation R of $A \wedge B$ and a *labeling function* L, computes an interpolant I for A based on R. The refutation together with the partitioning A, B is called an *interpolation instance* (R, A, B). The labeling function L assigns a label from the set $\{a, b, ab\}$ to every variable occurrence (p, C) in the clauses of the refutation R. A variable is *shared* if it occurs both in A and B; otherwise it is *local*. For all variable occurrences (p, C) in R, $L(p, C) = a$ if p is local to A and $L(p, C) = b$ if p is local to B. For occurrences of shared variables in the source clauses the label may be chosen freely. The label of a variable occurrence in a resolvent C is determined by the label of the variable in its antecedents. For a variable occurring in both its antecedents with different labels, the label of the new occurrence is ab, and in all other cases the label is equivalent to the label in its antecedent or both antecedents.

An interpolation algorithm based on LIS computes an interpolant with a dynamic algorithm by annotating each clause of R with a *partial interpolant* starting from the source clauses. The partial interpolant of a source clause C is

$$I(C) = \begin{cases} \bigvee\{l \mid l \in C \text{ and } L(var(l), C) = b\} & \text{if } C \in A, \text{ and} \\ \bigwedge\{\neg l \mid l \in C \text{ and } L(var(l), C) = a\} & \text{if } C \in B, \end{cases} \qquad (2)$$

The partial interpolant of a resolvent clause C with pivot p and antecedents C^+ and C^-, where $p \in C^+$ and $\neg p \in C^-$, is

$$I(C) = \begin{cases} I(C^+) \vee I(C^-) & \text{if } L(p, C^+) = L(p, C^-) = a, \\ I(C^+) \wedge I(C^-) & \text{if } L(p, C^+) = L(p, C^-) = b, \text{ and} \\ (I(C^+) \vee p) \wedge (I(C^-) \vee \neg p) & \text{otherwise.} \end{cases} \qquad (3)$$

The interpolation algorithms M_s, P, and M_w mentioned in the introduction can be obtained as special cases of LIS by providing a labeling function returning b, ab, and a for the shared variables, respectively.

In some applications it is useful to consider different interpolants constructed from a fixed interpolation instance, but using different interpolation algorithms [10]. For such cases the LIS framework provides a convenient tool for analyzing whether the interpolants generated by one interpolation algorithm always imply the interpolants generated by another algorithm. If we order the three labels so that $b \leq ab \leq a$, it can be shown that given two labeling functions L and L' resulting in the interpolants I_L and $I_{L'}$ in LIS and having the property that $L(p, C) \leq L'(p, C)$ for all occurrences (p, C), it is true that $I_L \to I_{L'}$.

In this case we say that the interpolation algorithm obtained from LIS using the labeling L' is *weaker* than the interpolation algorithm that uses the labeling L.

We define here two concepts that will be useful in the next section: the class of *uniform* labeling functions, and the *internal size* of an interpolant.

Definition 1. *A labeling function is* uniform *if for all pairs of clauses $C, D \in R$ containing the variable p, $L(p, C) = L(p, D)$, and no occurrence is labeled ab. Any interpolation algorithm with uniform labeling function is also called uniform.*

An example of non-uniform labeling function is D_{min}, presented in [8]. D_{min} is proven to produce interpolants with the least number of distinct variables.

Definition 2. *The* internal size *IntSize(I) of an interpolant I is the number of connectives in I excluding the connectives contributed by the partial interpolants associated with the source clauses.*

Typically, an interpolant constructed by a LIS-based algorithm will contain a significant amount of subformulas that are syntactically equivalent. The *structural sharing*, i.e., maintaining a unique copy of the syntactically equivalent subformulas, while completely transparent to the satisfiability, is of critical practical importance. Similarly important for performance is the *constant simplification*, consisting of four simple rewriting rules: $\top \wedge \phi \rightsquigarrow \phi$, $\perp \wedge \phi \rightsquigarrow \perp$, $\top \vee \phi \rightsquigarrow \top$, and $\perp \vee \phi \rightsquigarrow \phi$, where ϕ is an arbitrary Boolean formula.

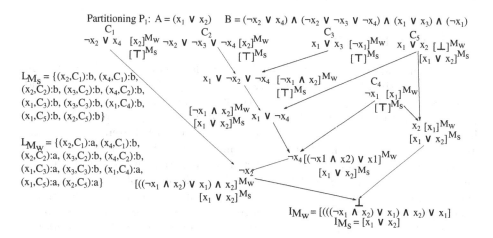

Fig. 1. Different interpolants obtained from the refutation using the partitioning P_1.

The following example illustrates the concepts discussed in this section by showing how LIS can be used to compute interpolants with two different uniform algorithms M_s and M_w.

Example 1. Consider the unsatisfiable formula $\phi = A \wedge B$ where ϕ is from Eq. (1) and $A = (x_1 \vee x_2)$ and $B = (\neg x_2 \vee x_4) \wedge (\neg x_2 \vee \neg x_3 \vee \neg x_4) \wedge (x_1 \vee x_3) \wedge (\neg x_1)$. Figure 1 shows a resolution refutation for ϕ and the partial interpolants computed by the interpolation algorithms M_s and M_w. Each clause in the refutation is associated with a partial interpolant ψ generated by labeling L_{M_s} (denoted by $[\psi]^{M_s}$) and a partial interpolant ψ' generated by labeling L_{M_w} (denoted by $[\psi']^{M_w}$). The generated interpolants are $I_{M_s} = x_1 \vee x_2$ and $I_{M_w} = (((\neg x_1 \wedge x_2) \vee x_1) \wedge x_2) \vee x_1$. Now consider a different partitioning $\phi' = A' \wedge B'$ for the same formula where the partitions have been swapped, that is, $A' = B$ and $B' = A$. Using the same refutation (figure omitted for lack of space), we get the interpolants $I'_{M_s} = (((x_1 \vee \neg x_2) \wedge \neg x_1) \vee \neg x_2) \wedge \neg x_1 = \neg I_{M_w}$ and $I'_{M_w} = \neg(x_1 \vee x_2) = \neg I_{M_s}$ We use both structural sharing and constant simplification in the example. The internal size of I_{M_s} is 0, whereas the internal size of I_{M_w} is 4.

The two partitionings illustrate a case where the interpolation algorithm M_s, in comparison to M_w, produces a small interpolant for one and a large interpolant for another interpolation instance. Since the goal in this work is to develop LIS-based interpolation algorithms that consistently produce small interpolants, the labeling function of choice cannot be L_{M_s} or L_{M_w}. Note that while in this case the interpolants I_{M_s} and I_{M_w} are equivalent, the representation of I_{M_w} is considerably smaller than the representation of I_{M_s}. Since minimizing a propositional formula is an NP-complete problem, producing interpolants that are small in the first place is a very important goal.

3   Labeling Functions for LIS

This section studies the algorithms based on the labeled interpolation system in an analytic setting. Our main objective is to provide a basis for developing and understanding labeling functions that construct interpolants having desirable properties. In particular, we will concentrate on three syntactic properties of the interpolants: the number of distinct variables; the number of literal occurrences; and the internal size of the interpolant. In most of the discussion in this section we will ignore the two optimizations on structural sharing and constraint simplification. While both are critically important for practicality of interpolation, our experimentation shows that they mostly have similar effect on all the interpolation algorithms we studied, and therefore they can be considered orthogonally (see Sect. 4.4). The exception is that *the non-uniform labeling functions allow a more efficient optimization compared to the uniform labeling functions* through constraint simplification. More specifically, the main results of the section are the following theorems.

(i) If an interpolation instance is not *p*-annihilable (see Definition 3), which in our experimentation turns out almost always to be the case, then all LIS interpolants constructed from the refutation have the same number of distinct variables (Theorem 1);

(ii) For a given interpolation instance, the interpolants I_n obtained with any non-uniform labeling function and I_u obtained with any uniform labeling function satisfy $IntSize(I_u) \leq IntSize(I_n)$. (Theorem 2); and

(iii) Among uniform labeling functions, the *proof-sensitive* labeling function (see Definition 4) results in the least number of variable occurrences in the partial interpolants associated with the source clauses (Theorem 3).

From the three theorems we immediately have the following:

Corollary 1. *For not p-annihilable interpolation instances, the proof-sensitive labeling function will result in interpolants that have the smallest internal size, the least number of distinct variables, and least variable occurrences in the source partial interpolants.*

The proof-sensitive interpolant strength can only be given the trivial guarantees: it is stronger than I_{M_w} and weaker than I_{M_s}. At the expense of the minimality in the sense of the above corollary, we introduce in Eqs. (6) and (7) the weak and strong versions of the proof-sensitive labeling functions.

3.1 Analysing Labeling Functions

An interesting special case in LIS-based interpolation algorithms is when the labeling can be used to reduce the number of distinct variables in the final interpolant. To make this explicit we define the concepts of a *p*-pure resolution step and a *p*-annihilable interpolation instance.

Definition 3. *Given an interpolation instance (R, A, B), a variable $p \in var(A) \cup var(B)$ and a labeling function L, a resolution step in R is p-pure if at most one of the antecedents contain p, or both antecedents C, D contain p but $L(p, C) = L(p, D) = a$ or $L(p, C) = L(p, D) = b$. An interpolation instance (R, A, B) is p-annihilable if there is a non-uniform labeling function L such that $L(p, C) = a$ if $C \in A$, $L(p, C) = b$ if $C \in B$, and all the resolution steps are p-pure.*

The following theorem shows the value of *p*-annihilable interpolation instances in constructing small interpolants.

Theorem 1. *Let (R, A, B) be an interpolation instance, $p \in var(A) \cap var(B)$, and I an interpolant obtained from (R, A, B) by means of a LIS-based algorithm. If $p \notin var(I)$, then (R, A, B) is p-annihilable.*

Proof. Assume that (R, A, B) is not *p*-annihilable, $p \in var(A) \cap var(B)$, but there is a labeling L which results in a LIS-based interpolation algorithm that constructs an interpolant not containing p. The labeling function cannot have $L(p, C) = b$ if $C \in A$ or $L(p, C) = a$ if $C \in B$ because p would appear in the partial interpolants associated with the sources by Eq. (2). No clause C in R can have $L(p, C) = ab$ since all literals in the refutation need to be used as a pivot on the path to the empty clause, and having an occurrence of p labeled ab

in an antecedent clause would result in introducing the literal p to the partial interpolant associated with the resolvent by Eq. (3) when used as a pivot. Every resolution step in the refutation R needs to be p-pure, since if the antecedents contain occurrences (p, C) and (p, D) such that $L(p, C) \neq L(p, D)$ either the label of the occurrence of p in the resolvent clause will be ab, violating the condition that no clause can have $L(p, C) = ab$ above, or, if p is pivot on the resolution step, the variable is immediately inserted to the partial interpolant by Eq. (3). □

While it is relatively easy to artificially construct an interpolation instance that is p-annihilable, they seem to be rare in practice (see Sect. 4.4). Hence, while instances that are p-annihilable would result in small interpolants, it has little practical significance at least in the benchmarks available to us. However, we have the following practically useful result which shows the benefits of labeling functions producing p-pure resolution steps in computing interpolants with low number of connectives.

Theorem 2. *Let (R, A, B) be an interpolation instance. Given a labeling function L such that the resolution steps in R are p-pure for all $p \in var(A \wedge B)$, and a labeling function L' such that at least one resolution step in R is not p-pure for some $p \in var(A \wedge B)$, we have $IntSize(I_L) \leq IntSize(I_{L'})$.*

Proof. For a given refutation R, the number of partial interpolants will be the same for any LIS-based interpolation algorithm. By Eq. (3) each resolution step will introduce one connective if both occurrences in the antecedents are labeled a or b and three connectives otherwise. The latter can only occur if the labeling algorithm results in a resolution step that is not p-pure for some p. □

Clearly, p-pure steps are guaranteed with uniform labeling functions. Therefore we have the following corollary:

Corollary 2. *Uniform labeling functions result in interpolants with smaller internal size compared to non-uniform labeling functions.*

The main result of this work is the development of a labeling function that is uniform, therefore producing small interpolants by Corollary 2, and results in the smallest number of variable occurrences among all uniform labeling functions. This *proof-sensitive labeling function* works by considering the refutation R when assigning labels to the occurrences of the shared variables.

Definition 4. *Let R be a resolution refutation for $A \wedge B$ where A and B consist of the source clauses, $f_A(p) = |\{(p, C) \mid C \in A\}|$ be the number of times the variable p occurs in A, and $f_B(p) = |\{(p, C) \mid C \in B\}|$ the number the variable p occurs in B. The proof-sensitive labeling function L_{PS} is defined as*

$$L_{PS}(p, C) = \begin{cases} a & \text{if } f_A(p) \geq f_B(p) \\ b & \text{if } f_A(p) < f_B(p). \end{cases} \tag{4}$$

Note that since L_{PS} is uniform, it is independent of the clause C. Let Sh_A be the set of the shared variables occurring at least as often in clauses of A as in B and Sh_B the set of shared variables occurring more often in B than in A:

$$Sh_A = \{p \in var(A) \cap var(B) \mid f_A(p) \geq f_B(p)\} \text{ and} \tag{5}$$
$$Sh_B = \{p \in var(A) \cap var(B) \mid f_A(p) < f_B(p)\}$$

Theorem 3 states the optimality with respect to variable occurrences of the algorithm PS among uniform labeling functions.

Theorem 3. *For a fixed interpolation instance (R, A, B), the interpolation algorithm PS will introduce the smallest number of variable occurrences in the partial interpolants associated with the source clauses of R among all uniform interpolation algorithms.*

Proof. The interpolation algorithm PS is a uniform algorithm labeling shared variables either as a or b. Hence, the shared variables labeled a will appear in the partial interpolants of the source clauses from B of R, and the shared variables labeled b will appear in the partial interpolants of the source clauses from A of R. The sum of the number of variable occurrences in the partial interpolants associated with the source clauses by PS is

$$n_{PS} = \sum_{v \in Sh_B} f_A(v) + \sum_{v \in Sh_A} f_B(v).$$

We will show that swapping uniformly the label of any of the shared variables will result in an increase in the number of variable occurrences in the partial interpolants associated with the source clauses of R compared to n_{PS}. Let v be a variable in Sh_A. By (4) and (5), the label of v in PS will be a. Switching the label to b results in the size $n' = n_{PS} - f_B(v) + f_A(v)$. Since v was in Sh_A we know that $f_A(v) \geq f_B(v)$ by (5), and therefore $-f_B(v) + f_A(v) \geq 0$ and $n' \geq n_{PS}$. An (almost) symmetrical argument shows that swapping the label for a variable $v \in Sh_B$ to a results in $n' > n_{PS}$. Hence, swapping uniformly the labeling of PS for any shared variable will result in an interpolant having at least as many variable occurrences in the leaves. Assuming no simplifications, the result holds for the final interpolant. □

Example 2. Figure 2 shows the interpolants that PS would deliver if applied to the same refutation R of ϕ and partitionings $A \wedge B$ and $A' \wedge B'$ given in Example 1. Notice that PS adapts the labeling to the best one depending on the refutation and partitions, and gives small interpolants for both cases.

Because of the way L_{PS} labels the variable occurrences, we cannot beforehand determine the strength of PS relative to, e.g., the algorithms M_s, P, and M_w. Although it is often not necessary that interpolants have a particular strength, in some applications this has an impact on performance or even soundness [17]. To be able to apply the idea in applications requiring specific interpolant strength,

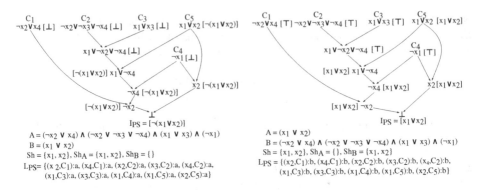

Fig. 2. Interpolants obtained by PS.

for example tree interpolation, we propose a weak and a strong version of the proof-sensitive interpolation algorithm, PS_w and PS_s. The corresponding labeling functions L_{PS_w} and L_{PS_s} are defined as

$$
L_{PS_w}(p, C) = \begin{cases} a & \text{if } p \text{ is not shared and } C \in A \text{ or } p \in Sh_A \\ b & \text{if } p \text{ is not shared and } C \in B \\ ab & \text{if } p \in Sh_B \end{cases} \tag{6}
$$

$$
L_{PS_s}(p, C) = \begin{cases} a & \text{if } p \text{ is not shared and } C \in A \\ b & \text{if } p \text{ is not shared and } C \in B, \text{ or } p \in Sh_B \\ ab & \text{if } p \in Sh_A \end{cases} \tag{7}
$$

Finally, it is fairly straightforward to see based on the definition of the labeling functions that the strength of the interpolants is partially ordered as shown in the diagram below.

$$ M_s \leq PS_s \leq \begin{matrix} D_{min} \\ PS \\ P \end{matrix} \leq PS_w \leq M_w $$

4   Experimental Results

We implemented the three interpolation algorithms within the PERIPLO [17] toolset and compare them with the D_{min} algorithm, as well as with the popular algorithms M_s, P and M_w in the context of three different model-checking tasks: (*i*) incremental software model checking with function summarization using FUNFROG [20]; (*ii*) checking software upgrades with function summarization using EVOLCHECK [10]; and (*iii*) pre-image overapproximation for hardware model checking with PDTRAV [5]. The wide range of experiments permits the study of the general applicability of the new techniques. In experiments (*i*) and

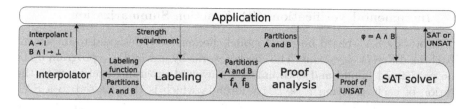

Fig. 3. Overall verification/interpolation framework.

(ii) the new algorithms are implemented within the verification process allowing us to evaluate their effect on the full verification run. Experiment (iii) focuses on the size of the interpolant, treating the application as a black box. Unlike in the theory presented in Sect. 3, all experiments use both structural sharing and constraint simplification, since the improvements given by these practical techniques are important. Experiments (i) and (ii) use a large set of benchmarks each containing a different call-tree structure and assertions distributed on different levels of the tree. For (iii), the benchmarks consisted of a set of 100 interpolation problems constructed by PDTRAV. All experiments use PERIPLO both as the interpolation engine and as the SAT solver.

Figure 3 shows a generic verification framework employing the new labeling mechanism for interpolation. Whenever the application needs an interpolant for the problem $A \wedge B$, it first requests the refutation from the SAT solver. After the refutation is generated, the application provides the partitioning to the proof analyser, which will generate functions f_A and f_B (Definition 4). The labeling engine then creates a labeling function based on the partitions A and B, the functions f_A and f_B, and a possible strength requirement from the application, and then passes it to the interpolator. The latter will finally construct an interpolant and return it to the application.

As mentioned in Sect. 1, different verification tasks may require different kinds of interpolants. For example, [17] reports that the FUNFROG approach works best with strong interpolants, whereas the EVOLCHECK techniques rely on weaker interpolants that have the tree-interpolation property. As shown in [18], only interpolation algorithms stronger than or equal to P are guaranteed to have this property. Therefore, we evaluated only M_s, P and PS_s for (ii), and M_s, P, M_w, PS, PS_w and PS_s for (i) and (iii). D_{min} was evaluated against the other algorithms for (i), but couldn't be evaluated for (ii) because it does not preserve the tree interpolation property. For (iii), D_{min} was not evaluated due to its poor performance in (i).

In the experiments (i) and (ii), the overall verification time of the tools and average size of interpolants were analysed. For (iii) only the size was analysed. In all the experiments the size of an interpolant is the number of connectives in its DAG representation.

The tool and experimental data are available at http://verify.inf.usi.ch/periplo.

4.1   Incremental Verification with Function Summarization

FUNFROG is a SAT-based bounded-model-checker for C designed to incrementally check different assertions. The checker works by unwinding a program up to some predefined bound and encoding the unwound program together with the negation of each assertion to a *BMC* formula which is then passed to a SAT solver. If the result is unsatisfiable, FUNFROG reports that the program is safe with respect to the provided assertion. Otherwise, it returns a counter-example produced from the model of the BMC formula.

Craig interpolation is applied in FUNFROG to extract *function summaries* (relations over input and output parameters of a function that over-approximate its behavior) to be reused between checks of different assertions with the goal of improving overall verification efficiency. Given a program P, and an assertion π, let $\phi_{P,\pi}$ denote the corresponding BMC formula. If $\phi_{P,\pi}$ is unsatisfiable, FUNFROG uses Craig Interpolation to extract function summaries. This is an iterative procedure for each function call f in P. Given f, the formula $\phi_{P,\pi}$ is partitioned as $\phi_{P,\pi} \equiv A_f \wedge B_\pi$, where A_f encodes f and its nested calls, B_π the rest of the program and the negated assertion π. FUNFROG then calls PERIPLO to compute an interpolant $I^{f,\pi}$ for the function f and assertion π.

While checking the program with respect to another assertion π', FUNFROG constructs the new BMC formula $\phi_{P,\pi'}, \equiv I^{f,\pi} \wedge B_{\pi'}$; where $I^{f,\pi}$ is used to over-approximate f. If $\phi_{P,\pi'}$ is unsatisfiable then the over-approximation was accurate enough to prove that π' holds in P. On the other hand, satisfiability of $\phi_{P,\pi'}$ could be caused by an overly weak over-approximation of $I^{f,\pi}$. To check this hypothesis, $\phi_{P,\pi'}$ is refined to $\phi_{P,\pi'}^{ref}$, in which $I^{f,\pi}$ is replaced by the precise encoding of f and the updated formula is solved again. If $\phi_{P,\pi'}^{ref}$ is satisfiable, the error is real. Otherwise, the unsatisfiable formula $\phi_{P,\pi'}^{ref}$ is used to create new function summaries in a similar manner as described above.

In our previous work [17,20] FUNFROG chooses the interpolation algorithm from the set $\{M_s, P, M_w\}$ and uses it to create summaries for all function calls in the program. In this paper, we add the algorithms PS, PS_w and PS_s to the portfolio of the interpolation algorithms and show that in particular the use of PS and PS_s improves quality of function summaries in FUNFROG and therefore makes overall model checking procedure more efficient.

Experiments. The set of benchmarks consists of 23 C programs with different number of assertions. FUNFROG verified the assertions one-by-one incrementally traversing the program call tree. The main goal of ordering the checks this way is to maximize the reuse of function summaries and thus to test how the labeling functions affect the overall verification performance. To illustrate our setting, consider a program with the chain of nested function calls

$$main()\{f()\{g()\{h()\{\}assert_g\}assert_f\}assert_{main}\},$$

where $assert_F$ represents an assertion in the body of function F. In a successful scenario, (a) $assert_g$ is detected to hold and a summary I^h for function h is

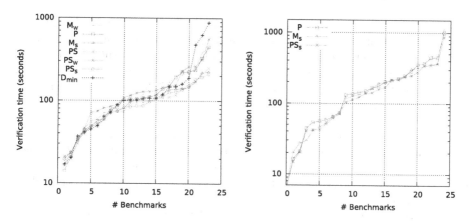

Fig. 4. Overall verification time of FUNFROG (*left*) and EVOLCHECK (*right*) using different interpolation algorithms.

Table 1. Sum of overall verification time and average interpolants size for the FUN-FROG (left) and EVOLCHECK (right) using the applicable labeling functions.

	FUNFROG							EVOLCHECK		
	M_s	P	M_w	PS	PS_w	PS_s	D_{min}	M_s	PS_s	P
Time (s)	2333	3047	3207	2272	3345	**2193**	3811	4867	**4422**	5081
Increase %	6	39	46	3	52	0	74	10	0	16
Avg size	48101	79089	86831	43781	95423	**40172**	119306	246883	**196716**	259078
Increase %	20	97	116	9	137	0	197	26	0	32

created; (b) $assert_f$ is efficiently verified by exploiting I^h, and I^g is then built over I^h; and (c) finally $assert_{main}$ is checked against I^g.

Figure 4 (left) shows FUNFROG's performance with each interpolation algorithm. Each curve represents an interpolation algorithm, and each point on the curve represents one benchmark run using the corresponding interpolation algorithm, with its verification time on the vertical axis. The benchmarks are sorted by their run time. The PS and PS_s curves are mostly lower than those of the other interpolation algorithms, suggesting they perform better. Table 1 (left) shows the sum of FUNFROG verification time for all benchmarks and the average size of all interpolants generated for all benchmarks for each interpolation algorithm. We also report the relative time and size increase in percents. Both PS and PS_s are indeed competitive for FUNFROG, delivering interpolants smaller than the other interpolation algorithms.

4.2 Upgrade Checking Using Function Summarization

EVOLCHECK is an Upgrade Checker for C, built on top of FUNFROG. It takes as an input an original program S and its upgrade T sharing the set of functions calls $\{f\}$. EVOLCHECK uses the interpolation-based function summaries

$\{I^{S,f}\}$, constructed for S as shown in Sect. 4.1 to perform upgrade checking. In particular, it verifies whether for each function call f the summary $I^{S,f}$ over-approximates the precise behavior of T. This local check is turned into showing unsatisfiability of $\neg I^{S,f} \wedge A_{T,f}$, where $A_{T,f}$ encodes f and its nested calls in T. If proven unsatisfiable, EVOLCHECK applies Craig Interpolation to refine the function summary with respect to T.

Experiments. The benchmarks consist of the ones used in the FUNFROG experiments and their upgrades. We only experiment with M_s, P and PS_s since EVOLCHECK requires algorithms at least as strong as P. Figure 4 (right) demonstrates that PS_s, represented by the lower curve, outperforms the other algorithms also for this task. Table 1 (right) shows the total time EVOLCHECK requires to check the upgraded versions of all benchmarks and average interpolant size for each of the three interpolation algorithms. Also for upgrade checking, the interpolation algorithm PS_s results in smaller interpolants and lower run times compared to the other studied interpolation algorithms.

4.3   Overapproximating Pre-image for Hardware Model Checking

PDTRAV [5] implements several verification techniques including a classical approach of unbounded model checking for hardware designs [13]. Given a design and a property, the approach encodes the existence of a counterexample of a fixed length k into a SAT formula and checks its satisfiability. If the formula is unsatisfiabile, proving that no counterexample of length k exists, Craig interpolation is used to over-approximate the set of reachable states. If the interpolation finds a fixpoint, the method terminates reporting safety. Otherwise, k is incremented and the process is restarted.

Experiments. For this experiment, the benchmarks consist of interpolation instances generated by PDTRAV. We compare the effect of applying different interpolation algorithms on the individual steps of the verification procedure.[1]

Table 2. Average size and increase relative to the winner for interpolants generated when interpolating over A (top) and B (bottom) in $A \wedge B$ with PDTRAV.

	M_s	P	M_w	PS	PS_w	PS_s
Avg size	683233	724844	753633	**683215**	722605	685455
Increase %	0.003	6	10	0	6	0.3
Avg size	699880	694372	649149	**649013**	650973	692434
Increase %	8	7	0.02	0	0.3	7

---

[1] The forthcoming research question is how interpolants generated using PS affect the convergence. This study is however orthogonal to ours and left for future work.

Table 2 (top) shows the average size of the interpolants generated for all the benchmarks using each interpolation algorithm, and the relative size compared to the smallest interpolant. Also for these approaches the best results are obtained from M_s, PS and PS_s, with PS being the overall winner. We note that M_s performs better than M_w likely due to the structure of the interpolation instances in these benchmarks: the partition B in $A \wedge B$ is substantially larger than the partition A. This structure favors algorithms that label many literals as b, since the partial interpolants associated with the clauses in B will be empty while the number of partial interpolants associated with the partition A will be small. To further study this phenomenon we interchanged the partitions, interpolating this time over B in $A \wedge B$ for the same benchmarks resulting in problems where the A part is large. Table 2 (bottom) shows the average size of the interpolants generated for these benchmarks and the relative size difference compared to the winner. Here M_w and PS_w perform well, while PS remains the overall winner.

We conclude that the experimental results are compatible with the analysis in Sect. 3. In the FUNFROG and EVOLCHECK experiments, PS_s outperformed the other interpolation systems with respect to verification time and interpolant size. PDTRAV experiments confirm in addition that PS is very capable in adapting to the problem, giving best results in both cases while the others work well in only one or the other.

4.4   Effects of Simplification

It is interesting to note that in our experiments the algorithm PS was not always the best, and the non-uniform interpolation algorithm PS_s sometimes produced the smallest interpolant, seemingly contradicting Corollary 1. A possible reason for this anomaly could be in the small difference in how constraint simplification interacts with the interpolant structure. Assume, in Eq. (3), that $I(C^+)$ or $I(C^-)$ is either constant true or false. As a result in the first and the second case respectively, the resolvent interpolant size decreases by one in Eq. (3). However in the third case, potentially activated only for non-uniform algorithms, the simplification if one of the antecedents' partial interpolants is false decreases the interpolant size by two, resulting in partial interpolants with smaller internal size. Therefore, in some cases, the good simplification behavior of non-uniform algorithms such as PS_s seems to result in slightly smaller interpolants compared to PS. We believe that this is also the reason why P behaves better than M_s and M_w in some cases.

We also observed (detailed data not shown) that in only five of the benchmarks a labeling function led to interpolants with less distinct variables, the difference between the largest and the smallest number of distinct variables being never over 3 %, suggesting that p-annihilable interpolation instances are rare. Finally, we measured the effect of structural sharing. The results (see Appendix A) show that there is no noticeable, consistent difference between any of the algorithms, suggesting that the theory developed in Sect. 3 suffices to explain the experimental observations.

5   Conclusion and Future Work

This paper studies the *labeled interpolation system* (LIS), a framework for constructing interpolation algorithms for propositional proofs. In particular, we study how different labeling functions influence the resulting interpolants by analyzing how the choice of labeling affects several size metrics. Based on the results we construct three new interpolation algorithms: the algorithm PS that decides the labeling based on the resolution refutation, and its strong and weak variants. We show that under certain practical assumptions PS results in the smallest interpolants among the framework. Experimentally, when fully integrated with two software model checkers, PS or its stronger variant outperforms widely used algorithms. The results are similarly encouraging when we overapproximate pre-image in unbounded model checking with PS. We believe that this result is due to the size reduction obtained by the new algorithms.

In the future we plan to study why p-annihilable proofs are rare and how to make them common. We also plan to integrate our framework more tightly with other model checkers through efficiently exchanging proofs and interpolants.

Acknowledgements. We thank our colleagues Professor Gianpiero Cabodi and Danilo Vendraminetto from the University of Turin, Italy for the benchmarks and instructions related to PDTRAV. This work was funded by the Swiss National Science Foundation (SNSF), under the project #200021_138078.

Appendix A   Experiments on Simplifications by Structural Sharing

To investigate the effect of structural sharing on simplifications, we analysed two parameters: the number of connectives in an interpolant on its pure tree representation ($Size_{Tree}$), and the number of connectives in an interpolant on its DAG representation ($Size_{DAG}$), which is the result of the application of structural sharing. Thus, we believe that the ratio $Size_{Tree}/Size_{DAG}$ is a good way to measure the amount of simplifications due to structural sharing.

Figure 5 shows the results of this analysis on FunFrog benchmarks. Each vertical line represents a benchmark, and each point on this line represents the ratio $Size_{Tree}/Size_{DAG}$ of the interpolant generated by each of the interpolation algorithms for the first assertion of that benchmark. The reason why only the first assertion is considered is that from the second assertion on, summaries (that is, interpolants) are used instead of the original code, and therefore it is not guaranteed that the refutations will be the same when different interpolation algorithms are applied.

It is noticeable that the existence of more/less simplifications is not related to the interpolation algorithms, since all of them have cases where many/few simplifications happen. Therefore, there is no difference between any of the algorithms with respect to structural sharing.

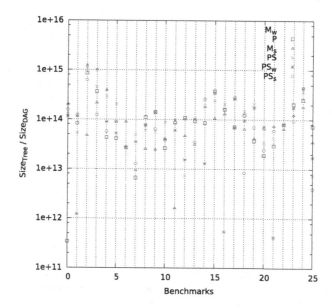

Fig. 5. Relation $Size_{Tree}/Size_{DAG}$ on FunFrog benchmarks for different interpolation algorithms

References

1. Albarghouthi, A., McMillan, K.L.: Beautiful interpolants. In: Sharygina, N., Veith, H. (eds.) CAV 2013. LNCS, vol. 8044, pp. 313–329. Springer, Heidelberg (2013)
2. Alberti, F., Bruttomesso, R., Ghilardi, S., Ranise, S., Sharygina, N.: Lazy abstraction with interpolants for arrays. In: Bjørner, N., Voronkov, A. (eds.) LPAR-18 2012. LNCS, vol. 7180, pp. 46–61. Springer, Heidelberg (2012)
3. Bloem, R., Malik, S., Schlaipfer, M., Weissenbacher, G.: Reduction of resolution refutations and interpolants via subsumption. In: Yahav, E. (ed.) HVC 2014. LNCS, vol. 8855, pp. 188–203. Springer, Heidelberg (2014)
4. Cabodi, G., Lolacono, C., Vendraminetto, D.: Optimization techniques for Craig interpolant compaction in unbounded model checking. In: DATE, pp. 1417–1422 (2013)
5. Cabodi, G., Murciano, M., Nocco, S., Quer, S.: Stepping forward with interpolants in unbounded model checking. In: ICCAD, pp. 772–778 (2006)
6. Cabodi, G., Palena, M., Pasini, P.: Interpolation with guided refinement: revisiting incrementality in SAT-based unbounded model checking. In: FMCAD, pp. 43–50 (2014)
7. Chockler, H., Ivrii, A., Matsliah, A.: Computing interpolants without proofs. In: Biere, A., Nahir, A., Vos, T. (eds.) HVC. LNCS, vol. 7857, pp. 72–85. Springer, Heidelberg (2013)
8. D'Silva, V.: Propositional interpolation and abstract interpretation. In: Gordon, A.D. (ed.) ESOP 2010. LNCS, vol. 6012, pp. 185–204. Springer, Heidelberg (2010)
9. D'Silva, V., Kroening, D., Purandare, M., Weissenbacher, G.: Interpolant strength. In: Barthe, G., Hermenegildo, M. (eds.) VMCAI 2010. LNCS, vol. 5944, pp. 129–145. Springer, Heidelberg (2010)

10. Fedyukovich, G., Sery, O., Sharygina, N.: eVolCheck: incremental upgrade checker for C. In: Piterman, N., Smolka, S.A. (eds.) TACAS 2013 (ETAPS 2013). LNCS, vol. 7795, pp. 292–307. Springer, Heidelberg (2013)
11. Fontaine, P., Merz, S., Woltzenlogel Paleo, B.: Compression of propositional resolution proofs via partial regularization. In: Bjørner, N., Sofronie-Stokkermans, V. (eds.) CADE 2011. LNCS, vol. 6803, pp. 237–251. Springer, Heidelberg (2011)
12. Jancík, P., Kofron, J., Rollini, S.F., Sharygina, N.: On interpolants and variable assignments. In: FMCAD, pp. 123–130 (2014)
13. McMillan, K.L.: Interpolation and SAT-based model checking. In: Hunt Jr. W.A., Somenzi, F. (eds.) CAV 2003. LNCS, vol. 2725, pp. 1–13. Springer, Heidelberg (2003)
14. McMillan, K.L.: An interpolating theorem prover. In: Jensen, K., Podelski, A. (eds.) TACAS 2004. LNCS, vol. 2988, pp. 16–30. Springer, Heidelberg (2004)
15. McMillan, K.L.: Lazy annotation revisited. In: Biere, A., Bloem, R. (eds.) CAV 2014. LNCS, vol. 8559, pp. 243–259. Springer, Heidelberg (2014)
16. Pudlák, P.: Lower bounds for resolution and cutting plane proofs and monotone computations. J. Symbolic Logic **62**(3), 981–998 (1997)
17. Rollini, S.F., Alt, L., Fedyukovich, G., Hyvärinen, A.E.J., Sharygina, N.: PeRIPLO: a framework for producing effective interpolants in SAT-based software verification. In: McMillan, K., Middeldorp, A., Voronkov, A. (eds.) LPAR-19 2013. LNCS, vol. 8312, pp. 683–693. Springer, Heidelberg (2013)
18. Rollini, S.F., Sery, O., Sharygina, N.: Leveraging interpolant strength in model checking. In: Madhusudan, P., Seshia, S.A. (eds.) CAV 2012. LNCS, vol. 7358, pp. 193–209. Springer, Heidelberg (2012)
19. Rümmer, P., Subotic, P.: Exploring interpolants. In: FMCAD, pp. 69–76 (2013)
20. Sery, O., Fedyukovich, G., Sharygina, N.: FunFrog: bounded model checking with interpolation-based function summarization. In: Chakraborty, S., Mukund, M. (eds.) ATVA 2012. LNCS, vol. 7561, pp. 203–207. Springer, Heidelberg (2012)
21. Vizel, Y., Ryvchin, V., Nadel, A.: Efficient generation of small interpolants in CNF. In: Sharygina, N., Veith, H. (eds.) CAV 2013. LNCS, vol. 8044, pp. 330–346. Springer, Heidelberg (2013)

Recursive Games for Compositional Program Synthesis

Tewodros A. Beyene[1]($\boxtimes$), Swarat Chaudhuri[2],
Corneliu Popeea[1], and Andrey Rybalchenko[3]

[1] TU München, Munich, Germany
beyene@in.tum.de
[2] Rice University, Texas, USA
[3] Microsoft Research, Cambridge, UK

Abstract. Compositionality, i.e., the use of procedure summarization instead of code inlining, is key to scaling automated verification to large code bases. In this paper, we present a way to exploit compositionality in the context of *program synthesis*.

The goal in our synthesis problem is to instantiate missing expressions in a procedural program so that the resulting program satisfies a safety or termination requirement in spite of an adversarial environment. The problem is modeled as a game between two players — the program and the environment — that take turns changing the program's state and stack. The objective of the program is to ensure that all executions of this *recursive game* satisfy the requirement. Synthesis involves the modular computation of a strategy under which the program meets this objective. Our solution is based on the notion of *game summaries*, which generalize traditional procedure summaries, and relate program states in a procedural context with sets of states at which the game can return from that context. Our method for compositional reasoning about game summaries is embodied in a set of deductive proof rules. We prove these rules sound and relatively complete. We also show that a sound approximation of these rules can be automated using a Horn constraint solver that utilizes SMT-solving, counterexample-guided abstraction refinement, and interpolation. An experimental evaluation over a set of systems code benchmarks demonstrates the practical promise of the approach.

1 Introduction

The last decade has seen remarkable advances in automated software verification [6,39]. An essential lesson from these developments is that to be scalable, techniques for reasoning about software need to be *compositional*. In other words, an analysis for a large program needs to be constructed from analyses for modules (commonly, procedures) in the program.

Specifically, successful software analysis tools like SLAM [6] and SATURN [39] use *procedure summarization* [32] to compositionally analyze large systems code bases. The idea here is to compute, for each procedure p in a program, a *summary*: a reachability relation between the input and output states of p. If p calls

© Springer International Publishing Switzerland 2016
A. Gurfinkel and S.A. Seshia (Eds.): VSTTE 2015, LNCS 9593, pp. 19–39, 2016.
DOI: 10.1007/978-3-319-29613-5_2

a procedure q, then the summary of q is used to compute the summary of p. The approach can handle recursion: if p and q are mutually recursive, then the relationship between the summaries of p and q is given by a system of recursive equations. To compute summaries of p and q, we find a fixpoint of this system.

The use of summaries in automated verification of programs is, by now, well-understood [2, 13]. Less is known about the use of summarization in the emerging setting of *automated program synthesis* [7, 25, 34, 35]. The goal in synthesis is to generate missing expressions in a partial program so that a set of requirements are satisfied. The problem is naturally framed in terms of a *graph game* [15]. This game involves two players — the program and its environment — who take turns changing the state and stack of the program. The program wins the game if all executions of the game satisfy a user-defined requirement, no matter how the environment behaves. Synthesis amounts to the computation of a *strategy* that ensures victory for the program.

There is a large literature, going back to the 1960s, on game-theoretic program synthesis [11, 30, 36]. However, most of these approaches are: (1) restricted to the synthesis of programs over finite data domains; and (2) do not support compositional reasoning about procedural programs. While a recent paper [7] offers a synthesis method that permits programs over unbounded data, it does not support compositional reasoning. An approach for *recursive infinite-state games* — games played on the configuration graphs of programs with recursion and unbounded data — has remained elusive so far.

In this paper, we present such an approach. The key idea here is a generalization of traditional summaries, called *game summaries*, that allow compositional reasoning about strategies in the presence of procedures and recursion. Our contributions include a set of sound and complete rules for compositional, deductive synthesis using game summaries, and a way to automate a sound approximation to these rules on top of an existing automated deduction system.

Concretely, a game summary *sum* for a program is a relation that relates states of the program to *sets of states*. For a state s and a set of states f, we have $sum(s, f)$ whenever:

1. s is a reachable state.
2. Suppose the game starts from s in a certain procedural context. Then the program has a strategy to ensure that in all executions of game, the *first unmatched return state* — the state to which the game returns from the initial context — is in f.

The genereralization to game summaries is called for as the use of traditional summaries leads to incompleteness in the game setting. Game summaries were previously explored in branching-time model checking of pushdown systems [3–5], but their use in synthesis, or for that matter analysis of infinite-state programs, is new.

Our proof rules for compositional inference of game summaries utilize quantifier alternation: an existential quantifier is used to nondeterministically guess moves for the program, and a universal quantifier is used to capture the adversarial environment. The quantifiers are second-order because summaries are higher-order relations relating states to sets. As in the traditional verification setting, a summary *sum* is propagated across procedure calls and returns through inductive reasoning. The computation exploits compositionality: to generate the parts of *sum* involving states of a procedure q, the rule generates the parts of the summary that involve procedures that q calls, and adds these summaries to *sum* once and for all. Like the corresponding proof rules for verification, the rule is agnostic to whether the input transition relations encode recursion.

To verify that a safety property p is satisfied in all executions of the game, we show that for all s, f such that $sum(s, f)$, s satisfies p. A winning strategy for the program is obtained as an instantiation of the existential quantifiers used in the deduction. Synthesis with respect to termination requirements necessitates the additional use of a disjunctively well-founded transition invariant [31].

We show that our rules are sound, meaning that if they derive a strategy, then the program actually wins under the strategy. They are also relatively complete, meaning that the rules can always derive a winning strategy when one exists, assuming a suitably powerful language of assertions over local and global program variables. Importantly, this completeness proof does not require an encoding of the stack using auxiliary program variables.

We present an implementation RECSYNTH of a sound approximation to our rules on top of an existing automated deduction engine. Specifically, our implementation RECSYNTH feeds our proof rules to the EHSF engine for solving constraints in the form of Horn-like clauses that permit existential quantification in clause heads [8]. Solving the repair problem now amounts to finding an interpretation to unknown sets and relations over program variables. EHSF performs this task with some guidance from user-provided templates, and by using a combination of counterexample-guided abstraction-refinement (CEGAR), interpolation and SMT-solving.

We evaluate RECSYNTH on an array of systems programs, including device driver benchmarks drawn from the SV-COMP software verification competition [9]. Some of our benchmarks contain up to 11 K lines of C code structured into up to 181 procedures. For each of these benchmarks, we set up a synthesis problem by starting with a device driver that satisfies its requirements and eliding certain expressions from the code. Our tool is now used to find values of these expressions so that the resulting code satisfies its specification.

The experimental results are promising: in most cases, RECSYNTH is able to return successfully within a minute, depending on amount of nondeterminism to be resolved. The exploitation of compositionality is essential to these results, as inlining procedures in these examples would lead to programs that are so large as to be beyond the reach of existing program verifiers, let alone known repair/synthesis techniques.

Now we summarize the main contributions of the paper:

- We present an approach to the compositional, deductive synthesis of programs with infinite data domains as well as recursion. The method is based on the use of the new notion of *game summaries*. We give a set of sound and complete proof rules for synthesis using game summaries under safety and termination requirements.

– We offer an implementation (called RECSYNTH) of a sound but incomplete approximation of our inference rules on top of the EHSF deduction engine. We illustrate the promise of the system using an array of challenging benchmarks running into thousands of lines of code.

2 Motivation

Our program synthesis problem can be viewed as a game [15] between two players: a *program player*, whose goal is to satisfy the program's correctness requirements, and an *environment player*, which aims to prevent the program player from doing so. The two players take turns changing the configuration (state and stack) of the program. The transitions of the program come from the user-supplied partial program, with nondeterminism used to capture our lack of knowledge of certain expressions. The environment's transitions model inputs that a hostile outside world feeds to the program. As the game is played on the configuration graph of a recursive program, we call it a *recursive game*. Our goal is to find a winning *strategy* for the program player, i.e., to reduce the nondeterminism in the program's transitions so that the resulting program satisfies the requirements no matter what the environment does.

Now we show that the standard notion of summaries, ubiquitous in verification of programs with procedures, can be inadequate when solving recursive games.

We consider the source code in Fig. 1 that describes an interaction between an environment player that controls all statement except at line P and the program player that only controls the non-deterministic assignment statement at line P. The goal of the program player is to find a strategy that resolves the non-determinism at line P such that regardless of how the environment player resolves the non-determinism at line E the assertion is always satisfied.

We observe that a standard summary for foo can only relate values of the variables in scope foo at the start and exit states of its execution. That is, if a triple (x, y, pc) represents a program state then we obtain the following summary for foo.

$$sum((x, y, pc), (x', y', pc)) = (pc = P \wedge x' = x \wedge (y' = 0 \vee y' = 1) \wedge pc' = S)$$

```
        void main(void) {              int x=-1, y=-1;
    E:      if (env_nondet()) {          int foo() {
    A:          foo();               P:      if (prog_nondet()) {
    B:          x = 0;               Q:          y = 0;
            } else {                         } else {
    C:          foo();               R:          y = 1;
    D:          x = 1;                       }
            }                        S: }
    F:      assert( x == y );
        }
```

Fig. 1. Program that exhibits inadequacy of summaries used for verification purposes for solving games.

Hence, when reasoning about the (existence of) winning strategy for the program player we lack crucial information about the calling context in which foo is executed. As a result, the summary for foo cannot distinguish if the top of the stack stores the value A or C for the program counter of main. That is, when applying $sum((x, y, pc), (x', y', pc))$ in the calling context with $pc = $ A, we obtain a state in which $y = 0 \lor y = 1$. Hence the subsequent assignment x = 1; leads to an assertion violation.

In contrast, when applying the notion of game summaries we relate each entry state of foo with states of main at the return sites A and C. Thus, the game summary can discriminate between the call site on the branch that executes x = 0; and the call site on the branch with x = 1;. As a result out method is able to identify a winning strategy for the program player.

3 Preliminaries

In this section, we formally define programs, games, and our synthesis problem.

Procedural Programs. A program consists of a finite set of procedures P, where $main \in P$ is a distinguished main procedure. For simplicity we assume that the program has no global variables (yet these can be easily added at the expense of lengthier presentation). Let v be a tuple of local variables that are in scope of each procedure.

We use an assertion $init(v)$ to describe the initial valuation of the local variables of *main*, that is, we assume there is only one such evaluation. We use $step(v, v')$ to represent intra-procedural transitions of all program procedures, i.e., the union of intra-procedural transition relations of all procedures. An assertion $call(v, v')$ represents argument passing transitions of all call sites, i.e., the union of argument passing transition relations at all call sites in the program. The left diagram below shows how the valuation of the program variables in scope changes during a call transition. For simplicity, we assume that the valuation of global variables can be modified during the argument passing.

$$call(v, v') \qquad\qquad ret(v, v'', v')$$

For return value passing we use the relation $ret(v, v'', v')$ where v represents the callee state at the exit location, v'' represents caller's state at the corresponding call site, and v' is result of passing the return value (while keeping caller's local variables unchanged) and advancing the caller's program counter value beyond the call site. To model the fact that only local states are put on the stack, we assume that only the local variables of v'' occur in the return value passing relation. The right diagram above shows how the valuation of the program variables in scope changes during a return transition. We assume that an assertion $safe(v)$ represents a set of safe valuations, and thus provides the means for specifying temporal safety properties.

Recursive Games. We model the interaction between the program and its environment as a *recursive game*: a game where two players Prog and Env (standing respectively for the program and the environment) take turns in performing computation steps[1]. In this paper, we assume that Env executes call and return transitions, as well as some of the intra-procedural steps. We capture two-player games by modifying our definition of programs as follows. We assume that instead of the monolithic intraprocedural transition relation $step(v, v')$, we are given two separate transition relations, $prog(v, v')$ and $env(v, v')$, respectively belonging to Prog and Env. Among the intra-procedural steps we assume a strict alternation between Prog and Env. That is, when considering an intra-procedural segment of the computation we assume that the first step executed in the environment, the second step is executed by the program, and so on.

Our partition of computation steps into program and environment steps is chosen to simplify the presentation in the following sections, however it does not restrict the applicability of our results. For example, in a similar way we can model the scenario where the roles of the program and the environment are exchanged, i.e., the program controls calls and returns while the environment controls some of the intra-procedural steps.

Strategies and Plays. Let S be a set of valuations of v. We refer to each $s \in S$ as a state. A stack st is a finite sequence of states, i.e., $st \in S^*$. We use "$\cdot$" for sequence concatenation. We represent the empty stack by ϵ. A configuration $(s, st) \in S \times S^*$ consists of a state and a stack. A configuration (s, ϵ) such that $init(s)$ is called an initial configuration. A configuration that is in the domain of the program transition relation $prog$ is called a program configuration, otherwise it is an environment configuration. Note that the sets of program and environment configurations are mutually disjoint.

We define a transition relation $next$ on configurations that takes into account both program and environment transitions below.

$$
\begin{aligned}
next((s, st), (s', st')) =& (prog(s, s') \lor env(s, s')) \land st = st' \lor \\
& call(s, s') \land st' = (s \cdot st) \lor \\
& \exists s'' : ret(s, s'', s') \land st = (s'' \cdot st')
\end{aligned}
$$

We define a computation tree as a node-labeled tree that satisfies the following conditions. The root is labeled by an initial configuration. Every pair of parent/child nodes (s, st) and (s', st') is related by $next((s, st), (s', st'))$.

A play π is a sequence of configurations that labels a branch of a computation tree. We write π_i, s_i and st_i to refer to the i-th configuration, the i-th state, and the i-th stack of the play, respectively. A play is safe if each of its states s satisfies $safe(s)$.

---

[1] The name *recursive game* captures the fact that our games are played on the configuration graphs of recursive programs, which can be infinite even when program variables range over finite data domains.

A safe strategy for Prog (respectively, Env) is a computation tree such that each node that is labeled by an environment (respectively, program) configuration (s, st) contains the entire set $\{(s', st') \mid next((s, st), (s', st'))\}$ as its children, and each play is safe. A terminating strategy for Prog (respectively, Env) is defined similarly and requires that each play is finite.

4   Solving Recursive Games

In this section, we present a set of deductive proof rules for synthesizing safe and terminating strategies for compositional program synthesis. These proof rules determine whether Prog has a winning strategy by solving implication and well-foundedness constraints on auxiliary assertions over system variables. The rules are based on the notion of *game summaries*, which generalize summaries used in program verification and analysis and permit compositional reasoning in the setting of games. Finally, the rules are sound as well as relatively complete.

4.1   Game Summaries

Given a play π, we define a reachability relation $\leadsto_\pi$ that connects positions whose configurations are in the same calling context. Formally, we define

$$i \leadsto_\pi j = (i \le j \wedge st_i = st_j \wedge \forall k : i < k < j \rightarrow \exists st' : st' \cdot st_i = st_k).$$

For a configuration π_i we define the set of first unmatched returns (FUR) as the set of configurations that are obtained by following the return transition out the π_i's calling context. Formally, we obtain the following set.

$$\{\pi'_{j+1} \mid \exists \pi' : \pi_1 = \pi'_1 \wedge \ldots \wedge \pi_i = \pi'_i \wedge i \leadsto_{\pi'} j \wedge \exists s : st_j = s \cdot st_{j+1}\}$$

In the set comprehension above, we ensure that π'_{j+1} is the FUR configuration by asking for a play π' that overlaps with π until the position i, connects π'_{j+1} with π_i within the same calling context, and actually results from a return transition.

A *game summary* relates states with (over-approximations of) sets of states occuring in their FUR configurations.

4.2   Safe Strategies

We consider a synthesis problem where Prog has a winning strategy if only states from $safe(v)$ are visited by all plays.

We present the corresponding proof rule in Figure 2. The proof rule relies on a game summary sum. We connect the game summary with the reachable states by resorting to reasoning by induction on the number of steps required to reach a state from its entry state. S1 requires that for any initial state s_0 of the program, i.e., $init(s_0)$, we have $sum(s_0, \emptyset)$. S2 represent the induction step for intra-procedural steps. Let us assume a state s_1 is given together with a set of states R_1 such that $sum(s_1, R_1)$. We require that for every state s_2 satisfying

$env(s_1, s_2)$ there exists a set of states R_2 such that $sum(s_2, R_2)$ and $R_1 \supseteq R_2$, and there exist a state s_3 such that $prog(s_2, s_3)$. We also require that there exists a set of states R_3 such that $sum(s_3, R_3)$ and $R_2 \supseteq R_3$. Let us assume a state s_1 is given together with a set of states R_1 such that $sum(s_1, R_1)$. For any state s_2 such that $call(s_1, s_2)$, S3 requires that there exists a set of states R_2 such that $sum(s_2, R_2)$. S4 represent the induction step for a call step. Given states s_1 and s_2 together with sets of states R_1 and R_2, let us assume $call(s_1, s_2)$, $sum(s_1, R_1)$ and $sum(s_2, R_2)$. For any $s_3 \in R_2$, we require that there exists a set of states R_3 such that $sum(s_3, R_3)$ and $R_1 \supseteq R_3$. S1 and S3 ensure that $sum(v, X)$ is defined at entry states of the program and each procedural level. S2 and S4 ensure that the set of states associated with each reachable state shrinks while traversing on the same procedural level. S5 represent the induction step for a return step. Given the states s_1 and s_2 and a set of states R_1 such that $sum(s_1, R_1)$ and $ret(s_1, s_2)$, we require that s_2 is in R_1. Since the winning condition requires all states to satisfy $safe(v)$, each state s such that $sum(s, R)$ needs to satisfy $safe(s)$. This condition is enforced by S6.

Example 1. We show how the safety proof rule can be applied using the example in Fig. 1.

Since the inital state of `main` is $(E, -1, -1)$, by S1 we have $sum((E, -1, -1), \emptyset)$. Assuming Env decides to move from E to A, we apply S2 to derive $sum((A, -1, -1), \emptyset)$. To strictly adhere with the alternation of players, we assume that Prog does a skip. From $pc = A$, Env makes a call to `foo` and the program control will go to the state $(P, -1, -1)$. S3 ensures that there exists a set of states R_1 such that $sum((P, -1, -1), R_1)$. From $sum((P, -1, -1), R_1)$, let Env make a skip and let Prog move to R thereby reaching the state $(R, -1, -1)$. S3 ensures that there exists a set of states R_2 such that $sum((R, -1, -1), R_2)$ and $R_1 \supseteq R_2$. From $sum((R, -1, -1), R_2)$, let once again Env make a skip and let Prog move to S by updating value of y to 1 thereby reaching the state $(S, -1, 1)$. S3 ensures that there exists a set of states R_3 such that $sum((S, -1, 1), R_3)$ and $R_2 \supseteq R_3$. The return step from $(S, -1, 1)$ in `foo` to $(B, -1, 1)$ in `main` together with S5 ensures that $(B, -1, 1)$ is in R_3 and by transitivity in R_2 and R_1. From $sum((E, -1, -1), \emptyset)$, $call((E, -1, -1), (P, -1, -1))$, and $sum((P, -1, -1), \{(B, -1, 1)\})$, S4 ensures that there exists R_4 such that $sum((B, -1, 1), R_4)$. Continuing in a similar way from $sum((B, -1, 1), R_4)$ by applying S2, we reach a state $(F, 0, 1)$ which violates the assertion.

However, from $sum((P, -1, -1), R_1)$, if Env makes a skip and Prog moves to Q instead R, the assertion will be eventually satisfied. If Env decides to move from E to B (instead of E to A), Prog needs to move to R instead Q for the assertion to be satisfied. Therefore, the safe strategy for Prog should use information on the top of the stack to know if it should move to Q or R from P. For example, replacing `prog_nondet()` by $pc = A$ provides a winning strategy for Prog.

Theorem 1 (Correctness of Rule RuleSafe). *The proof rule* RuleSafe *is sound and relatively complete.* ■

Find *sum* such that:

S1: $init(v)$	$\rightarrow sum(v, \emptyset)$
S2: $sum(v_1, X_1) \wedge env(v_1, v_2)$	$\rightarrow \exists X_2 : sum(v_2, X_2) \wedge X_1 \supseteq X_2 \wedge$
	$\exists v_3 : prog(v_2, v_3) \wedge \exists X_3 : sum(v_3, X_3) \wedge X_2 \supseteq X_3$
S3: $sum(v_1, X_1) \wedge call(v_1, v_2)$	$\rightarrow \exists X_2 : sum(v_2, X_2)$
S4: $sum(v_1, X_1) \wedge call(v_1, v_2) \wedge sum(v_2, X_2) \wedge X_2(v_3)$	$\rightarrow \exists X_3 : sum(v_3, X_3) \wedge X_1 \supseteq X_3$
S5: $sum(v_1, X) \wedge ret(v_1, v_2)$	$\rightarrow X(v_2)$
S6: $sum(v, X)$	$\rightarrow safe(v)$

Fig. 2. Proof rule RULESAFE for synthesis with respect to a safety requirement given by assertion $safe(v)$.

A complete proof of the theorem is given below. But first, we define the following auxilary predicate S that imposes a certain totality and monotonicity condition on game summaries. When considering a pair of configurations in the same calling context, the game summary *sum* needs to provide corresponding state sets and these state sets need to be non-increasing.

$$S(\pi, i, j) = i \leadsto_\pi j \rightarrow \exists R_i \exists R_j : sum(s_i, R_i) \wedge sum(s_j, R_j) \wedge R_i \supseteq R_j)$$

We extend the predicate to range over a prefix of a play as follows.

$$H(\pi, k) = (\forall i \forall j : 0 \leq i \leq j \leq k \rightarrow S(\pi, i, j))$$

The following lemma is crucial for proving the soundness of the proof rule for proving the existence of safe strategies.

Lemma 1. *For each play π and each of its positions k we have $H(\pi, k)$.*

Proof. Let π be a play and k be a position in this play. We prove the lemma by induction over k.

First, we consider the base case $k = 0$. Since $init(s_0)$, from S1 follows $S(\pi, 0, 0)$ via $R_0 = R_0 = \emptyset$.

For the induction step we assume $H(\pi, k)$ and prove $H(\pi, k + 1)$. After expanding definitions of H the proof goal is $\forall i \forall j : 0 \leq i \leq j \leq k+1 \rightarrow S(\pi, i, j)$. For i and j such that $0 \leq i \leq j \leq k$ we obtain $S(\pi, i, j)$ from $H(\pi, k)$ directly. In the rest of this proof we consider the case $0 \leq i \leq j = k + 1$, i.e., our proof goal becomes

$$\exists R_i \exists R_{k+1} : sum(s_i, R_i) \wedge sum(s_{k+1}, R_{k+1}) \wedge R_i \supseteq R_{k+1}$$

for arbitrary $0 \leq i \leq k + 1$ such that $i \leadsto_\pi k + 1$. We proceed by performing a case destinction on how π_k transitions to π_{k+1}.

In case $env(s_k, s_{k+1})$ we rely on the induction hypothesis to obtain R_i and R_k such that $sum(s_i, R_i)$, $sum(s_k, R_k)$, and $R_i \supseteq R_k$. The consequence of S2 yields R_{k+1} such that $sum(s_{k+1}, R_{k+1})$ and $R_k \supseteq R_{k+1}$, which together with $R_i \supseteq R_k$ proves our goal.

For $prog(s_k, s_{k+1})$ we first consider that $env(s_{k-1}, s_k)$ since the program step is always preceded by an environment step, so we have $k - 1 \geq 0$. From the induction hypothesis we obtain corresponding $R_i \supseteq R_{k-1}$. Thus, the premise of S2 holds, as $sum(s_{k-1}, R_{k-1}) \wedge env(s_{k-1}, s_k)$. Hence there exists R_k such that $sum(s_k, R_k)$ and $R_{k-1} \supseteq R_k$, as well as there exists R_{k+1} such that $sum(s_{k+1}, R_{k+1})$ and $R_k \supseteq R_{k+1}$. Hence, we meet our proof goal.

If $call(s_k, s_{k+1})$ then $i = k + 1$ since π_{k+1} is an entry configuration. Hence from $S(\pi, k, k)$ and S3 we directly prove our goal.

With $ret(s_k, s_{k+1})$ we first observe that there is a call configuration π_c and an entry configuration π_e such that $call(\pi_c, \pi_e)$. This call yields the exit configuration π_k and the return configuration π_{k+1}. Since $c \leadsto_\pi k + 1$ we have $i \leadsto_\pi c$. From the induction hypothesis we obtain corresponding R_i and R_c such that $R_i \supseteq R_c$. Similarly, from $e \leadsto_\pi k$ we obtain corresponding $R_e \supseteq R_k$. For S5 we obtain the premise $sum(s_k, R_k) \wedge ret(s_k, s_{k+1})$, and hence $R_k(s_{k+1})$. By transitivity, we have $R_e(s_{k+1})$. We instantiate the premise of S4 as follows.

$$sum(s_c, R_c) \wedge call(s_c, s_e) \wedge sum(s_e, R_e) \wedge R_e(s_{k+1})$$

As a consequence we get R_{k+1} such that $sum(s_{k+1}, R_{k+1})$ and $R_c \supseteq R_{k+1}$. Hence, we have $R_i \supseteq R_{k+1}$, which proves the goal.   □

Coming back to RULESAFE, we split the correctness proof into two parts: soundness and relative completeness.

Soundness. If there exists sum that satisfies premises of RULESAFE then the program has a strategy to win the safety game.

Proof. For a proof by contradiction we assume that sum satisfies the premises of RULESAFE and the program does not have a safe strategy. Hence, there exists a strategy for the environment in which every play eventually violates the safety condition. Let us take one such play π and its position p in which the safety condition is violated. By Lemma 1 for the position p we obtain R_p such that $sum(s_p, R_p)$. Hence from S6 follows $safe(s_p)$, which is a contradiction to our assumption that sum satisfies the premises of RULESAFE.   □

Relative Completeness. If the program has a strategy to win the safety game then there exists sum that satisfies premises of RULESAFE.

Proof. Let us assume that Prog has a safe strategy, i.e., the conclusion of RULE-SAFE holds. This strategy σ alternates between universal choices of Env and existential choices of Prog. We prove the completeness claim by showing how to construct sum satisfying the premises of the rule. Let $sum(s, R)$ holds for each state s that occurs in a configuration (s, st) of some play where R is the corresponding set of first unmatched return states.

Since the initial state, say s, occurs in the strategy, $sum(s, R)$ is defined such that $R = \emptyset$ and hence S1 is satisfied.

Now we consider an arbitrary pair (s_0, R_0) such that $sum(s_0, R_0)$. The strategy guarantees that for every successor s_1 of s_0 wrt. Env there exists a successor s_2 wrt. Prog. For every such s_2, there exists a set of FURs R_2 such that $sum(s_2, R_2)$ since s_2 is an Env state. In addition, $R_2 \subseteq R_0$ since the set of FURs may only shrink across intra-procedural steps. i.e., sum satisfies S2.

Let us take an arbitrary pair (s_0, R_0) such that $sum(s_0, R_0)$, and a state s_1 such that $call(s_0, s_1)$. For the set of FURs R_1 of s_1, we have $sum(s_1, R_1)$ since s_1 is an Env state. This shows $sum(v, R)$ satisfies S3.

Next, let us assume that for arbitrary states s_0 and s_1, we have $sum(s_0, R_0)$ and $sum(s_1, R_1)$, and $call(s_0, s_1)$. It follows that for any $s_2 \in R_1$ and a set of its FURs R_2, $sum(s_2, R_2)$ holds since s_2 is an Env state. In addition, since s_2 is in the same procedural level as s_0, $R_2 \subseteq R_0$, i.e. S4 is satisfied.

Now let us assume that for arbitrary states s_0 and s_1, we have $ret(s_0, s_1)$ and $sum(s_0, R_0)$. By definition of FURs, we see that s_1 should be in R_0, satisfying S5.

Finally, for all pairs (s, R) such that $sum(s, R)$, we have $safe(s)$ since we consider a safe strategy. Therefore, sum also satisfies S6.   □

5   Terminating Strategies

Let us now consider a synthesis problem where Prog has a winning strategy if a state from which no further move can be made is eventually reached by each play. Reasoning about such eventuality properties demands the use of well-founded orders.

We connect the invariant assertion with the reachable states by resorting to reasoning by induction on the number of steps required to reach a state from its entry state.

T1 requires that for any initial state s_0 of the program, $sum(s_0, s_0, \emptyset)$. T2 represent the induction step for intra-procedural steps. Let us assume a state s_1 is given together with its entry state s_0 and a set of states R_1 such that $sum(s_0, s_1, R_1)$. We require that for every state s_2 satisfying $env(s_1, s_2)$ there exists a set of states R_2 such that $sum(s_0, s_2, R_2)$ and $R_1 \supseteq R_2$, and there exist a state s_3 such that $prog(s_2, s_3)$. We also require that there exists a set of states R_3 such that $sum(s_0, s_3, R_3)$ and $R_2 \supseteq R_3$. We also require that (s_1, s_3) is in $round$. Assume for a state s_1, $sum(s_0, s_1, R_1)$ is given. For any state s_2 such that $call(s_1, s_2)$, T3 requires that there exists a set of states R_2 such that $sum(s_2, s_2, R_2)$. T4 represent the induction step for a call step. Given states s_1 and s_2 together with sets of states R_1 and R_2, let us assume $call(s_1, s_2)$, $sum(s_0, s_1, R_1)$ and $sum(s_2, s_2, R_2)$. For any $s_3 \in R_2$, we require that there exists a set of states R_3 such that $sum(s_0, s_3, R_3)$ and $R_1 \supseteq R_3$. We also require that (s_1, s_3) is in $round$. T1 and T3 ensure that sum is defined at entry states of the program and each procedural level. T2 and T4 ensure that the set of states associated with each reachable state shrinks while traversing on the same procedural level. T5 represent the induction step for a return step. For a return step (s_1, s_2) such that $sum(s_0, s_1, R_1)$, we require that s_2 is in R_1. To ensure that the game progresses when aiming at termination, we keep track of pairs of states across every call site in *descent*. This is done in T3. Finally, to ensure termination by each play we require that both *descent* and *round* represent a well-founded relation. Thus, it is impossible to return to *sum* infinitely many times. This is captured by T6 and T7 (Fig. 3).

Find *sum*, *round*, and *descent* such that:

T1: $init(v)$ $\qquad\qquad\qquad\qquad \rightarrow sum(v, v, \emptyset)$

T2: $sum(v_1, v_2, R_1) \wedge env(v_2, v_3) \rightarrow \exists R_2 : sum(v_1, v_3, R_2) \wedge R_1 \supseteq R_2$

$$\wedge\ \exists v_4 : prog(v_3, v_4) \wedge round(v_2, v_4)$$

$$\wedge\ \exists R_3 : sum(v_1, v_4, R_3) \wedge R_3 \supseteq R_2$$

T3: $sum(v_1, v_2, R_1) \wedge call(v_2, v_3) \rightarrow \exists R_2 : sum(v_3, v_3, R_2) \wedge descent(v_1, v_3)$

T4: $sum(v_1, v_2, R_1) \wedge call(v_2, v_3)$

$\quad \wedge\ sum(v_3, v_3, R_2) \wedge R_2(v_4) \quad \rightarrow \exists R_3 : sum(v_1, v_4, R_3) \wedge R_1 \supseteq R_3 \wedge round(v_2, v_4)$

T5: $sum(v_1, v_2, R) \wedge ret(v_2, v_3) \quad \rightarrow R(v_3)$

T6: *well-founded*(*round*)

T7: *well-founded*(*descent*)

Fig. 3. Proof rule RULETERM for synthesis with respect to the termination requirement.

Theorem 2 (Correctness of Rule RuleTerm). *The proof rule* RULETERM *is sound and relatively complete.* ■

The complete proof of the theorem can be found in the appendix section.

6   Evaluation

In this section we describe an experimental evaluation of our compositional synthesis approach on infinite-state programs. The evaluation relies on a solver of Horn clauses with alternating quantification, so we first describe this class of clauses.

Implementation. Our prototype implementation RECSYNTH is based on two modules. The first module is a C frontend, derived from the CIL library [28], that transforms C code into verification conditions represented as Horn clauses. This transformation is based on a sound approximation of our proof rules. The second module of RECSYNTH is a solver for Horn clauses that is based on predicate abstraction and counterexample guided abstraction refinement [8]. The Horn clause solver EHSF is implemented in SICStus Prolog and uses the CLP(Q) solver for handling linear constraints [22] and the Z3 solver [14] for handling non-linear constraints.

We skip the syntax and semantics of the clauses targeted by this system — see [8] for more details. Instead, we illustrate these clauses with the following example:

$$x \geq 0 \rightarrow \exists y : x \geq y \wedge rank(x, y), \quad rank(x, y) \rightarrow ti(x, y),$$
$$ti(x, y) \wedge rank(y, z) \rightarrow ti(x, z), \quad dwf(ti).$$

These clauses represent an assertion over the interpretation of "query symbols" *rank* and *ti* (the second order predicate *dwf* represents disjunctive well-foundedness [31], and is not a query symbol). The semantics of these clauses maps each predicate symbol occurring in them into a constraint over v. Specifically, the above set of clauses has a solution that maps both $rank(x, y)$ and $ti(x, y)$ to the constraint $(x \geq 0 \wedge y \leq x - 1)$.

EHSF resolves clauses like the above using a CEGAR scheme to discover witnesses for existentially quantified variables. The refinement loop collects a global constraint that declaratively determines which witnesses can be chosen. The chosen witnesses are used to replace existential quantification, and then the resulting universally quantified clauses are passed to a solver over decidable theories, e.g., HSF [16] or μZ [21]. Such a solver either finds a solution, i.e., a model for uninterpreted relations constrained by the clauses, or returns a counterexample, which is a resolution tree (or DAG) representing a contradiction. EHSF turns the counterexample into an additional constraint on the set of witness candidates, and continues with the next iteration of the refinement loop.

For the existential clause above, EHSF introduces a witness/skolem relation sk over variables x and y, i.e., $x \geq 0 \wedge sk(x, y) \rightarrow x \geq y \wedge rank(x, y)$. In addition, since for each x such that $x \geq 0$ holds we need a value y, we require that such x is in the domain of the Skolem relation using an additional clause $x \geq 0 \rightarrow \exists y : sk(x, y)$. In the EHSF approach, the search space of a skolem relation $sk(x, y)$ is restricted by a template function $\mathrm{TEMPL}(sk)(x, y)$. To conclude this example, we note that one possible solution returned by EHSF is the skolem relation $sk(x, y) = (y = x - 1)$.

Benchmarks. For evaluation, we used benchmarks from the repository of the SV-COMP verification competition [9]. We selected 10 driver files from the directories `ntdrivers` and `ntdrivers-simplified` with sizes ranging between 576 and 11 K lines of code. Each benchmark contains assertions that correspond to safety specifications. Due to their complexity and size, these driver benchmarks have been considered a litmus test for verification tools during the last decade [1, 10, 20].

For each benchmark file, our experiments consist of 3 conceptual steps: **(1)** We mark a C expression in the input file where non-determinism is to be resolved. (We call the code region that contains this expression a *hole*.) **(2)** We use the frontend to generate a program representation in Horn clause form. **(3)** We solve the Horn clauses using EHSF and the solution returned by EHSF corresponds to synthesised-code to fill the hole in the code. If EHSF succeeds in finding a solution for the Horn clauses, our approach guarantees that the device driver code with the hole replaced by the EHSF's solution satisfies the safety specification present in the original benchmark.

First, we describe in detail the SV-COMP example kbfiltr_simpl1, however in an abridged form due to space reasons. Similar to other C benchmark files, kbfiltr_simpl1 contains code corresponding to the driver and the test harness.

```
419:   NTSTATUS IofCallDriver(PDEVICE_OBJECT DvObj, PIRP Irp) {
420:     NTSTATUS returnVal2 ;
         ...
456:     if (?) { /* expression to synthesize */
457:       s = IPC;
458:       lowerDriverReturn = returnVal2;
459:     } else {
460:       if (s == MPR1) {
461:         if (returnVal2 == 259L) {
462:           s = MPR3;
463:           lowerDriverReturn = returnVal2;
464:         } else {
465:           s = NP;
466:           lowerDriverReturn = returnVal2;
467:         }
468:       } else {
469:         if (s == SKIP1) {
470:           s = SKIP2;
471:           lowerDriverReturn = returnVal2;
472:         } else { assert(0); }
473:       }
474:     }
475:     return (returnVal2);
476:   }
```

Fig. 4. Part of function IofCallDriver.

See Fig. 4 for the function IofCallDriver, a function that is invoked repeatedly on many execution paths of the driver. This function has two arguments and some of the variables accessed in its body have global scope, i.e., the variables s, IPC, lowerDriverReturn, MPR1, MPR3, NP, SKIP1 and SKIP2. The safety requirement is instrumented in the code using a finite-state automaton representation, where the variable s corresponds to the current state of the automaton. The variable s is assigned integer values corresponding to different states of the automaton, i.e., UNLOADED = 0, NP = 1, DC = 2, SKIP1 = 3, SKIP2 = 4,

MPR1 = 5, MPR3 = 6 and IPC = 7. The file contains 10 assertions, including the assertion shown on line 472. For our experiment, we marked the code region from line 456 as non-deterministic. (The original SV-COMP benchmark file contained the conditional test s==NP on line 456.)

For applying RECSYNTH we provide a template corresponding to the hole expression that reflects the choice of automaton states

$$\text{TEMPL}(sk)(v) =$$

$$(?_{\text{UNLOADED}} * \text{UNLOADED} + ?_{\text{NP}} * \text{NP} + ?_{\text{DC}} * \text{DC} + ?_{\text{SKIP1}} * \text{SKIP1}$$

$$+ ?_{\text{SKIP2}} * \text{SKIP2} + ?_{\text{MPR1}} * \text{MPR1} + ?_{\text{MPR3}} * \text{MPR3} + ?_{\text{IPC}} * \text{IPC} = \text{s})$$

together with a template constraint

$$0 \leq ?_{\text{UNLOADED}} \leq 1 \wedge 0 \leq ?_{\text{NP}} \leq 1 \wedge 0 \leq ?_{\text{DC}} \leq 1 \wedge 0 \leq ?_{\text{SKIP1}} \leq 1$$

$$\wedge 0 \leq ?_{\text{SKIP2}} \leq 1 \wedge 0 \leq ?_{\text{MPR1}} \leq 1 \wedge 0 \leq ?_{\text{MPR3}} \leq 1 \wedge 0 \leq ?_{\text{IPC}} \leq 1$$

$$\wedge ?_{\text{UNLOADED}} + ?_{\text{NP}} + ?_{\text{DC}} + ?_{\text{SKIP1}} + ?_{\text{SKIP2}} + ?_{\text{MPR1}} + ?_{\text{MPR3}} + ?_{\text{IPC}} = 1$$

that reflects a comparison with an automaton state and excludes arithmetic operations on them.

The task of EHSF is to find suitable values for the template parameters, i.e., the unknown coefficients $?_{\text{UNLOADED}}$, $?_{\text{NP}}$, $?_{\text{DC}}$, $?_{\text{SKIP1}}$, $?_{\text{SKIP2}}$, $?_{\text{MPR1}}$, $?_{\text{MPR3}}$, and $?_{\text{IPC}}$, and thus determine the *hole* expression. RECSYNTH returns in 1 s with the solution NP = s.

Results. For our experiments we used a computer with an Intel Core i7 2.3 GHz CPU and 16 GB of RAM. See Table 1 for our experimental results. For each of the 10 SV-COMP benchmark files, we list the benchmark name and three synthesis scenarios named after a function where the synthesis region is located (Column 1). We also report the size of the file (Column 2) and results of running RECSYNTH (Column 4,5,6). For each file we also report verification results using the complete driver code. For example, the result from the first row of the benchmark **parport** indicates that verifying the driver code succeeds after 19s. (The benchmark indeed satisfies its safety specification.) For the three code regions, IofCalldriver, PptDispatch, and KeSetEvent, our tool synthesises a solutions after 26s, 27s, and 33s, respectively.

In all cases, RECSYNTH is able to succeed within 2-3 times overhead compared to the verification time. We inspected the synthesized expressions and observed that in most cases we obtain the original expressions that was erased when constructing the benchmark. In the remaining cases the synthesized expressions were logically equivalent to the original expressions.

Overall, our results indicate the feasibility of our synthesis approach across a range of different drivers and code regions to synthesize.

Table 1. Application of RECSYNTH on 10 drivers.

Benchmark	LOC	Time (sec)		Steps	Benchmark	LOC	Time (sec)		Steps
		Total	SMT				Total	SMT	
kbfiltr_simpl1	576	0.9			cdaudio_simpl1	2124	8.1		
IofCallDriver		1.1	0.5	3	IofCallDriver		11.7	3.7	13
StubDriverInit		1.4	0.6	12	HPCdrDevice		11.9	3.9	12
KbFilterPnP		1.3	0.5	4	KeSetEvent		12.9	4.1	16
kbfiltr_simpl2	1001	1.2			diskperf	4462	3.2		
IofCallDriver		1.9	0.9	3	IofCallDriver		3.6	0.9	10
StubDriverInit		2.1	0.6	12	FwdIrpSync		4.4	1.2	14
KbFilterPnP		1.9	0.5	4	KeSetEvent		4.2	1.1	14
diskperf_simpl1	1095	2.7			floppy	8285	6.3		
IofCallDriver		3.6	1.5	8	IofCallDriver		7.8	2.8	11
FwdIrpSync		3.9	1.2	12	FloppyPnp		7.7	2.9	11
KeSetEvent		3.6	1.1	11	KeSetEvent		9.2	3.1	16
floppy_simpl3	1123	3.8			cdaudio	8827	11.3		
IofCallDriver		3.3	0.9	1	IofCallDriver		14.2	4.1	22
FloppyPnp		3.4	1.0	1	HPCdrDevice		10.9	3.4	19
KeSetEvent		4.1	1.4	6	KeSetEvent		11.6	4.3	24
floppy_simpl4	1598	5.6			parport	10934	13.5		
IofCallDriver		6.7	1.2	1	IofCallDriver		17.7	4.2	14
FloppyPnp		6.8	1.3	1	PptDispatch		18.7	3.8	13
KeSetEvent		7.5	1.9	6	KeSetEvent		22.1	4.4	18

7   Related Work

The last few years have seen much work on constraint-based software synthesis [25,34,35,37]. Like our paper, these approaches advocate synthesis from partial programs, and leverage modern SMT-solving and invariant generation techniques. However, most of these approaches are not compositional. Exceptions include work on *component-based* synthesis, where programs are synthesized by composing routines from a software library in an example-driven way [23], and modular sketching [33]. The former work is restricted to the synthesis of loop-free programs. The latter work allows the use of summaries for library functions called from a procedure with missing expressions, but requires that the library procedures do not contain unknown expressions themselves. In contrast, our approach synthesizes programs with procedures that call each other in arbitrary ways.

There is a rich literature on synthesis and repair of finite-state reactive systems based on game-theoretic techniques [11,24,27,30,36], using both explicit-state [36] and symbolic [29] approaches. Also well-known are algorithms for *pushdown games* [12,38], which can be expanded into synthesis algorithms for reactive programs with procedures and finite-domain variables [17]. Synthesis of finite-state reactive systems from components has also been studied [26].

The elemental distinction between these approaches and ours is that our programs can handle data from infinite domains.

Game summaries have previously been explored in the context of branching-time model checking of pushdown systems [3–5]. Pushdown systems can be viewed as recursive programs over finite data domains. Branching-time model checking of pushdown systems is a computationally hard problem — EXPTIME-complete in the size of the pushdown system. This is why the traditional definition of summaries, which gives an algorithm that is polynomial in the system size, does not suffice here. [3,5] give an algorithm for this problem based on game summaries. However, this algorithm relies on the fact that pushdown systems have a finite number of control states and stack symbols, and assumes an explicit, rather than symbolic, representation of summaries. Two keys contribution of our work are an extension of the idea of game summaries to a setting with infinite data domains, and its application in synthesis.

8 Conclusion

We have presented a constraint based approach to computing winning strategies in infinite-state games. The approach consists of: (1) a set of sound and relatively complete proof rules for solving such games, and (2) automation of the rules on top of an existing automated deduction engine. We demonstrate the practical promise of our approach through several case studies using examples derived from prior work on program repair and synthesis.

Many avenues for future work remain open. The system we have presented is a prototype. Much more remains to be done on engineering it for greater scalability. In particular, we are especially interested in applying the system to reactive synthesis questions arising out of embedded systems and robotics. On the theoretical end, exploring opportunities of synergy between our approach and abstraction-based [18,19] and automata-theoretic approaches to games [36] remains a fascinating open question.

A Correctness Proofs for RuleTerm

Proof. We split the proof into two parts: soundness and relative completeness.

Soundness. We prove the soundness by contradiction.

Assume that there exist an assertions $sum(v_1, v_2, R)$, $round(v_1, v_2)$ and $descent(v_1, v_2)$ that satisfy the premises of the rule, yet the conclusion of the rule does not hold. That is, there is no winning strategy for Prog.

Hence, there exists a strategy σ for Env in which each play does not terminates. This strategy σ alternates between existential choices of Env and universal choices of Prog. Let $aux(v)$ be a set of states for which σ provides existentially chosen successors wrt. Prog. Note that no play terminates from any $s \in aux(v)$ since no play determined by σ terminates.

We derive a contradiction by relying on a certain play π that is determined by σ. The play π is constructed iteratively. We start from some root state s_0 of σ, which satisfies the initial condition $init(v)$. Note that $sum(s_0, s_0, R_0)$, due to T1, and $aux(s_0)$ due to σ.

Each iteration round extends the matched play $s_0..s$ obtained so far in three ways:

- by two states, say s_1 and s_2 where $env(s, s_1)$ and $prog(s_1, s_2)$,
- by a state, say s_1 where $call(s, s_1)$, or
- by a sequence of states $s_1..s_2$ where we have $call(s, s_1)$, $sum(s_1, R_1)$, and $s_1..s_2$ is a play from s_1 to one of its FURs $s_2 \in R_1$.

We maintain a condition that for the last state s of each such play, $sum(s_0, s, R)$ and $aux(s)$ where $s_0 = entry(s)$, i.e., s_0 is the entry state of the calling context of s.

Let s be the last state of the play π constructed so far, and $s_0 = entry(s)$. Due to our condition, we have $sum(s_0, s, R)$ and $aux(s)$. We iteratively construct a play π taking one of the following steps at a time:

- σ determines a successor state s_1 such that $env(s, s_1)$, and T2 guarantees that there exists a state s_2 such that $prog(s_1, s_2)$, $round(s, s_2)$, and $sum(s_0, s_2, R_2)$ such that $R_2 \subseteq R$. The play is extended by s_1, s_2. Furthermore, $aux(s_2)$ due to G.
- σ determines a successor state s_1 such that $call(s, s_1)$, and T3 guarantees that there exists a set of FURs R_1 of s_1 such that $sum(s_1, s_1, R_1)$, and also $descent(s_0, s_1)$. The play is extended by s_1. Furthermore, $aux(s_1)$ due to σ.
- σ determines a sequence of successor state s_1 such that $call(s, s_1)$, where $sum(s_1, s_1, R_1)$ is given together with some $s_2 \in R_1$. Here, T4 guarantees that there exists a set of FURs R_2 for s_2 such that $sum(s_0, s_2, R_2)$ where $R_2 \subseteq R$, and also $round(s, s_2)$. The play is extended by $s_1..s_2$. Furthermore, $aux(s_2)$ due to σ.

By iteratively constructing π following the above steps, we obtain a play that satisfies the strategy σ. Hence, one of the following follows:

- there exists an infinite sequence of Env states at some procedural level if the infinite play is due to infinite intra-procedural steps by Env which contradicts with T6.
- there exists an infinite sequence of entry states if the infinite play is due to infinite call steps by Env which contradicts with T7

Relative Completeness. Let us assume that Prog has a winning strategy, say σ. We show how to construct $sum(v_1, v_2, R)$, $round(v_1, v_2)$ and $descent(v_1, v_2)$ satisfying the premises of the rule by taking an arbitrary play π determined by σ.

Let $sum(v_1, v_2, R)$ be the set of all triplets (s_0, s, R) such that s is a state in π for which σ provides a universally chosen successor w.r.t. Env, $s_0 = entry(s)$, and R is the set of FURs in σ starting at s. Let $round(v_1, v_2)$ be the set of all pairs of states (s_1, s_2) such that s_1 and s_2 are consecutive Env states on the same procedural level. Let $descent(v_1, v_2)$ be the set of all pairs of states (s_1, s_2) such that s_1 and s_2 are entry states of two consecutive procedural levels.

Since an initial state is an Env state, $sum(v_1, v_2, R)$ is defined for any initial state, satisfying T1.

Let us take an arbitrary summary $sum(s_0, s_1, R_1)$. σ guarantees that for every successor s_2 of s_1 wrt. Env there exists a successor s_3 wrt. Prog. For every such s_3, $sum(s_0, s_3, R_3)$. Since the set of FURs may only shrink across intra-procedural steps, $R_3 \subseteq R_1$. In addition, we have $round(s_1, s_3)$ since s_1 and s_3 are consecutive Env states on the same procedural level, i.e. $sum(v_1, v_2, R)$ and $round(v_1, v_2)$ satisfy T2.

For an arbitrary Env state s_1 with $sum(s_0, s_1, R_1)$ and a state s_2 such that $call(s_1, s_2)$, we get $sum(s_2, s_2, R_2)$ since s_2 is an Env state. Since s_0 and s_2 are entry states to the caller and callee context respectively, we have $descent(s_0, s_2)$,i.e. T3 is satisfied.

Let us consider a pair of states s_1 and s_2 such that $sum(s_0, s_1, R_1)$, $sum(s_2, s_2, R_2)$, and $call(s_1, s_2)$. For any $s_3 \in R_2$, we have $sum(s_0, s_3, R_3)$ since s_3 is an Env state by definition of FURs, and s_0 is in the same procedural level with all states in R_1 including s_2. It follows that any FUR of s_2 is also FUR of s_0 implying $R_2 \subseteq R_0$. In addition, we have $round(s_1, s_3)$ since s_1 and s_3 are consecutive Env states on the same procedural level, i.e. T4 is satisfied.

Now let us consider a state s_1 such that $sum(s_0, s_1, R_1)$ for $s_0 = entry(s_1)$ and $ret(s_1, s_2)$ for some state s_2. By definition of FURs, we see that s_2 is in R_1, satisfying T5.

Now we show by contradiction that $round(v_1, v_2)$ is well-founded. Assume otherwise, i.e., there exists an infinite sequence of states $s1, s2, \ldots$ induced by $round(v_1, v_2)$ and Prog still terminates. As noted previously, for each pair of consecutive Env states s_i and s_{i+1} there exists an intermediate sequence of state $s_i'\ldots s_i''$ such that the sequence $s_1, s_1', \ldots, s_1'', s_2, \ldots, s_i, s_i', \ldots, s_i'', s_{i+1}, \ldots$ is a play. Since this play does not terminate, we obtain a contradiction to the assumption. Hence, we conclude that $round(v_1, v_2)$ is well-founded, satisfying T6.

Similarly, we show by contradiction that descent(u, v) is well-founded, satisfying T7. □

References

1. Albarghouthi, A., Li, Y., Gurfinkel, A., Chechik, M.: UFO: a framework for abstraction- and interpolation-based software verification. In: CAV (2012)
2. Alur, R., Chaudhuri, S.: Temporal reasoning for procedural programs. In: Barthe, G., Hermenegildo, M. (eds.) VMCAI 2010. LNCS, vol. 5944, pp. 45–60. Springer, Heidelberg (2010)
3. Alur, R., Chaudhuri, S., Madhusudan, P.: A fixpoint calculus for local and global program flows. In: POPL, pp. 153–165 (2006)
4. Alur, R., Chaudhuri, S., Madhusudan, P.: Languages of nested trees. In: Ball, T., Jones, R.B. (eds.) CAV 2006. LNCS, vol. 4144, pp. 329–342. Springer, Heidelberg (2006)

5. Alur, R., Chaudhuri, S., Madhusudan, P.: Software model checking using languages of nested trees. ACM Trans. Program. Lang. Syst. **33**(5), 15 (2011)
6. Ball, T., Rajamani, S.K.: The SLAM project: debugging system software via static analysis. In: POPL (2002)
7. Beyene, T.A., Chaudhuri, S., Popeea, C., Rybalchenko, A.: A constraint-based approach to solving games on infinite graphs. In: POPL (2014)
8. Beyene, T.A., Popeea, C., Rybalchenko, A.: Solving existentially quantified horn clauses. In: Sharygina, N., Veith, H. (eds.) CAV 2013. LNCS, vol. 8044, pp. 869–882. Springer, Heidelberg (2013)
9. Beyer, D.: Second competition on software verification. In: Piterman, N., Smolka, S.A. (eds.) TACAS 2013 (ETAPS 2013). LNCS, vol. 7795, pp. 594–609. Springer, Heidelberg (2013)
10. Beyer, D., Keremoglu, M.E.: CPACHECKER: a tool for configurable software verification. In: CAV (2011)
11. Büchi, J.R., Landweber, L.: Solving sequential conditions by finite-state strategies. Trans. Amer. Math. Soc. **138**, 295–311 (1969)
12. Cachat, T.: Symbolic strategy synthesis for games on pushdown graphs. In: Widmayer, P., Triguero, F., Morales, R., Hennessy, M., Eidenbenz, S., Conejo, R. (eds.) ICALP 2002. LNCS, vol. 2380, pp. 704–715. Springer, Heidelberg (2002)
13. Cook, B., Podelski, A., Rybalchenko, A.: Summarization for termination: no return!. Formal Methods Syst. Design **35**(3), 369–387 (2009)
14. de Moura, L., Bjørner, N.S.: Z3: an efficient SMT solver. In: Ramakrishnan, C.R., Rehof, J. (eds.) TACAS 2008. LNCS, vol. 4963, pp. 337–340. Springer, Heidelberg (2008)
15. Grädel, E., Thomas, W., Wilke, T. (eds.): Automata, Logics, and Infinite Games. LNCS, vol. 2500. Springer, Heidelberg (2002)
16. Grebenshchikov, S., Lopes, N.P., Popeea, C., Rybalchenko, A.: Synthesizing software verifiers from proof rules. In: PLDI (2012)
17. Griesmayer, A., Bloem, R., Cook, B.: Repair of boolean programs with an application to C. In: Ball, T., Jones, R.B. (eds.) CAV 2006. LNCS, vol. 4144, pp. 358–371. Springer, Heidelberg (2006)
18. Grumberg, O., Lange, M., Leucker, M., Shoham, S.: *Don't Know* in the μ-Calculus. In: Cousot, R. (ed.) VMCAI 2005. LNCS, vol. 3385, pp. 233–249. Springer, Heidelberg (2005)
19. Gurfinkel, A., Chechik, M.: Why waste a perfectly good abstraction? In: Hermanns, H., Palsberg, J. (eds.) TACAS 2006. LNCS, vol. 3920, pp. 212–226. Springer, Heidelberg (2006)
20. Henzinger, T.A., Jhala, R., Majumdar, R., McMillan, K.L.: Abstractions from proofs. In: POPL (2004)
21. Hoder, K., Bjørner, N., de Moura, L.: μZ– an efficient engine for fixed points with constraints. In: Gopalakrishnan, G., Qadeer, S. (eds.) CAV 2011. LNCS, vol. 6806, pp. 457–462. Springer, Heidelberg (2011)
22. Holzbaur, C.: OFAI clp(q, r) Manual, 1.3.3(edn.). Austrian Research Institute for Artificial Intelligence, Vienna, TR-95-09 (1995)
23. Jha, S., Gulwani, S., Seshia, S.A., Tiwari, A.: Oracle-guided component-based program synthesis. In: ICSE (2010)
24. Jobstmann, B., Griesmayer, A., Bloem, R.: Program repair as a game. In: Etessami, K., Rajamani, S.K. (eds.) CAV 2005. LNCS, vol. 3576, pp. 226–238. Springer, Heidelberg (2005)
25. Kuncak, V., Mayer, M., Piskac, R., Suter, P.: Complete functional synthesis. In: PLDI (2010)

26. Lustig, Y., Vardi, M.Y.: Synthesis from component libraries. STTT **15**(5–6), 603–618 (2013)
27. Madhusudan, P.: Synthesizing reactive programs. In: CSL, pp. 428–442 (2011)
28. Necula, G.C., McPeak, S., Rahul, S.P., Weimer, W.: CIL: Intermediate language and tools for analysis and transformation of C programs. In: CC (2002)
29. Piterman, N., Pnueli, A., Sa'ar, Y.: Synthesis of reactive(1) designs. In: Emerson, E.A., Namjoshi, K.S. (eds.) VMCAI 2006. LNCS, vol. 3855, pp. 364–380. Springer, Heidelberg (2006)
30. Pnueli, A., Rosner, R.: On the synthesis of a reactive module. In: POPL, pp. 179–190. ACM (1989)
31. Podelski, A., Rybalchenko, A.: Transition invariants. In: LICS (2004)
32. Sharir, M., Pnueli, A.: Two approaches to interprocedural data flow analysis. In: Program Flow Analysis: Theory and Applications, pp. 189–234 (1981)
33. Singh, R., Singh, R., Xu, Z., Krosnick, R., Solar-Lezama, A.: Modular synthesis of sketches using models. In: McMillan, K.L., Rival, X. (eds.) VMCAI 2014. LNCS, vol. 8318, pp. 395–414. Springer, Heidelberg (2014)
34. Solar-Lezama, A., Tancau, L., Bodík, R., Seshia, S.A., Saraswat, V.A.: Combinatorial sketching for finite programs. In: ASPLOS, pp. 404–415 (2006)
35. Srivastava, S., Gulwani, S., Foster, J.S.: From program verification to program synthesis. In: POPL, pp. 313–326 (2010)
36. Thomas, W.: On the synthesis of strategies in infinite games. In: STACS, pp. 1–13 (1995)
37. Vechev, M.T., Yahav, E., Yorsh, G.: Abstraction-guided synthesis of synchronization. In: POPL (2010)
38. Walukiewicz, I.: Pushdown processes: games and model-checking. Inf. Comput. **164**(2), 234–263 (2001)
39. Xie, Y., Aiken, A.: SATURN: A scalable framework for error detection using boolean satisfiability. ACM TOPLAS, 29(3) (2007)

Testing the IPC Protocol for a Real-Time Operating System

Achim D. Brucker[1]([✉]), Oto Havle[3], Yakoub Nemouchi[2], and Burkhart Wolff[2]

[1] SAP SE, Vincenz-Priessnitz-Str. 1, 76131 Karlsruhe, Germany
achim.brucker@sap.com
[2] LRI, Université Paris Sud, CNRS, Centrale Supélec,
Université Saclay, Orsay, France
{nemouchi,wolff}@lri.fr
[3] SYSGO AG, Am Pfaffenstein 14, 55270 Klein-Winternheim, Germany
oto.havle@sysgo.com

Abstract. In this paper, we adapt model-based testing techniques to concurrent code, namely for test generations of an (industrial) OS kernel called PikeOS. Since our data-models are complex, the problem is out of reach of conventional model-checking techniques. Our solution is based on symbolic execution implemented inside the interactive theorem proving environment Isabelle/HOL extended by a plugin with test generation facilities called HOL-TestGen.

As a foundation for our symbolic computing techniques, we refine the theory of monads to embed interleaving executions with abort, synchronization, and shared memory to a general but still optimized behavioral test framework.

This framework is instantiated by a model of PikeOS inter-process communication system-calls. Inheriting a micro-architecture going back to the L4 kernel, the system calls of the IPC-API are internally structured by atomic actions; according to a security model, these actions can fail and must produce error-codes. Thus, our tests reveal errors in the enforcement of the security model.

Keywords: Test program generation · Symbolic test case generations · Black box testing · Testing operating systems · Certification · CC · Concurrency · Interleaving

1 Introduction

The verification of systems combining soft- and hardware, such as modern avionics systems, asks for combined efforts in test and proof: In the context of certifications such as EAL5 in Common Criteria [14], the required formal security models have to be linked to system models via refinement proofs, and system models to code-level implementations via testing techniques. Tests are required for methodological reasons ("did we get the system model right? Did we adequately model the system environment?") as well as economical reasons (state

© Springer International Publishing Switzerland 2016
A. Gurfinkel and S.A. Seshia (Eds.): VSTTE 2015, LNCS 9593, pp. 40–60, 2016.
DOI: 10.1007/978-3-319-29613-5_3

of the art deductive verification techniques of machine-level code are *practically* limited to systems with ca. 10 kLOC of size, see [11]).

This paper stands in the context of an EAL5+ certification project [7] of the commercial PikeOS operating system used in avionics applications; PikeOS [18–20] is a virtualizing separation kernel in the tradition of L4-microkernels [10]. Our work complements the testing initiative by a model-based testing technique linking the formal system model of the PikeOS inter-process communication against the real system. This is a technical challenge for at least the following reasons:

- the system model is a transaction machine over a very rich state,
- system calls were implemented by internal, uninterruptible "atomic actions" reflecting the L4-microkernel concept; atomic actions define the granularity of our concurrency model, and
- the security model is complex and, in case of aborted system calls, leads to non-standard notions of execution trace interleaving.

To meet these challenges, we need to revise conceptual and theoretical foundations.

- We use symbolic execution techniques to cope with the large state-space; their inherent drawback to be limited to relatively short execution traces is outweighed by their expressive power,
- we extend the "monadic test-sequence approach" proposed in [2, 4] to a test-method for concurrent code. It combines an IO-automata view [13] with extended finite state machines [9] using abstract states and abstract transitions, and
- we need an adaption of concurrency notions, a "semantic view" on partial-order reduction and its integration into interleaving-based coverage criteria.

This sums up to a novel, tool-supported, integrated test methodology for concurrent OS-system code, ranging from an abstract system model in Isabelle/HOL which was not *not authored by us*, complemented by *our* embedding of the latter into our monadic sequence testing framework, *our* setups for symbolic execution down to generation of test-drivers and the code instrumentation.

2 Theoretical and Technical Foundations

2.1 HOL-TestGen: From Formal Specifications to Testing

HOL-TestGen [3, 4] is a specification-based test case generation environment that integrates seamlessly formal verification and testing in a very unique way:

1. it is an extension of Isabelle/HOL [16] and, thus, inherits all its features (e.g., formal modeling and verification, code generation),
2. its test case generation algorithm is based on the symbolic computation engine of Isabelle and, thus, can count as highly trustworthy,

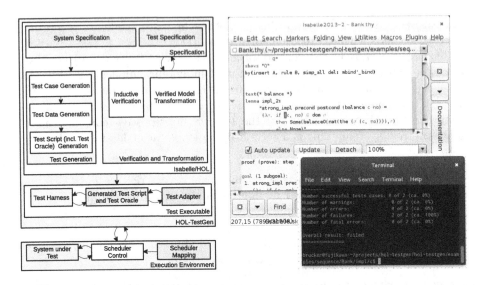

Fig. 1. The HOL-TestGen workflow.

3. it generates automatically test hypothesis such as the uniformity hypothesis and thus establish a formal link between test and proof (see [4] for details).

Besides test data, HOL-TestGen also generates test drivers including the test oracles for the system under test (SUT) verifying it against the HOL specification. Figure 1 shows on the left the HOL-TestGen architecture, and on the right a screen shot of its user interface and a test execution. The usual workflow is:

1. we model the SUT using Isabelle/HOL (*system specification*). This modeling process can leverage the full power and methodology of Isabelle, for example, the system specification can build upon the rich library of datatypes provided by Isabelle or properties of the system specification can be formally proven.
2. we specify the set of test goals (*test specification*), again, in Isabelle/HOL.
3. we use the test case generation implementation of HOL-TestGen to automatically generate abstract *test cases* (that may still contain, e.g., constraints of the form $0 < x < 10$) from the system specification and test specification.
4. we use constraint solvers generating *test data*, i.e., we construct ground instances for the constraints in the test cases (e.g., we choose x to be 4).
5. we generate automatically *test scripts* that execute the SUT as well as validate the test output (by *test oracles*)
6. we compile the test script, together with a generic *test harness*, which controls the test execution and collects statistics about the number of successful or failed tests, to actually execute the test.

Depending on the SUT, we might need to manually write a small *test adapter* that, e.g., converts data types between the representation in the generated test scripts and the one actually used in the SUT. Moreover, for multi-threaded implementations, a *scheduler mapping* has to be provided that maps abstract threads to the critical infrastructures in the implementation. Usually, the manually written code is orders or magnitude smaller than the generated code of the testers and often reusable between different scenarios.

2.2   A Gentle Introduction to Sequence Testing Theory

Sequence testing is a well-established branch of formal testing theory having its roots in automata theory. The methodological assumptions (sometimes called *testability hypothesis* in the literature) are summarized as follows:

1. The tester can reset the system under test (the *SUT*) into a known initial state,
2. the tester can stimulate the SUT only via the *operation-calls* and *input* of a known interface; while the internal state of the SUT is hidden to the tester, the SUT is assumed to be *only* controlled by these stimuli, and
3. the SUT behaves deterministic with respect to an observed sequence of input-output pairs (it is *input-output deterministic*).

The latter two assumptions assure the reproducibility of test executions. The latter condition does *not* imply that the SUT is deterministic: for a given input ι, and in a given state σ, SUT may non-deterministically choose between the successor states σ' and σ'', provided that the pairs (o', σ') and (o'', σ'') are distinguishable. Thus, a SUT may behave non-deterministically, but must make its internal decisions observable by appropriate output. In other words, the relation between a sequence of input-output pairs and the resulting system state must be a function.

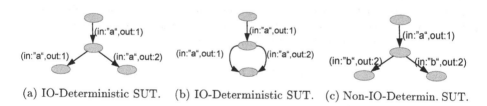

(a) IO-Deterministic SUT.   (b) IO-Deterministic SUT.   (c) Non-IO-Determin. SUT.

Fig. 2. IO-Determinism and Non-IO-Determinism

There is a substantial body of theoretical work replacing the latter testability hypothesis by weaker or alternative ones (and avoiding the strict alternates of input and output, and adding asynchronous communication between tester and SUT, or adding some notion of time), but most practical approaches do assume it as we do throughout this paper. Moreover note, that there are approaches (including our own paper [5]) that allow at least a limited form of access to the final (internal) state of the SUT.

A sequence of input-output pairs through an automaton A is called a *trace*, the set of traces is written *Trace(A)*. The function *In* returns for each trace the set of inputs for which A is enabled after this trace; in Fig. 2c for example, $In\ [(``a",1)]$ is just $\{``b"\}$. Dually, Out yields for a trace t and input $\iota \in In(t)$ the set of outputs for which A is enabled after t; in Fig. 2b for example, $Out([(``a",1)], ``a")$ this is just $\{1, 2\}$.

Equipped with these notions, it is possible to formalize the intended *conformance relation* between a system specification (given as automaton SPEC labelled with input-output pairs) and a SUT. The following notions are known in the literature:

- *inclusion conformance* [6]: all traces in SPEC must be possible in SUT,
- *deadlock conformance* [8]: for all traces $t \in Traces(\text{SPEC})$ and $b \notin In(t)$, b must be refused by SUT, and
- *input/output conformance (IOCO)* [21]: for all traces $t \in Traces(\text{SPEC})$ and all $\iota \in In(t)$, the observed output of SUT must be in $Out(t, \iota)$.

2.3   Using Monadic Testing Theory

The obvious way to model the state transition relation of an automaton A is by a relation of the type $(\sigma \times (\iota \times o) \times \sigma)$ set; isomorphically, one can also model it via:

$$\iota \Rightarrow (\sigma \Rightarrow (o \times \sigma)\, \text{set})$$

or for a case of a deterministic transition function:

$$\iota \Rightarrow (\sigma \Rightarrow (o \times \sigma)\, \text{option})$$

In a theoretic framework based on classical higher-order logic (HOL), the distinction between "deterministic" and "non-deterministic" is actually much more subtle than one might think: since the transition function can be underspecified via the Hilbert-choice operator, a transition function can be represented by

$$step\ \iota\ \sigma = \{(o, \sigma') \mid \text{post}(\sigma, o, \sigma')\}$$

or:

$$step\ \iota\ \sigma = Some(\text{SOME}(o, \sigma').\ \text{post}(\sigma, o, \sigma'))$$

for some post-condition post. While in the former "truly non-deterministic" case *step* can and will at run-time choose different results, the latter "underspecified deterministic" version will decide in a given model (so to speak: the implementation) always the same way: a choice that is, however, unknown at specification level and only declaratively described via post. For the system in this paper and our prior work on a processor model [5], it was possible to opt for an underspecified deterministic stepping function.

We abbreviate functions of type $\sigma \Rightarrow (o \times \sigma)\,\text{set}$ or $\sigma \Rightarrow (o \times \sigma)\,\text{option}$ $\text{MON}_{\text{SBE}}(o, \sigma)$ or $\text{MON}_{\text{SE}}(o, \sigma)$, respectively; thus, the aforementioned state transition functions of io-automata can be typed by $\iota \to \text{MON}_{\text{SBE}}(o, \sigma)$ for the general and $\iota \to \mathrm{MON}_{SE}(o, \sigma)$ for the deterministic setting. If these function spaces were extended by the two operations *bind* and *unit* satisfying three algebraic properties, they form the algebraic structure of a *monad* that is well known to functional programmers as well as category theorists. Popularized by [22], monads became a kind of standard means to incorporate stateful computations into a purely functional world.

Since we have an underspecified deterministic stepping function in our system model, we will concentrate on the latter monad which is called the *state-exception monad* in the literature.

The operations *bind* (representing sequential composition with value passing) and *unit* (representing the embedding of a value into a computation) are defined for the special-case of the state-exception monad as follows:

```
definition bindSE :: "('o,'σ)MONSE ⇒('o ⇒('o','σ)MONSE) ⇒('o','σ)MONSE"
where      "bindSE f g = (λσ. case f σof None ⇒None
                                | Some (out, σ') ⇒g out σ')"
```

```
definition unitSE :: "'o ⇒('o,'σ)MONSE" ("(return _)" 8)
where      "unitSE e = (λσ. Some(e,σ))"
```

We will write $x \leftarrow m_1;\ m_2$ for the sequential composition of two (monad) computations m_1 and m_2 expressed by $\mathrm{bind}_{SE}\ m_1(\lambda\,x.m_2)$. Moreover, we will write "return" for unit_{SE}.

This definition of bind_{SE} and unit_{SE} satisfy the required monad laws:

```
bind_left_unit:  (x ←return c; P x) = P c
bind_right_unit: (x ←m; return x) = m
bind_assoc:      (y ← (x ←m; k x); h y) = (x ←m; (y ←k x; h y))
```

On this basis, the concept of a *valid monad execution*, written $\sigma \models m$, can be expressed: an execution of a Boolean (monad) computation m of type $(\mathrm{bool}, \sigma)\ \mathrm{MON}_{SE}$ is valid iff its execution is performed from the initial state σ, no exception occurs and the result of the computation is true. More formally, $\sigma \models m$ holds iff $(m\ \sigma \neq \mathrm{None} \wedge \mathrm{fst}(\mathrm{the}(m\ \sigma)))$, where fst and snd are the usual *first* and *second* projection into a Cartesian product and the the projection in the Some-variant of the option type.

We define a *valid test-sequence* as a valid monad execution of a particular format: it consists of a series of monad computations $m_1 \ldots m_n$ applied to inputs $\iota_1 \ldots \iota_n$ and a post-condition P wrapped in a return depending on observed output. It is formally defined as follows:

$$\sigma \models o_1 \leftarrow m_1\ \iota_1; \ldots; o_n \leftarrow m_n\ \iota_n; \mathrm{return}(P\ o_1 \cdots o_n)$$

The notion of a valid test-sequence has two facets: On the one hand, it is executable, i.e., a *program*, iff $m_1, \ldots, m_n, P$ are. Thus, a code-generator can map a valid test-sequence statement to code, where the m_i where mapped to operations of the SUT interface. On the other hand, valid test-sequences can be treated by a particular simple family of symbolic executions calculi, characterized by the schema (for all monadic operations m of a system, which can be seen as the its step-functions):

$$\frac{}{(\sigma \models \text{return } P) = P} \tag{1a}$$

$$\frac{C_m \ \iota \ \sigma \qquad m \ \iota \ \sigma = None}{(\sigma \models ((s \leftarrow m \ \iota; m' \ s))) = False} \tag{1b}$$

$$\frac{C_m \ \iota \ \sigma \qquad m \ \iota \ \sigma = Some(b, \sigma')}{(\sigma \models s \leftarrow m \ \iota; m' \ s) = (\sigma' \models m' \ b)} \tag{1c}$$

This kind of rules is usually specialized for concrete operations m; if they contain pre-conditions C_m (constraints on ι and state), this calculus will just accumulate those and construct a constraint system to be treated by constraint solvers used to generate concrete input data in a test.

An Example: MyKeOS. To present the effect of the symbolic rules during symbolic execution, we present a toy OS-model (our functional PikeOS including our symbolic execution process, theories on interleaving, memory and test scenarios has a length of more than 12 000 lines of Isabelle/HOL code; a complete presentation is therefore out of reach). MyKeOS provides only three atomic actions for *allocation* and *release* of a resource (for example a descriptor of a communication channel or a file-descriptor). A *status* operation returns the number of allocated resources. All operations are assigned to a thread (designated by thread_id) belonging to a task (designated by task_id, a Unix/POSIX-like *process*); each thread has a thread-local counter in which it stores the number (the status) of the allocated resources. The input is modeled by the data-type:

```
datatype in_c = alloc task_id thread_id nat
              | release task_id thread_id nat
              | status task_id thread_id
```

```
datatype out_c = alloc_ok | release_ok | status_ok nat
```

where out_c captures the return-values. Since alloc and release do not have a return value, they signalize just the successful termination of their corresponding system steps. The global table var_tab (corresponding to our symbolic state σ) of thread-local variables is modeled as partial map assigning to each active thread (characterized by the pair of task and thread id) the current status:

```
type_synonym thread_local_var_tab ="(task_id ×thread_id) ⇀int"
```

The operation have the precondition that the pair of task and thread id is actually defined and, moreover, that resources can only be released that have been allocated; the initial status of each defined thread is set to 0.

Depicted as an extended finite state-machine (EFSM), the operations of our system model SPEC are specified as shown in Fig. 3. A transcription of an EFSM to HOL is straight-forward and omitted here. However, we show a concrete symbolic execution rule derived from the definitions of the SPEC system transition function, e.g., the instance for Eq. 1c:

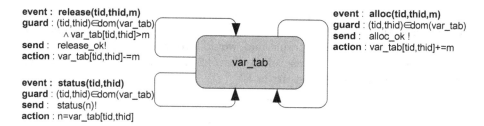

event : release(tid,thid,m)
guard : (tid,thid)∈dom(var_tab)
                ∧ var_tab[tid,thid]>m
send :   release_ok!
action : var_tab[tid,thid]-=m

event : status(tid,thid)
guard : (tid,thid)∈dom(var_tab)
send :   status(n)!
action : n=var_tab[tid,thid]

event : alloc(tid,thid,m)
guard : (tid,thid)∈dom(var_tab)
send :   alloc_ok !
action : var_tab[tid,thid]+=m

var_tab

Fig. 3. SPEC: an extended finite state machine for MyKeOS.

$$\frac{(tid,\, thid) \in \mathrm{dom}(\sigma) \qquad \text{SPEC (alloc } tid\ thid\ m)\ \sigma = \mathit{Some}(\text{alloc \_ok}, \sigma')}{(\sigma \models s \leftarrow \text{SPEC (alloc } tid\ thid\ m); m'\ s) = (\sigma' \models m'\ \text{alloc \_ok})}$$

where $\sigma = var\_tab$ and $\sigma' = \sigma((tid,\, thid) := (\sigma(tid,\, thid) + m))$. Thus, this rule allows for computing σ, σ' in terms of the free variables var_tab, tid, $thid$ and m. The rules for release and status are similar. For this rule, SPEC (alloc $tid\ thid\ m$) is the concrete stepping function for the input event alloc $tid\ thid\ m$, and the corresponding constraint C_{SPEC} of this transition is $(tid,\, thid) \in \mathrm{dom}(\sigma)$.

Conformance Relations Revisited. We state a family of test conformance relations that link the specification and abstract test drivers. The trick is done by a coupling variable res that transport the result of the symbolic execution of the specification SPEC to the attended result of the SUT.

$$\sigma \models o_1 \leftarrow \text{SPEC } \iota_1; \ldots; o_n \leftarrow \text{SPEC } \iota_n; \text{return}(res = [o_1 \cdots o_n])$$
$$\longrightarrow$$
$$\sigma \models o_1 \leftarrow \text{SUT } \iota_1; \ldots; o_n \leftarrow \text{SUT } \iota_n; \text{return}(res = [o_1 \cdots o_n])$$

Successive applications of symbolic execution rules allow to reduce the premise of this implication to $C_{\mathrm{SPEC}}\ \iota_1\ \sigma_1 \longrightarrow \ldots \longrightarrow C_{\mathrm{SPEC}}\ \iota_n\ \sigma_n \longrightarrow res = [a_1 \cdots a_n]$ (where the a_i are concrete terms instantiating the bound output variables o_i), i.e., the constrained equation $res = [a_1 \cdots a_n]$. The latter is substituted into the conclusion of the implication. In our previous example, case-splitting over input-variables ι_1, ι_2 and ι_3 yields (among other instances) $\iota_1 = $ alloc $t_1\ th_1\ m$, $\iota_2 = $ release $t_2\ th_2\ n$ and $\iota_3 = $ status $t_3\ th_3$, which allows us to derive automatically the constraint:

$$(t_1, th_1) \in \mathrm{dom}(\sigma) \longrightarrow (t_2, th_2) \in \mathrm{dom}(\sigma') \wedge n < \sigma'(t_2, th_2) \longrightarrow$$
$$(t_3, th_3) \in \mathrm{dom}(\sigma'') \longrightarrow res = [\text{alloc \_ok}, \text{release \_ok}, \text{status \_ok}(\sigma''(t_3, th_3)]$$

where $\sigma' = \sigma((t_1, th_1) := (\sigma(t_1, th_1) + m)))$ and $\sigma'' = \sigma'((t_2, th_2) := (\sigma(t_2, th_2) - n)))$.

In general, the constraint $C_{\mathrm{SPEC}_i}\ \iota_i\ \sigma_i$ can be seen as an *symbolic abstract test execution*; instances of it (produced by a constraint solver such as Z3 integrated into Isabelle) will provide concrete input data for the valid test-sequence statement over SUT, which can therefore be compiled to test driver code. In our example here, the witness $t_1 = t_2 = t_3 = 0$, $th_1 = th_2 = th_3 = 5$, $m = 4$ and $n = 2$ satisfies the constraint and would produce (predict) the output sequence $res = [\text{alloc\_ok}, \text{release\_ok}, \text{status\_ok2}]$ for SUT according to SUT. Thus, a resulting (abstract) test-driver is:

$$\sigma \models o_1 \leftarrow \text{SUT } \iota_1; \ldots; o_3 \leftarrow \text{SUT } \iota_3;$$
$$\text{return}([\text{alloc\_ok}, \text{release\_ok}, \text{status\_ok2}] = [o_1 \cdots o_3])$$

This schema of a test-driver synthesis can be refined and optimized. First, for iterations of stepping functions an 'mbind' operator can be defined, which is basically a fold over bind_{SE}. It takes a list of inputs $\iota s = [i_1, \ldots, i_n]$, feeds it subsequently into SPEC and stops when an error occurs. Using mbind, valid test sequences for a stepping-function (be it from the specification SPEC or the SUT) evaluating an input sequence ιs and satisfying a post-condition P can be reformulated to:

$$\sigma \models os \leftarrow \text{mbind } \iota s \, \text{SPEC}; \text{return}(P \, os)$$

Second, we can now formally define the concept of a test-conformance notion:

$$(\text{SPEC} \sqsubseteq_{\langle \text{Init}, \text{CovCrit}, \text{conf} \rangle} \text{SUT}) =$$
$$(\forall \sigma_0 \in \textit{Init}. \, \forall \iota \, s \in \textit{CovCrit}. \, \forall res.$$
$$\sigma_0 \models os \leftarrow \text{mbind } \iota s \, \text{SPEC}; \, \text{return}(\textit{conf } \iota s \, os \, res)$$
$$\longrightarrow$$
$$\sigma_0 \models (os \leftarrow \text{mbind } \iota s \, \textit{SUT}; \, \text{return}(\textit{conf } \iota s \, os \, res)))$$

For example, if we instantiate the conformance predicate conf by:

$$\text{conf } \iota s \, os \, res = (\text{length}(\iota s) = \text{length}(os) \wedge res = os)$$

we have a precise characterization of inclusion conformance introduced in the previous section: We constrain the tests to those test sequences where no exception occurs in the symbolic execution of the model. Symbolic execution fixes possible output-sequence (which must be as long as the input sequence since no exception occurs) in possible symbolic runs with possible inputs, which must be exactly observed in the run of the SUT in the resulting abstract test-driver.

Using pre- and postcondition predicates, it is straight-forward to characterize deadlock conformance or IOCO mentioned earlier (recall that our framework assumes synchronous communication between tester and SUT; so this holds only for a IOCO-version without quiescence). Further, we can characterize a set of initial states or express constraints on the set of input-sequences by the *coverage criteria CovCrit*, which we will discuss in the sequel.

2.4   Coverage Criteria for Interleaving

In the following, we consider input sequences ιs which were built as interleaving of one or more inputs for different processes; for the sake of simplicity, we will assume that it is always possible to extract from an input event the thread and task id it belongs to. It is possible to represent this interleaving, for example, by the following definition:

```
fun interleave :: "'a list ⇒'a list ⇒'a list set"
where "interleave [] [] = {[]}"
    |"interleave A [] = {A}"
    |"interleave [] B = {B}"
    |"interleave (a # A) (b # B) =
       (λx. a # x) 'interleave A (b # B) ∪
       (λx. b # x) 'interleave (a # A) B"
```

and by requiring for the input sequence ιs to belong to the set of interleavings of two processes P1 and P2: $\iota s \in$ interleave P1 P2.

It is well known that the combinatorial explosion of the interleaving space represents fundamental problem of concurrent program verification. Testing, understood as the art of creating finite, well-chosen subspaces for large input-output spaces, offers solutions based on adapted coverage criteria [17] of these spaces, which refers to particular instances of CovCrit in the previous section. A well-defined coverage criterion [1,23] can reduce a large set of interleavings to a smaller and manageable one. For example, consider the executions of the two threads in MyKeOS: T = [alloc 3 1 2, release 3 1 1, status 3 1] and T' = [alloc 2 5 3, release 3 1 1, status 2 5]. Since our simplistic MyKeOS has no shared memory, we simulate the effect by allowing T' to execute a **release**-action on the local memory of task 3, thread 1 by using its identity. In general, we are interested in all possible values of a shared program variable x at position l after the execution of a process P. To this end we will define two sets of interleavings under two different known criteria.

- **Criterion1: standard interleaving** (SIN) *the interleaving space of actions sequences gets a complete coverage iff all feasible interleavings of the actions of P are covered.*
- **Criterion2: state variable interleaving** (SVI) *the interleaving space of actions sequences gets a complete coverage iff all possible states of x at l in P are covered.*

The number of interleavings increases exponentially with the length of traces (for bounds of the combinatorial explosion, see [17]). Under SIN we derive 10 possible actions sequences, which is reduced under SVI to 3 sequences (where one leads to a crash; recall our assumption that the memory is initially 0). Unlike to SIN, SVI has provided a smaller interleaving set that cover all possible states. If we consider var_tab[3,1] for x when executing status 3 1, the possible results may be undefined, O or 1. While SIN has provided a bigger set, that cover all possible 3 states of x with redundant sequences representing the same value.

In model-checking, this reduction technique is also known as partial order reduction. It is now part of the beauty of our combined test and proof approach, that we can actually formally prove that the test-sets resulting from the test-refinements:

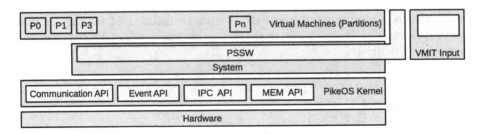

Fig. 4. PikeOS architecture.

$$\text{SPEC} \sqsubseteq_{\langle Init,SIN,conf \rangle} \text{SUT} \quad \text{and} \quad \text{SPEC} \sqsubseteq_{\langle Init,SVN,conf \rangle} \text{SUT}$$

are equivalent for a given SPEC. The core of such an equivalence proof is, of course, a proof of commutativity of certain step executions, so properties of the form:

$$o \leftarrow \text{SPEC } \iota_i; o' \leftarrow \text{SPEC } \iota_j; M \, o \, o' = o' \leftarrow \text{SPEC } \iota_j; o \leftarrow \text{SPEC } \iota_i; M \, o \, o',$$

which are typically resulting from the fact that these executions depend on disjoint parts of the state. In MyKeOS, for example, such a property can be proven automatically for all ι_i = release t th and ι_j = release t' th' with $t \neq t' \lor th \neq th'$; such reordering theorems justify a partial order on inputs to reduce the test-space. We are implicitly applying the testability hypothesis that SUT is input-output deterministic; if a input-output sequence is possible in SPEC, the assumed input-output determinism gives us that repeating the test by an equivalent one will produce the same result.

3 Application: Testing PikeOS

In the following, we will outline the PikeOS model (the full-blown model developed as part of the EUROMILS project is about 20 kLOC of Isabelle/HOL code), and demonstrate how the this model is embedded into our monadic testing theory.

3.1 PikeOS System Architecture

PikeOS is an operating system that supervises and ensures the execution and separation between software applications running on the top of various hardware platforms [19]. It stands in the tradition of so-called *separation kernels* and follows ideas of the influential L4 kernel project [12]. The PikeOS architecture comprises four layers (see Fig. 4). The *virtual machine initialization table* (VMIT) is a data-base containing the global configuration of the system and its application structure. In the VMIT, *partitions* (virtual machines), *tasks* (POSIX-like processes), their *threads*, their memory-, processor-, and time resources, communication channels as well as access-control rights on these resources were defined.

Only at boot-time, partitions, processes and threads can be created via *PikeOS System Software* (PSSW); at run-time the application structure and its time-scheduling is fixed: PikeOS has no dynamic process creation. In other words: based on the VMIT configuration, the *PikeOS system software* (PSSW) will generate a set of virtual machines in the *Partitions layer* during the boot-phase. In this layer each resource partition is composed from a set of applications, and can be executed under the predefined policy and use the predefined resources of the VMIT. Applications in the resource partitions can also be used for system calls of *PikeOS kernel*. In kernel layer, the set of resource partitions is seen as a set of PikeOS *tasks*, that contain PikeOS *threads* and shares kernel resources (memory, files, processors, communication channels ...).

The kernel provides a set of APIs used by the threads and tasks. As in Unix-like systems, special hardware—the MMU—gives application-level *tasks* the illusion to live in an own separate memory space: the virtual memory. However, all *threads* belonging to a task live in the same memory space, namely the memory space of the task they belong to. In contrast, system-level tasks can also access the physical memory and the MMU. Besides memory separation, PikeOS also offers time-separation and multi-core support.

Our work focuses on a particular part of the kernel layer providing inter-process communication (IPC), the PikeOS IPC API.

3.2   PikeOS IPC API

The IPC mechanism [19, 20] is the primary means of thread communication in PikeOS. Historically, its efficient implementation in L4 played a major role in the micro-kernel renaissance after the early 1990s. Microkernels had received a bad reputation, as systems built on top were performing poorly, culminating in the billion-dollar failure of the IBM Workplace OS. A combination of shared memory techniques—the MMU is configured such that parts of virtual memory space are actually represented by identical parts of the physical memory—and a radical redesign of the IPC primitives in L4 resulted in an order-of-magnitude decrease in IPC cost. Also in PikeOS, IPC message transfer can operate between threads which may belong to different tasks. However, the kernel controls the scope of IPC by determining, in each instance, whether the two threads are permitted to communicate with each other. IPC transfer is based on shared memory, which requires an agreement between the sender and receiver of an IPC message. If either the sending or the receiving thread is not ready for message transfer, then the other partner must wait. Both threads can specify a timeout for the maximum time they are prepared to wait and have appropriate access-control rights. Our IPC model includes eight *atomic actions*, corresponding more-or-less to code sections in the API system calls `p4_ipc_buf_send()` and `p4_ipc_buf_recv()` protected by a global system lock. If errors in these actions occur—for example for lacking access-rights—the system call is *aborted*, which means that all atomic actions belonging to the running system call as well as the call of the communication partner were skipped and execution after the system calls on both sides is continuing as normal. It is the responsibility of the application to act appropriately on error-codes reported as a result of a call.

3.3   PikeOS Model Organization

We model the protocol as composition of several operational semantics; this composition is represented by monad-transformers adding, for example, to the basic transition semantics the semantics for abort behavior. The execution of IPC system calls is supervised by a protocol containing a number of stages corresponding to atomic actions.

3.4   Embedding the PikeOS Functional Model into the Monadic Framework

System State. In our model, the system state is an abstraction of the VMIT (which is immutable) and mutable task specific resources. It is presented by the (polymorphic) record type:

```
record ('memory,'thread_id,'thread,'sp_th_th,'sp_th_res,'errors)kstate=
   resource              :: 'memory
   current_thread        :: 'thread_id
   thread_list           :: "'thread list"
   communication_rights  :: 'sp_th_th
   access_rights         :: 'sp_th_res
   error_codes           :: 'errors
   errors_tab            :: 'thread_id ⇀ 'errors
```

Note that the syntax is very close to functional programming languages such as SML or OCaml or F#. The parameterization is motivated by the need of having different abstraction layers throughout the entire theory; thus, for example, the *resource* field will be instantiated at different places by abstract shared memory, physical memory, physical memory and devices, etc.—from the viewpoint of an operating system, devices are just another implementation of memory. In the entire theory, these different instantiations of kstate were linked by abstraction relations establishing formal refinements. Similarly, the field *current_thread* will be instantiated by the model of the *ID* of the thread in the execution context and more refined versions thereof. *thread_list* represents information on threads and there executions. The *communication_rights* field represent the communication policy defined between the active entities (i.e., threads and tasks). The field *access_rights* represent the access policy defined between active entities and passive entities (i.e., system resources).

For the purpose of test-case generation, we favor instances of kstate which are as abstract as possible and for which we derived suitable rules for fast symbolic execution.

Shared Memory Model. Shared memory is the key for the L4-like IPC implementations: while the MMU is usually configured to provide a separation of memory spaces for different tasks (a separation that does not exist on the level of physical memory with its physical memory pages, page tables, ...), there is an important exception: physical pages may be attributed to two different tasks allowing to transfer memory content directly from one task to another.

We will use an abstract model for memory with a sharing relation between addresses. The sharing relation is used to model the IPC map operation, which establishes that memory spaces of different tasks were actually shared, such that writes in one memory space were directly accessed in the other. Under the sharing relation, our memory operations respect two properties:

1. Read memory on shared addresses returns the same value.
2. All shared addresses has the same value after writing.

We will present just the key properties of our shared memory model, where *write* is denoted by $\_ :=\$ \_$ and *read* by $\_ \$ \_$:

```
typedef (α, β) memory = "..."
```

```
x shares(σ) x       x shares(σ) y ⟹ y shares(σ) x   ...
```

```
x shares(σ) y ⟹ y ∈ Domain σ ⟹ σ (x :=$ (σ $ y)) = σ
x ∈ Domain σ   ⟹  σ $ x = z ⟹ σ (x:=$ z) = σ
z shares(σ) x ⟹ σ (x :=$ a) $ z = a
¬(z shares(σ) x) ⟹ σ (x :=$ a) $ z = σ$ z
x shares(σ) x' ⟹ σ (x :=$ y)(x' :=$ z) = (σ(x' :=$ z))
```

or, in other words, a memory theory where addresses were considered modulo sharing.

Atomic Actions. As mentioned earlier, the execution of the system call can be interrupted or *aborted* at the border-line of code-segments protected by a lock. To avoid the complex representation of interruption points, we model the effect of these lock-protected code-segments as atomic actions. Thus, we will split any system call into a sequence of atomic actions (the problem of addressing these code-segments and influencing their execution order in a test is addressed in the next section). Atomic actions are specified by datatype as follows:

```
datatype ('ipc_stage,'ipc_dir)action_ipc = IPC 'ipc_stage 'ipc_dir
datatype p4_stage_ipc = PREP | WAIT | BUF | MAP | DONE

datatype ('thread_id ,'adresses) p4_direct_ipc =
            SEND "'thread_id" "'thread_id" "'adresses"
          | RECV "'thread_id" "'thread_id" "'adresses"

type_synonym
    ACTION_ipc = (p4_stage_ipc,(nat×nat×nat,nat list)p4_direct_ipc)action_ipc
```

Where $ACTION_{ipc}$ is type abbreviation for IPC actions instantiated by $p4\_direct_{ipc}$. The type $ACTION_{ipc}$ models exactly the input events of our monadic testing framework. Thread IDs are triples of natural numbers that specify the resource partition the thread belongs to as well as the task and the individual id. The stepping function as a whole is too complex to be presented here; we refrain on the presentation of a portion of an auxilliary function of it that models just the PREP_SEND stage of the IPC protocol; it must check if the task and thread id of the communication partner is allowed in the VMIT, if the memory is shared to this partner, if the sending thread has in fact writing permission to the shared memory, etc. The VMIT is part of the resource, so the memory configuration, and auxiliary functions like is_part_mem_th allow for extracting the relevant information from it. The semantic of the different stages is described using a total functions:

```
definition PREP_SEND :: "ACTION_ipc state_id⇒ ACTION_ipc ⇒ACTION_ipc state_id"
where "PREP_SEND σ act =
      (case act of (IPC PREP (SEND caller partner msg)) ⇒
        ...
          if is_part_mem_th (get_thread_by_id'' partner σ) (resource σ)
          then
            if IPC_params_c1 (get_thread_by_id'' partner σ)
            then ...)
```

Where PREP_SEND, WAIT_SEND, BUF_SEND, and DONE_SEND define an operational semantic for the stages of the PikeOS IPC protocol.

Traces, Executions and Input Sequences. During our experiments, we will generate *input sequences* rather than traces. An input sequence is a list of a datatype capturing atomic action input syntactically. An *execution* is the application of a transition function over a given input sequence. Using mbind, the execution over a given input sequence *is* can be immediately constructed.

```
definition execution = (λis ioprog σ. mbind is ioprog σ)
```

IPC Execution Function. The execution semantic of the IPC protocol is expressed using a total function:

```
fun exec_action :: "ACTION_ipc state_id⇒ ACTION_ipc ⇒ACTION_ipc state_id"
where
  PREP_SEND_run:"exec_action σ(IPC PREP (SEND caller partner msg)) =
              PREP_SEND σ (IPC PREP (SEND caller partner msg))"|
  (...)
```

The function is adapted to the monads using the following definition:

```
definition exec_action_Mon
where    "exec_action_Mon = (λact σ. Some (error_codes(exec_action σact),
                                          exec_action σ act))"
```

System Calls. As mentioned earlier, PikeOS system calls are seen as sequence of atomic actions that respect a given ordering. Actually, each system call can perform a set of *operations*. PikeOS IPC API provides seven different calls, the most general one is the call $P4\_ipc()$. Using $P4\_ipc()$, five operations can be performed:

1. Send a copied message,
2. Receive a copied message,
3. Receive an event (not modeled),
4. Send a mapped message (not used in this paper), and
5. Receive a mapped message (not used in this paper).

The corresponding Isabelle model for the call is:

```
datatype ('thread_id,'msg) P4_IPC_call =
   P4_IPC_call     'thread_id'thread_id'msg
 | P4_IPC_BUF_call 'thread_id'thread_id'msg
 | P4_IPC_MAP_call 'thread_id'thread_id'msg
   (...)
```

Communication Coverage Criterion. An IPC call defines a *communication* relation between two threads. In PikeOS, IPC communications can be symmetric, transitive but can not be reflexive (a thread can not send or receive an IPC message for himself). The transitivity or intransitivity of IPC communications depends mainly on the defined communication rights table and access rights table. In this section, we will define a set of Isabelle rules to derive input sequences for ipc calls. The derived input sequences express IPC communications between threads. Other rules, which are almost the same as the ones used for deriving input sequences, will be defined to derive the possible communications between threads after the execution of an IPC call. While IPC input sequences will be used in scenarios for testing information flow policy via IPC error codes, IPC communications let us to address scenarios on access control policy implemented via the two tables cited before.

To this end we define a new coverage criterion, i.e., the set of interleavings that satisfy all these constrains. The definition of the criterion is based on the functional model of PikeOS IPC (see Sect. 3.2) and our technique to reduce the set of interleaving if two actions can commute (see Sect. 2.4).

– **Criterion3: IPC communications** (IPC_{comm}) *the interleaving space of input sequences gets a complete coverage iff all IPC communications of a given SUT are covered.*

IPC communications are input sequences. An example of a communication derived under **IPC**$_{comm}$ is:

```
[IPC PREP (SEND th_id th_id' msg), IPC PREP (RECV th_id' th_id msg),
 IPC WAIT (SEND th_id th_id' msg), IPC WAIT (RECV th_id' th_id msg),
 IPC BUF (RECV th_id' th_id msg), IPC DONE (RECV th_id' th_id msg),
 IPC DONE (SEND th_id th_id' msg)]"
```

4   Test Generation

Test Scenarios. A test scenario is represented by a test specification and can have two main schemes: unit test or sequence test. An example of a test scenario is the specification TS_simple_example2:

```
test_spec TS_simple_example2:
  is ∈ IPC_communication ⟹
  σ₁ ⊨ (outs ←mbind is(abort_lift exec_action_Mon);return(outs = x)
  ⟶σ₁ ⊨ (outs ←mbind is SUT; return(outs = x))
```

For a σ_1 definition that contains a suitable VMIT configuration, a possible is is, e.g.:

```
[IPC PREP (RECV (0,0,1) (0,0,2) [0,4,5,8]),
 IPC PREP (SEND (0,0,2) (0,0,1) [0,4,5,8]),
 IPC WAIT (RECV (0,0,1) (0,0,2) [0,4,5,8]),
 IPC WAIT (SEND (0,0,2) (0,0,1) [0,4,5,8]),
 IPC BUF  (SEND (0,0,2) (0,0,1) [0,4,5,8]),
 IPC DONE (SEND (0,0,2) (0,0,1) [0,4,5,8]),
 IPC DONE (RECV (0,0,1) (0,0,2) [0,4,5,8])]
```

The sequence is an abstraction of an IPC communication between the thread with the $ID = (0,0,1)$ and the thread with $ID = (0,0,2)$ via a message $msg = [0,4,5,8]$. Natural numbers inside the message are abstractions on memory addresses. The execution semantic of the input sequence is represented by our execution function $exec\_action\_Mon$. We wrap around our execution function a monad transformer $abort_{lift}$ that express the behavior of an abort. The equality specify our conformance relation between SUT outputs and the model outputs. After using our symbolic execution process the out of this test case is:

```
[NO_ERRORS,
 NO_ERRORS,
 ERROR_IPC error_IPC_1_in_WAIT_RECV,
 ERROR_IPC error_IPC_1_in_WAIT_RECV,
 ERROR_IPC error_IPC_1_in_WAIT_RECV,
 ERROR_IPC error_IPC_1_in_WAIT_RECV,
 ERROR_IPC error_IPC_1_in_WAIT_RECV]
```

The error-codes observed in the sequence is related to IPC. The error-codes was returned in the stage $WAIT\_RECV$. The interpretation of this error-codes is that the thread has not the rights to communicate with his partner. We can observe the behavior of our abort operator in this sequence of error-codes; All stages following WAIT_RECV are purged (not executed), and the same error is returned instead. We focus on error-codes in our scenarios, since error-codes represent a potential for undesired information flow: for example, un-masked error-messages may reveal the structure of tasks and threads of a foreign partition in the system; a revelation that the operating system as separation kernel should prevent.

Generating Test Drivers. In this section we address the problem to compile "abstract test-drivers" as described in the previous sections into concrete code and code instrumentations that actually execute these tests.

HOL-TestGen can generate test scripts (recall Fig. 1) in SML, Haskell, Scala and F#. For our application, we generate SML test scripts and use MLton (www. mlton.org) for building the test executable: MLton 1. provides a foreign function interface to C and 2. is easily portable to small POSIX system.

In more detail, we generate two SML structures *automatically* from the Isabelle theories. The first structure, called `Datatypes`, contains the datatypes that are used by the interface of the SUT. In our example, this includes, e.g., `IPC_protocol` and `P4_IPC_call`. The second structure, called `TestScript`, contains a list of all generated test cases as well the *test oracle*, i.e., the algorithms necessary to decide if a test result complies to the specification or not.

In addition, for testing C code, we need to provide a small SML structure (ca. 20 lines of code), called `Adapter`, that serves two purposes: 1. the configuration of the foreign function, e.g., the mapping from SML datatypes to C datatypes and 2. the concretization of abstractions to bridge the gap between an abstract test model and the concrete SUT. The `Adapter` structure only needs to be updated after significant changes to either the system specification or the system under test.

For testing concurrent, i.e., multi-threaded, programs we need to solve a particular challenge: *enforcing certain thread execution orders* (a certain scheduling) during test execution. There are, in principle, three different options available to control the scheduler during test execution: 1. instrumenting the SUT to make the thread switching deterministic and controllable, 2. using a deterministic scheduler that can be controlled by test driver, or 3. using the features of debuggers, such as the GNU debugger (gdb), for multi-threaded programs.

In our prototype for POSIX compliant systems, we have chosen the third option: we execute the SUT within a gdb session and we use the gdb to switch between the different threads in a controlled way. We rely on two features of gdb (thus, out approach can be applied to any other debugger with similar features), namely: 1. the possibility to attach to break points in the object code scripting code that is executed if a break point is reached and 2. the complete control of the threading, i.e., gdb allows to switch explicitly between threads while ensuring that only the currently active thread is executed (using the option `set scheduler-locking on`).

This approach has the advantage that we neither need to modify the SUT nor do we need to develop a custom scheduler. We only need to generate a configuration for controlling the debugger. The necessary gdb command file is generated automatically by HOL-Testgen based on a mapping of the abstract thread switching points to break points in the object code. The break points at the entry points allows us to control the thread creation, while the remaining break points allow us to control the switching between threads. Thus, we only need the SUT compiled in debugging mode and this mapping. In this sense, we still have a "black-box" testing approach.

Moreover, Using gdb together with `taskset`, we ensure that all threads are executed on the same core; in our application, we can accept that the actual execution in gdb changes the timing behavior. Moreover, we assume a sequential memory model, so our approach does not cover TLB-related race conditions occurring in multi-core CPU's.

5 Conclusion

Related Work. There is a wealth of approaches for tests of behavioral models; they differ in the underlying modeling technique, the testability and test hypothesis', the test conformance relation etc.; in Sect. 2 we mention a few. Unfortunately, many works make the underlying testability hypothesis' not explicit which makes a direct comparison difficult and somewhat vague. For the space of testability assumptions used here (the system is input-output deterministic, is adequately modeled as underspecified deterministic system, synchronous coupling between tester and SUT suffices), to the best of our knowledge, our approach is unique in its integrated process from theory, modeling, symbolic execution down to test-driver generation.

With respect to the test-driver approach, this work undeniably owes a lot Microsoft's CHESS project [15], which promoted the idea to actually control the scheduler of real systems and use partial-order reduction techniques to test systematically concurrent executions for races in applications of realistic size (e.g., IE, Firefox, Apache). For our approach, controlling the scheduler is the key to justify the presentation of the system as underspecified-deterministic transition function.

Conclusion and Future Work. We see several conceptual and practical advantages of a *monadic approach* to sequence testing:

1. a monadic approach resists the tendency to surrender to finitism and constructivism at the first-best opportunity; a tendency that is understandably wide-spread in model-checking communities,
2. it provides a sensible shift from syntax to semantics: instead of a first-order, intentional view in *nodes* and *events* in automata, the heart of the calculus is on *computations* and their *compositions*,
3. the monadic theory models explicitly the difference between input and output, between data under control of the tester and results under control of the SUT,
4. the theory lends itself for a theoretical and practical framework of numerous conformance notions, even non-standard ones, and which gives
5. ways to new calculi of symbolic evaluation enabling symbolic states (via invariants) and input events (via constraints) as well as a seamless, theoretically founded transition from system models to test-drivers.

We see several directions for future work: On the model level, the formal theory of sequence testing (as given in the HOL-TestGen library theories

`Monad.thy` and `TestRefinements.thy`) providing connections between monads, rules for test-driver optimization, different test refinements, etc., is worth further development. On a test-theoretical level, our approach provides the basis for a comparison on test-methods, in particular ones based on different testability hypothesis'.

Pragmatically, our test driver setup needs to be modified to be executable on the PikeOS system level. For this end, we will need to develop a host-target setup (see Sect. 4). Finally, we are interested in extending our techniques to actually test information flow properties; since error-codes in applications may reveal internal information of partitions (as, for example, the number of its tasks and threads), this seems to be a rewarding target. For this purpose, not only action sequences need to be generated during the constraint solving process, but also (abstract) VMITs.

Acknowledgement. This work was partially supported by the Euro-MILS project funded by the European Union's Programme [FP7/2007-2013] under grant agreement number ICT-318353.

References

1. Hierons, R.M., Bowen, J.P., Harman, M. (eds.): FORTEST. LNCS, vol. 4949. Springer, Heidelberg (2008)
2. Brucker, A.D., Wolff, B.: Test-sequence generation with Hol-TestGen with an application to firewall testing. In: Gurevich, Y., Meyer, B. (eds.) TAP 2007. LNCS, vol. 4454, pp. 149–168. Springer, Heidelberg (2007)
3. Brucker, A.D., Wolff, B.: HOL-TESTGEN: an interactive test-case generation framework. In: Chechik, M., Wirsing, M. (eds.) FASE 2009. LNCS, vol. 5503, pp. 417–420. Springer, Heidelberg (2009)
4. Brucker, A.D., Wolff, B.: On theorem prover-based testing. Formal Aspects Comput. **25**, 683–721 (2012)
5. Brucker, A.D., Feliachi, A., Nemouchi, Y., Wolff, B.: Test program generation for a microprocessor. In: Veanes, M., Viganò, L. (eds.) TAP 2013. LNCS, vol. 7942, pp. 76–95. Springer, Heidelberg (2013)
6. Ponce de León, H., Haar, S., Longuet, D.: Conformance relations for labeled event structures. In: Brucker, A.D., Julliand, J. (eds.) TAP 2012. LNCS, vol. 7305, pp. 83–98. Springer, Heidelberg (2012)
7. Euro-Mils. http://www.euromils.eu/
8. Feliachi, A., Gaudel, M.-C., Wenzel, M., Wolff, B.: The *Circus* testing theory revisited in Isabelle/HOL. In: Groves, L., Sun, J. (eds.) ICFEM 2013. LNCS, vol. 8144, pp. 131–147. Springer, Heidelberg (2013)
9. Gill, A.: Introduction to the Theory of Finite-State Machines. McGraw-Hill, New York (1962)
10. Härtig, H., Hohmuth, M., Liedtke, J., Schönberg, S., Wolter, J.: The performance of microkernel-based systems. In: SOSP (1997)
11. Klein, G., Elphinstone, K., Heiser, G., Andronick, J., Cock, D., Derrin, P., Elkaduwe, D., Engelhardt, K., Kolanski, R., Norrish, M., Sewell, T., Tuch, H., Winwood, S.: seL4: formal verification of an OS kernel. In: SOSP, pp. 207–220 (2009)

12. Liedtke, J.: On μ-kernel construction. SOSP **29**(5), 237–250 (1995)
13. Lynch, N., Tuttle, M.: An introduction to input/output automata. CWI-Quart. **2**(3), 219–246 (1989)
14. Common criteria for information technology security evaluation. http://www.commoncriteriaportal.org/
15. Musuvathi, M., Qadeer, S., Ball, T.: Chess: a systematic testing tool for concurrent software. Technical report MSR-TR-2007-149, Microsoft Research (2007)
16. Nipkow, T., Paulson, L.C., Wenzel, M. (eds.): Isabelle/HOL. LNCS, vol. 2283. Springer, Heidelberg (2002)
17. Shan Lu, W.J., Zhou, Y.: A study of interleaving coverage criteria. In: ESEC-FSE Companion, pp. 533–536 (2007)
18. SYSGO: Pikeos. http://www.sysgo.com/products/pikeos-rtos-and-virtualization-concept/
19. SYSGO: PikeOS Fundamentals. SYSGO (2013)
20. SYSGO: PikeOS Kernel. SYSGO (2013)
21. Tretmans, J.: Model based testing with labelled transition systems. In: Hierons, R.M., Bowen, J.P., Harman, M. (eds.) FORTEST. LNCS, vol. 4949, pp. 1–38. Springer, Heidelberg (2008)
22. Wadler, P.: Comprehending monads. Math. Struct. Comput. Sci. **2**(4), 461–493 (1992)
23. Zhu, H., Hall, P.A.V., May, J.H.R.: Software unit test coverage and adequacy. ACM Comput. Surv. (CSUR) **29**(4), 366–427 (1997)

Pseudo-Random Number Generator Verification: A Case Study

Felix Dörre and Vladimir Klebanov[✉]

Karlsruhe Institute of Technology (KIT),
Am Fasanengarten 5, 76131 Karlsruhe, Germany
felix.doerre@student.kit.edu, klebanov@kit.edu

Abstract. In 2013, a monetarily moderate but widely noted bitcoin theft drew attention to a flaw in Android's pseudo random number generator (PRNG). A programming error affecting the information flow in the seeding code of the generator has weakened the security of the cryptographic protocol behind bitcoin transactions.

We demonstrate that logic-based verification can be efficiently applied to safeguard against this particular class of vulnerabilities, which are very difficult to detect otherwise. As a technological vehicle, we use the KeY verification system for Java. We show how to specify PRNG seeding with information flow contracts from the KeY's extension to the Java Modeling Language (JML) and report our experiences in verifying the actual implementation.

1 Introduction

In 2013 a security incident [3] resulting in theft of bitcoin gained significant public attention. While the total monetary damage was at \$5700 relatively modest, the ease and low risk of attack were notable. The perpetrators were never identified, and the exact circumstances of the attack remain to a degree speculation. Yet, the attack promptly raised public awareness of a vulnerability in the implementation of the pseudo-random number generator (PRNG) in Android [13]. Soon thereafter, Google replaced the Android PRNG.

The vulnerability in question is an instance of the "squandered entropy" problem, where entropy (i.e., information difficult to guess for an attacker) flows from a source to a destination, and some or all of it is lost (i.e., replaced by a constant or predictable value) underway due to a programming error. Concretely, out of 20 byte of entropy requested from the OS kernel to seed the PRNG, 12 did not reach the generator's internal state, significantly diminishing the quality of the PRNG output. This kind of problem is difficult to detect (as explained later on) and reoccurs periodically. Other notable instances include the Debian weak key disaster [5] (PRNG broken for two years), or the recent FreeBSD-current PRNG incident [7] (PRNG broken for four months), but there are also many others.

So far, entropy squandering is typically detected by manual code inspection, as, e.g., in [13]. With this paper, we present the first, to our knowledge, case

© Springer International Publishing Switzerland 2016
A. Gurfinkel and S.A. Seshia (Eds.): VSTTE 2015, LNCS 9593, pp. 61–72, 2016.
DOI: 10.1007/978-3-319-29613-5_4

study on formally verifying the implementation of a real-world PRNG.[1] We show that absence of entropy squandering can be efficiently specified (in terms of information flow) and practically verified with current deductive verification technology. In fact, we argue that formal verification is the tool of choice for addressing the problem.

We have chosen the above-mentioned Android PRNG as the subject of the case study as it allows us to illustrate how code verification can protect against bugs that have indeed occurred in the wild. On the technical side, the PRNG is implemented in Java, while we have experience in verification of Java programs.

The Bitcoin Theft Incident. The presumed genesis of the attack is as follows. Bitcoin operates a public database of all transactions, the *block chain*. Each transaction is cryptographically signed by its initiator using the ECDSA scheme [8]. Creating ECDSA signatures requires a per-transaction nonce. Partial predictability of nonces allows for attacks like [14], but using the same nonce for two transactions signed by the same key—which is what probably happened—constitutes a catastrophic security failure. Anyone can easily identify this case from the information recorded in the block chain, reconstruct the victim's private key, and divert their money to a bitcoin address of choice. No intrusion into the victim's system is necessary. A loss of seed entropy in the PRNG used for generating nonces increases the probability of the breach.

2   Inner Workings of the Android PRNG

The origin of the Android PRNG lies in the Apache Harmony project, a clean room reimplementation of the Java Core Libraries under the Apache License. The PRNG was part of the Android platform up to and including Android 4.1. The PRNG consists of the main class `org.apache.harmony.security.provider.crypto.SHA1PRNG_SecureRandomImpl` and the auxiliary class `SHA1Impl`.

Overall size of the PRNG is slightly over 300 LOC, though not all functionality was exercised in this case study. The code is monolithic, dense, and hard to follow. There are many comments, but these use jittering terminology, are not always clear, and are at times inconsistent with the code. The description in [13] was instrumental in facilitating our understanding of the implementation.

The main PRNG method `engineNextBytes(byte[] bytes)`, shown schematically in Listing 1.1, fills the caller-supplied array `bytes` with pseudo-random bytes. The PRNG operates in cycles, each cycle generating 20 pseudo-random bytes. If the caller requests more bytes, several cycles are performed; if the caller requests fewer bytes, the surplus generated bytes are stored for later usage.

The main component of the PRNG state is an `int[]` array of length 87, somewhat inappropriately named `seed` (Fig. 1). The front part of this array is populated with the externally-provided entropy (i.e., the actual seed). The PRNG can either be seeded manually by calling `setSeed()` or automatically.

---

[1] Artifacts available at http://formal.iti.kit.edu/~klebanov/pubs/vstte2015/.

In the latter case, the PRNG is seeded with 20 byte of entropy requested from the OS kernel on first invocation of `engineNextBytes()` (Listing 1.1, line 6). This so-called *self-seeding* mode was typically considered preferable as less error-prone, and it is indeed the scenario we are considering here.[2]

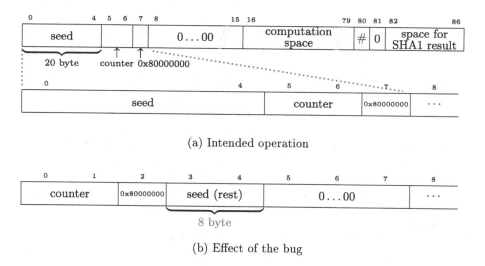

(a) Intended operation

(b) Effect of the bug

Fig. 1. Structure of the Android PRNG's main array (1 word = 1 `int` = 4 bytes)

In cycle k, the pseudo-random bytes are computed as the pseudo-SHA-1 hash of the seed (words 0–4 in Fig. 1a) concatenated with the cycle counter k (as a 64-bit integer in words 5–6). The computation (Listing 1.1, line 17) makes use of the scratch space in words 16–79, and its result is stored in words 82–86. The latter are subsequently unpacked into bytes that form the output of the cycle. The computed hash is not quite the standard SHA-1 hash, as only in cycle zero, the initialization vector defined in the SHA-1 standard is used. In a cycle $k > 0$, the initialization vector is formed by the 20 pseudo-random bytes generated in cycle $k - 1$.

To compute the hash, the seed and the cycle counter have to be suffixed by a standard-defined SHA-1 padding. Now, the PRNG keeps track of the length of the seed in word 80. The essence of the vulnerability is that a stale value of this length (i.e., zero) is used after initializing the seed in the self-seeding mode.[3] As a consequence, the cycle counter and the SHA-1 padding constant overwrite words 0–2, leaving only two words of the original seed (Fig. 1b). The effective inflow of entropy into the PRNG amounts thus to 8 instead of 20 bytes.[4]

---

[2] Google changed its stance on this matter several times, as the PRNG implementation was updated. As far as we are aware, self-seeding is the recommended mode again.

[3] There are more irregularities in the padding code, but they are irrelevant here.

[4] The PRNG also contains a native backup component in case the kernel does not provide an entropy source. Incidentally, this component contained two more instances of entropy squandering, though these were much simpler technically.

3   Information Flow Verification with the KeY System

The KeY Verification System. The case study has been carried out using the KeY deductive verification system for Java [1,9]. The reasons for choosing KeY are our familiarity with it due to our involvement with its development, good programming language support (KeY supports, for instance, 100 % of the Java Card standard), as well as a frontend for specifying information flow in programs. On the other hand, the approach that we apply is not tool-specific and could be reenacted with another deductive verification system.

The frontend of KeY takes as input a Java program annotated in the Java Modeling Language (JML) [12]. The backend is a theorem prover for *Dynamic Logic* (DL), which can be seen as a generalization of Hoare logic. Reasoning about programs is based on symbolic execution. Proof construction is guided by the user via program annotations and/or interacting with the prover GUI. All proof steps are recorded and can be inspected via an explicit proof object.

For loop- and recursion-free programs, symbolic execution is performed in a fully automated manner. Loops can either be unrolled or abstracted by a user-provided loop invariant. Similarly, method calls can be handled either by inlining the method body or by abstracting with a user-provided method specification. All user-provided abstractions are machine-checked for soundness.

Going beyond functional properties, KeY supports a language for specifying information flow in programs as part of its JML* extension of JML. The language was originally published in [16] though we refer the interested reader to the more up-to-date information source [15] for details.

$$\langle contract \rangle \quad ::= \text{determines } \langle determinandum \rangle \text{ \textbackslash by } \langle determinans \rangle \text{ ;}$$

$$\langle determinandum \rangle \quad ::= \langle expr\_seq \rangle \mid \text{\textbackslash pre}(\langle expr\_seq \rangle) \mid \text{\textbackslash post}(\langle expr\_seq \rangle)$$

$$\langle determinans \rangle \quad ::= \langle expr\_seq \rangle \mid \text{\textbackslash pre}(\langle expr\_seq \rangle) \mid \text{\textbackslash post}(\langle expr\_seq \rangle)$$

$$\langle expr\_seq \rangle \quad ::= \text{\textbackslash nothing} \mid \langle expression \rangle \mid \langle expression \rangle , \langle expr\_seq \rangle$$

where $\langle expression \rangle$ is an arbitrary JML expression (i.e., term or formula)

Fig. 2. Concrete grammar for information flow contracts in JML*

Specifying Information Flow with JML*. The main instrument for specifying information flow in JML* is an *information flow contract*. The contract can be attached—among other things—to method declarations, and its grammar is shown in Fig. 2.

Definition 1 (Semantics of information flow contracts). *Let m be a terminating sequential method with an attached information flow contract. Let (ds_i) and (dm_j) be the expression sequences of the determinans and the determinandum of the contract respectively. Let (s^a_{pre}, s^a_{post}) and (s^b_{pre}, s^b_{post}) be a pair of runs of the method m, where s^a_{pre} and s^b_{pre} are the initial (or pre) states and s^a_{post} and s^b_{post} are the final (or post) states respectively. The method m satisfies*

*the attached information flow contract, iff for each such pair of runs, the coincid-
ing evaluation of the determinans in both runs implies the coinciding evaluation
of the determinandum:*

$$\bigwedge_i\left((ds_i \ in \ s_x^a) = (ds_i \ in \ s_x^b)\right) \rightarrow \bigwedge_j\left((dm_j \ in \ s_y^a) = (dm_j \ in \ s_y^b)\right) \ ,$$

*where $x, y \in \{pre, post\}$ according to the state designators wrapping the determi-
nans and determinandum respectively. In absence of explicit state designators,
the defaults $x = pre$ and $y = post$ are used.*

For example, the specification

```
//@ determines \result \by l1, l2;
int f(int h, int l1, int l2) { ... }
```

says that the return value of the method f is completely determined by the
method parameters l1 and l2. This means that no information flows from the
method parameter h (or other data on the heap) to the return value of f. Note
that since it is not stated otherwise, the determinans l1, l2 is evaluated in
the initial state, while the determinandum is evaluated in the final state. This
convention follows the original design goal of JML* in specifying *absence* of
undesired information flow in programs.

More interesting for our purposes is the specification

```
//@ determines \pre(h) \by \post(\result);                    (*)
int f(int h) { ... }
```

describing, in a sense, the opposite situation. It is fulfilled when knowing the
result of f is sufficient to reconstruct the (initial) value of the parameter h.
Mathematically, this case amounts to injectivity of f and means intuitively that
the complete information contained in h flows to the return value. Contrary
to the JML* defaults, the explicit state designators \pre() and \post() force
the determinans to be evaluated in the final state and the determinandum in
the initial state. We have extended JML* with these designators specifically on
occasion of this case study.

In case one needs to speak about array content in contracts, the finite
sequence comprehensions of JML* allow this easily. For example, the JML* comprehension expression (\seq_def int i; 0; a.length; a[i]) is essentially a
shorthand for the expression sequence a[0],...,a[a.length-1] (for presentation in this paper, we also use the notation a[*] for this particular sequence).

Proof Obligations for Information Flow. To prove information flow contracts, KeY formalizes the condition of Definition 1 in Dynamic Logic. The formalization follows self-composition style and is straight-forward. The (schematic)
proof obligation for a contract like (*) is

$$\forall h^a, h^b. \ f(h^a) = f(h^b) \rightarrow h^a = h^b \ .$$

We refer the interested reader to [15,17] for details of the formalization in Dynamic Logic. The important fact is that information flow contracts of the callee method can be used—just like functional contracts—when verifying the caller method.

Listing 1.1. The main PRNG method (schematic)

```
1  void
2  engineNextBytes(byte[] bytes) {
3    ...
4    if (state == UNDEFINED) {
5      // entropy source
6      updateSeed(
7        RandomBitsSupplier
8          .getRandomBits(20));
9      ...
10   } else { ... }
11
12   ...
13
14   for (;;) {
15     ...
16     // entropy target
17     SHA1Impl.computeHash(seed);
18     ...
19   }
20 }
```

Listing 1.2. Modified source with top-level requirement specification (excerpt)

```
1  /*@
2    requires counter == 0;
3    requires state == UNDEFINED;
4
5    requires bytes.length == 20;
6    requires extSource.length == 20;
7
8    determines \pre (extSource[*])
9          \by \post(bytes[*]);
10 */
11 void
12 engineNextBytes(byte[] bytes,
13               byte[] extSource) {
14   ...
15   if (state == UNDEFINED) {
16     updateSeed(extSource);
17     ...
18   } else ...
19   ...
20 }
```

Listing 1.3. Specification of the pseudo-SHA1 method

```
1  /*@ public normal_behavior
2    requires arrW.length==87;
3    assignable arrW[16..79],arrW[82..86];
4    determines \pre ((\seq_def int i;  0;  5; arrW[i]))
5          \by \post((\seq_def int i; 82; 87; arrW[i]));
6  */
7  static void computeHash(int[] arrW) {...}
```

4   PRNG Specification and Correctness Proof

4.1   The Specification and Problems Attaching It

To show full flow of entropy (i.e., absence of squandering), we are instantiating the specification pattern (∗) for the main PRNG method shown in Listing 1.1.

Our original intent was to show that the entropy returned by the call to the RandomBitsSupplier.getRandomBits() method in line 7 of Listing 1.1 (the source) is preserved at least until the call to the SHA1Impl.computeHash() method in line 17 (the target). The problem is that the source is nested within another method call expression that is itself nested within an if-statement, while the target occurs in the middle of a loop body. Specification languages like

JML are, in contrast, designed to specify programs in a mostly block-structured way, i.e., pre- and postconditions can only be attached to complete blocks, loops, method declarations, etc. Facilities for point-to-point specification are less developed. To overcome this obstacle, we resorted to a minor source code modification as well as to extending the verified property as outlined in the following.

The Source. We removed the call to `RandomBitsSupplier.getRandomBits()` in line 7 and replaced it by an extra parameter `extSource`, which allows us to speak about the inflowing entropy in the method specification. The modified source is shown in Listing 1.2. The precondition `state == UNDEFINED` states that the PRNG is indeed in self-seeding mode. For the sake of clarity, we are not showing a few more trivial preconditions stating that the PRNG object is initially in a consistent state (fields are initialized with default values, etc.). These preconditions stem from (separate) symbolic execution of the object constructor.

The Target. We solve the problem with the inaccessible entropy target by stating a postcondition on the *whole* method. In other words, we are specifying not only that the 20 byte of entropy in `extSource` are safely transferred into the internal state of the PRNG but that they are contained in the 20 byte of output returned to the caller, which is a stronger property.

The Hash. The above strengthening also causes a complication: the call to `SHA1Impl.computeHash()` is now in the code path. Due to the (intended) computational complexity of SHA-1, it is not practicable to reason about this method either by inlining its code or stating a faithful functional specification. In contrast, it is possible to give an information flow specification, which can be used for the proof of `engineNextBytes()`.

We assume (but do not prove) the specification of `SHA1Impl.computeHash()` shown in Listing 1.3, stating that the method transfers all information (i.e., is injective) from the first five words of the main array into the last five words. While we do not know if this assumption is true (as disproving it would amount to finding a collision in SHA-1), it constitutes a fundamental proviso for the security of the PRNG. Unsurprisingly, proof inspection showed that it was indeed not disproved. A similar, if more obviously justifiable, contract was used for the sole standard library method used by the PRNG, `System.arraycopy()`.

4.2   The Proof

The vulnerability is unmissable when attempting the proof, so the following remarks apply to the fixed implementation incorporating the official patch.

The main proof consists of 21 882 proof steps, of which 95 were interactive. The majority of the latter are carrying out case distinctions, splitting the equality of sequences into five equalities over words and 20 over bytes. The rest are for weakening the proof goal to eliminate irrelevant information and reduce the search space, as well as applications of rules for byte packing and unpacking (see below). The automated proof search took altogether 45 min to complete the proof. All loops in the main code were unrolled (thus

also establishing termination), no invariants or auxiliary annotations were necessary. Trivial invariants were used to prove termination and assignable clause
of SHA1Impl.computeHash().

A significant portion of proof complexity stems from the code packing bytes
into words and a later converse unpacking. Figure 3 shows the code factored for
exposition purposes as synthetic methods. For the proof, we have defined two
custom rules that express the injectivity of these code fragments. The soundness
of the rules has been proven using KeY's rule justification mechanism and the
KeY's SMT bridge to Z3/CVC4 (the only place where an external SMT solver
was used). Each rule was applied five times, once for each word of the seed.

```
1  int pack(byte[] b) { return
2    ((b[0]&0xFF)<<24) | ((b[1]&0xFF)<<16) | ((b[2]&0xFF)<<8) | (b[3]&0xFF);}
3
4  byte[] unpack(int i) { return new byte[] {
5    (byte)(i>>>24), (byte)(i>>>16), (byte)(i>>>8), (byte)i };}
```

Fig. 3. Packing and unpacking code (illustration)

The KeY logic is based on the theory of integers and not bitvectors. To achieve
soundness, proof rules either generate proof obligations showing absence of overflow, or perform operations modulo machine integer range. The former option
was used for the majority of the code, while the latter option was necessary to
handle the packing and unpacking code.

5   Alternatives and Related Work

Functional Verification and Testing. Of course, it is possible to state and
verify a functional specification of the methods involved without resorting to
the concept of information flow. However, such a specification would have to
closely mimic the implementation and thus be complex and tedious to write
(the same reasoning also applies to functional testing). It would be difficult
to understand it and ascertain its adequacy; neither would it be possible to
reuse it for another PRNG. It would also be challenging to write down such a
specification in existing languages due to the structure of the code (see Sect. 4.1).
The information flow specification, on the other hand, directly expresses the
desired property, is compact and easy to understand, and is nearly independent
of the PRNG implementation in question.

Statistical Testing. Several statistical test suites exist for assessing the quality
of random numbers. Among the most popular are DIEHARD with its open
source counterpart DIEHARDER and the NIST test suite. The suites scan a
stream of pseudo-random numbers for certain predefined distribution anomalies.
At the same time, we are not aware of recommendations on how the stream is
to be produced. In practice, it appears customary to derive the stream from

a single seed. The tests are repeated multiple times (with different seeds) to increase the degree of confidence but the results between individual runs are not cross-correlated. In any case, distinguishing a PRNG seeded with 8 byte of entropy from a PRNG seeded with 20 byte of entropy would likely require a prohibitively high number of tests.

Quantitative Information Flow Analysis (QIF). Detecting entropy squandering can be seen as an instance of the Quantitative Information Flow problem (QIF) concerned with measuring leakage of secret information to an observer of the program output. Several methods and tools for QIF exist, including our own work [10,11]. Yet, the landscape of available QIF analyses is not well-suited for the specifics of the problem we face. Some techniques are only practicable for small leakage, or small/simple programs. Some are not implemented or do not support real-world programming languages. Some only establish upper bounds on the leakage, while we need lower bounds, as our observer is not an adversary. Given these limitations, the prospects of using current QIF techniques for practical PRNG verification remain unclear at best.

High-level PRNG Analysis. Apart from the above-mentioned [13], "modern" PRNGs have been studied in, e.g., [2,4,6]. The perspective taken in the latter works is based on elaborate attack models, where the attacker, for instance, can control the distribution of the inputs used to seed the PRNG, view or even corrupt the internal PRNG state. The analysis focuses primarily on design and high-level implementation aspects w.r.t. these models and is not mechanized. In contrast, we do not consider attackers with advanced capabilities, but our work closes the gap concerning low-level implementation aspects with mechanized reasoning.

6   Conclusions

A good design document and a high-level analysis are indispensable for a correct PRNG, but so is low-level verification. The problem of squandered entropy due to subtle code bugs is real and relevant, yet very difficult to detect by conventional means. At the same time, a concise and uniform specification of correctness can be given in terms of information flow. The JML* specification language proved its convenience in this regard.

Logic-based information flow reasoning is the tool of choice for PRNG verification, as other techniques (e.g., type systems, PDGs, etc.) inherently incorporate overapproximations that make them unsuitable. The correctness proofs are conceptually quite simple, and do not require ingenuity, but the complexity and monolithic nature of the code tax the verification system to a significant degree.

A large part of our effort went to understanding the details of the implementation. Besides referring to higher-level descriptions such as [4,13], we found verification technology in general (for establishing data footprints of code segments) and symbolic execution in particular (for identifying dead code on a given path) very helpful in this regard. While it is hard to quantify the total effort spent on the case study due to a learning process that occurred over a longer period of time, we conjecture that we could now verify a comparable PRNG within one or a few days.[5]

A   Source Code of the Android PRNG (Excerpt)

Source code below has been slightly edited for presentation purposes. Comments are removed. Constant declarations are elided or inlined. Code unreachable in the verification scenario presented in the paper is elided.

```
1   public class SHA1PRNG_SecureRandomImpl implements SHA1_Data {
2
3       private transient int[] seed;
4       private transient byte[] nextBytes;
5       private transient int nextBIndex;
6       private transient long counter;
7       private transient int state;
8
9       public SHA1PRNG_SecureRandomImpl() { ... }
10
11      protected synchronized void engineNextBytes(byte[] bytes) {
12
13          int i, n;
14          long bits;
15          int nextByteToReturn;
16          int lastWord;
17          final int extrabytes = 7;
18
19          if (bytes == null) throw new NullPointerException("bytes␣==␣null");
20
21          lastWord = seed[81] == 0 ? 0 : (seed[81] + extrabytes) >> 3 - 1;
22
23          if (state == UNDEFINED) {
24
25              updateSeed(RandomBitsSupplier.getRandomBits(20));
26              nextBIndex = 20;
27
28              // official patch for the vulnerability
29              lastWord = seed[81] == 0 ? 0 : (seed[81] + extrabytes) >> 3 - 1;
30
31          } else if (state == SET_SEED) { ... }
32          state = NEXT_BYTES;
33
34          if (bytes.length == 0) return;
35
36          nextByteToReturn = 0;
37
38          n = (20 - nextBIndex) < (bytes.length - nextByteToReturn) ?
39                  20 - nextBIndex :
40                  bytes.length - nextByteToReturn;
41          if (n > 0) { ... }
42
43          if (nextByteToReturn >= bytes.length) return;
44
45          n = seed[81] & 0x03;
46          for (;;) {
47              if (n == 0) {
48
49                  // the problem occurs here
50                  seed[lastWord    ] = (int) (counter >>> 32);
51                  seed[lastWord + 1] = (int) (counter & 0xFFFFFFFF);
52                  seed[lastWord + 2] = END_FLAGS[0];
53
54              } else { ... }
55              if (seed[81] > 48) { ... }
56
57              SHA1Impl.computeHash(seed);
58
59              if (seed[81] > 48) { ... }
60              counter++;
61
62              int j = 0;
```

[5] This work was in part supported by the German National Science Foundation (DFG) under the priority programme 1496 "Reliably Secure Software Systems – RS3." The authors would like to thank Christoph Scheben for help with the proof system, and Bernhard Beckert, Mattias Ulbrich, and Sylvain Ruhault for comments on the topic.

```
63              for (i = 0; i < 5; i++) {
64                  int k = seed[82 + i];
65                  nextBytes[j    ] = (byte) (k >>> 24);
66                  nextBytes[j + 1] = (byte) (k >>> 16);
67                  nextBytes[j + 2] = (byte) (k >>> 8);
68                  nextBytes[j + 3] = (byte) (k);
69                  j += 4;
70              }
71
72              nextBIndex = 0;
73              j = 20 < (bytes.length - nextByteToReturn) ?
74                  20 : bytes.length - nextByteToReturn;
75
76              if (j > 0) {
77                  System.arraycopy(nextBytes, 0, bytes, nextByteToReturn, j);
78                  nextByteToReturn += j;
79                  nextBIndex += j;
80              }
81
82              if (nextByteToReturn >= bytes.length) break;
83          }
84      }
85
86      private void updateSeed(byte[] bytes) {
87          SHA1Impl.updateHash(seed, bytes, 0, bytes.length - 1);
88          seedLength += bytes.length;
89      }
90  }
91
92  public class SHA1Impl implements SHA1_Data {
93
94      static void computeHash(int[] arrW) { /* elided for brevity */ }
95
96      static void updateHash(int[] intArray, byte[] byteInput, int fromByte, int toByte) {
97
98          int index = intArray[81];
99          int i = fromByte;
100         int maxWord;
101         int nBytes;
102
103         int wordIndex = index >>2;
104         int byteIndex = index & 0x03;
105
106         intArray[81] = ( index + toByte - fromByte + 1 ) & 077 ;
107
108         if ( byteIndex != 0 ) { ... }
109
110         maxWord = (toByte - i + 1) >> 2;
111
112         for ( int k = 0; k < maxWord ; k++ ) {
113
114             intArray[wordIndex] = (((int) byteInput[i    ] & 0xFF) <<24 ) |
115                                   (((int) byteInput[i + 1] & 0xFF) <<16 ) |
116                                   (((int) byteInput[i + 2] & 0xFF) <<8  ) |
117                                   (((int) byteInput[i + 3] & 0xFF)      ) ;
118             i += 4;
119             wordIndex++;
120
121             if ( wordIndex >= 16 ) { ... }
122         }
123
124         nBytes = toByte - i +1;
125         if ( nBytes != 0 ) { ... }
126     }
127 }
```

References

1. Ahrendt, W., et al.: The KeY platform for verification and analysis of Java programs. In: Giannakopoulou, D., Kroening, D. (eds.) VSTTE 2014. LNCS, vol. 8471, pp. 55–71. Springer, Heidelberg (2014)
2. Barak, B., Halevi, S.: A model and architecture for pseudo-random generation with applications to /dev/random. In: Proceedings of the 12th ACM Conference on Computer and Communications Security, CCS 2005, pp. 203–212. ACM (2005)
3. Bitcoin.org. Android security vulnerability (2013). https://bitcoin.org/en/alert/2013-08-11-android
4. Cornejo, M., Ruhault, S.: Characterization of real-life PRNGs under partial state corruption. In: Proceedings of the ACM SIGSAC Conference on Computer and Communications Security, CCS 2014, pp. 1004–1015. ACM (2014)

5. Debian Weak Key Vulnerability. CVE-2008-0166 (2008). https://cve.mitre.org/cgi-bin/cvename.cgi?name=CVE-2008-0166

6. Dodis, Y., Pointcheval, D., Ruhault, S., Vergniaud, D., Wichs, D.: Security analysis of pseudo-random number generators with input: /dev/random is not robust. In: Proceedings of the ACM SIGSAC Conference on Computer and Communications Security, CCS 2013, pp. 647–658. ACM (2013)

7. Gurney, J.-M.: URGENT: RNG broken for last 4 months (2015). https://lists.freebsd.org/pipermail/freebsd-current/2015-February/054580.html

8. Johnson, D., Menezes, A., Vanstone, S.: The elliptic curve digital signature algorithm (ECDSA). Int. J. Inf. Secur. 1(1), 36–63 (2001)

9. The KeY Tool. www.key-project.org

10. Klebanov, V.: Precise quantitative information flow analysis - a symbolic approach. Theoret. Comput. Sci. **538**, 124–139 (2014)

11. Klebanov, V., Manthey, N., Muise, C.: SAT-based analysis and quantification of information flow in programs. In: Joshi, K., Siegle, M., Stoelinga, M., D'Argenio, P.R. (eds.) QEST 2013. LNCS, vol. 8054, pp. 177–192. Springer, Heidelberg (2013)

12. Leavens, G.T., Baker, A.L., Ruby, C.: Preliminary design of JML: a behavioral interface specification language for Java. SIGSOFT Softw. Eng. Notes **31**(3), 1–38 (2006)

13. Michaelis, K., Meyer, C., Schwenk, J.: Randomly failed! the state of randomness in current Java implementations. In: Dawson, E. (ed.) CT-RSA 2013. LNCS, vol. 7779, pp. 129–144. Springer, Heidelberg (2013)

14. Nguyen, P.Q., Shparlinski, I.E.: The insecurity of the elliptic curve digital signature algorithm with partially known nonces. Des. Codes Crypt. **30**(2), 201–217 (2003)

15. Scheben, C.: Program-level specification and deductive verification of security properties. Ph.D. thesis, Karlsruhe Institute of Technology (2014)

16. Scheben, C., Schmitt, P.H.: Verification of information flow properties of Java programs without approximations. In: Beckert, B., Damiani, F., Gurov, D. (eds.) FoVeOOS 2011. LNCS, vol. 7421, pp. 232–249. Springer, Heidelberg (2012)

17. Scheben, C., Schmitt, P.H.: Efficient self-composition for weakest precondition calculi. In: Jones, C., Pihlajasaari, P., Sun, J. (eds.) FM 2014. LNCS, vol. 8442, pp. 579–594. Springer, Heidelberg (2014)

Inside a Verified Flash File System: Transactions and Garbage Collection

Gidon Ernst[✉], Jörg Pfähler, Gerhard Schellhorn, and Wolfgang Reif

Institute for Software and Systems Engineering,
University of Augsburg, Augsburg, Germany
{ernst,pfaehler,schellhorn,reif}@isse.de

Abstract. The work presented here addresses a long-standing conceptual gap in flash file system verification: We map an abstract graph-based representation down to the flat blocks of bytes of the storage medium. Specifically, we consider grouping of file system objects into atomic transactions together with layout, allocation and garbage collection of on-flash storage space. Two major concerns guide the design and verification: proper handling of errors and, more importantly, guaranteed recovery from unexpected power cuts. Finding *useful specifications* of intermediate interfaces to address these concerns realistically dominates the verification effort.

Keywords: Flash File Systems · Formal verification · Specification · Transactions · Garbage collection · Write buffer · KIV

1 Introduction

NASA's proposal [19] to build a verified file system (FS) for flash memory has been received with a lot of interest and has prompted a great body of work. Many file system concepts have been modeled, formalized and verified by different researchers, with varying degrees of abstraction, such as a path-based interface in [17], and a graph-based view in [8]. Most of these approaches study some selected aspects in isolation only. The inner workings of realistic flash file systems have received relatively little formal treatment in comparison to high-level concepts.

As part of our ongoing effort [26] to construct a verified flash FS,[1] we bridge the remaining conceptual gap between a high-level structured representation of file system objects towards an encoding within the erase blocks and pages of flash hardware. We present the specifications and verified implementations of two intermediate file system layers: A transactional *journal* provides atomic writes of groups of file system objects alongside free-space management by garbage collection of obsolete objects. A *persistence* layer provides the transition down to bytes, caching partial writes for efficiency. The two layers are fully integrated into

---

This work is part of the project "Verifikation von Flash-Dateisystemen" (RE828/13-1) sponsored by the Deutsche Forschungsgemeinschaft (DFG).

[1] http://isse.de/flashix.

© Springer International Publishing Switzerland 2016
A. Gurfinkel and S.A. Seshia (Eds.): VSTTE 2015, LNCS 9593, pp. 73–93, 2016.
DOI: 10.1007/978-3-319-29613-5_5

the rest of our development by mechanized proofs, conducted in the interactive verification system KIV [10].

Besides functional correctness, it is of great interest that the file system can deal with *power cuts* anytime during the run of an operation. Whenever an operation is aborted in an intermediate state, a designated recovery procedure can reconstruct a state sufficiently similar to the pre- resp. post-state of the respective operation. The journal and the persistence layer work in close cooperation to provide strong guarantees in the presence of such power cuts and similarly for nondeterministic hardware errors, which have to be taken into account as well.

Alongside the presentation of the formal models we will demonstrate that artifacts tend to leak through abstractions and interfaces, disrupting "obvious" verification approaches, even when the implementation concerns are cleanly separated. We will show how we have addressed such difficulties in this specific case study, especially focusing on power cuts.

Section 2 provides an overview of our approach and of the core concepts of flash file systems. Section 3 explains the formal models that represent the boundaries and capture the requirements for this work. Sections 4 to 7 present the formal models and some verification artifacts with the details necessary to expose several intricate aspects. Section 8 discusses related work and Sect. 9 draws insights from the verification. In summary, the contribution of this paper consists of a significant step towards a realistic, fully verified file system for flash memory.

2   Background

This section gives an overview over the project, the basic idea behind modern flash file system implementations and how the various parts of the system play together in Sect. 2.1. The formalism that backs the verification of functional correctness and power cut safety is summarized in Sect. 2.2.

2.1   Project Overview and Flash File System Concepts

This work is part of an ongoing long-term project to construct a verified, POSIX-compliant [29] file system for flash memory, taking up NASA's proposal [19]. We take the existing UBIFS [18] as a design blueprint, which realizes state-of-the-art techniques to address the inherent access limitations of flash hardware. To tackle such a complex verification task we follow an incremental, correct-by-construction approach: a top-level specification of the textual POSIX standard is gradually refined towards an implementation.

The resulting layers are (partially) visualized in Fig. 1. These correspond to the various logical parts of the file system, and to different levels of abstraction. Technically, each box represents an Abstract State Machines (ASMs) [4], which are used to encode both specifications (white) and the implementations (gray) in an operational way. The interface symbol —◉— denotes that one component uses another. Correctness is established by a series of nested refinements, depicted by dotted lines.

In the first refinement step [12,13] a formal top-level POSIX specification is broken down into generic concepts (such as path lookup) realized by a Virtual Filesystem Switch (VFS) and flash-specific concepts realized by the flash file system core. An abstract specification of the behavior of the latter decouples the two.

A POSIX-compliant file system can be thought of as a tree-like structure consisting of directories with files as leaves.[2] File and directory names are attached to the edges in the tree. As an example, Fig. 2 shows an excerpt of a typical file system hierarchy. Directories are visualized as grey circles, files as white ones. The root node at the top corresponds to the path /.

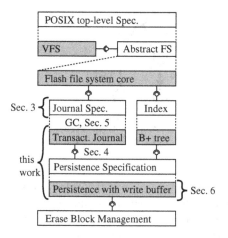

Fig. 1. System structure

The VFS decomposes the tree structure shown in Fig. 2 into three types of file system objects: One for directories and files (storing metadata, such as size, access rights and timestamps), one for directory entries (carrying a name and a reference to the target object) and one for each segment of file data. In response to each top-level POSIX operation, the VFS instructs the file system core to create, modify, or delete a number of these objects. Creating a new file /tmp/test.txt, for example, yields three updates, corresponding to the part of Fig. 2 with a dotted contour: one for the new file, one for the new directory entry, and one to update some metadata of the parent directory /tmp.

Storing these file system objects has to take into account the restricted access characteristics of flash memory already at a very high level. Flash memory is structured into erase blocks, each consisting of a number of pages. Random reads are supported, but writes must be page aligned and sequential within a block. Overwriting is not supported and space can be reclaimed by erasing whole blocks only, which is slow and physically wears out the flash memory cells over time. These difficulties are addressed incrementally by our models.

The flash file system core in Fig. 1 tackles the problem that updates need to be written out-of-place to flash. For uniformity, file system objects (and their updates) are encoded within so-called *nodes*, which are ultimately written to flash memory through the *journal* layer. An *index* (implemented as a B[+]-tree) tracks current versions of data by mapping *keys* to the respective addresses of the most recent node for a given object. The core relies on the index component to store this mapping in memory for efficient access and on flash (in an outdated version) to speed up startup time.

---

[2] With hard-links (which we support) this structure becomes an acyclic graph.

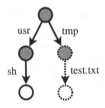

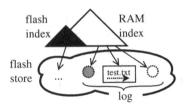

Fig. 2. File system tree, creation of /tmp/test.txt

Fig. 3. Conceptual view of the index, flash store, and log; showing the update corr. to Fig. 2.

The integration of the index and the journal is shown in Fig. 3. At the bottom the flash memory is visualized as an unstructured storage, except that "recent" writes are recorded in a sequential log. At the top, the index is shown: a current version in main memory encompasses all modifications, but there is also an outdated version stored on flash. Informally, the log corresponds exactly to the difference between the two indices. At specific points, called *commits*, the current index is stored on flash and the log is emptied.

The flash file system core thus already introduces the concepts necessary to deal efficiently with out-of-place updates and recovery from power failures (by replaying the log starting from the flash index). However, the following aspects are delegated to lower layers: the core assumes that the journal (1) can write several nodes atomically, (2) can perform a commit atomically together with the index and (3) takes the block structure and sequential writes into account. Furthermore, garbage collection is just specified abstractly, because an implementation is meaningful only once blocks are considered.

In this paper we show how this can be achieved in two steps: The transactional journal provides the atomicity of multiple updates based on blocks and includes garbage collection. The transition down to bytes is realized within the persistence layer, which in turn relies on the erase block management as a logical view of the flash hardware (which is similar to UBI [16], see [23]). It writes the nodes buffered and sequentially to flash. Additionally, atomicity of the commit and free space management is provided.

From the implementation ASMs (gray in Fig. 1) we generate executable Scala[3] code (for simulation and testing purposes) and C code, which is integrated into Linux via FUSE.[4]

2.2 Methodology

The formal foundations of our work are Abstract State Machines (ASMs) [4] and a corresponding refinement theory [3,25] with a recent extension [11] to support encapsulated submachines and the modular verification of power cuts.

---

[3] http://scala-lang.org.
[4] http://fuse.sourceforge.net.

Referring back to Fig. 1, the development follows a recurring pattern as shown on the right: an abstract model $\mathcal{A}$ is decomposed into an implementation part $\mathcal{C}$ which realizes a specific subtask, whereas some concepts remain

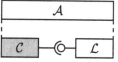

abstract, encoded by a (local) subcomponent $\mathcal{L}$. Such a hierarchical construction of systems is modular in the sense that any correct implementation of $\mathcal{L}$ can be plugged in instead without compromising the proof that $\mathcal{C}$ adheres to $\mathcal{A}$. The critical aspect wrt. power cuts is how persistent data is modeled as a not-necessarily separable part of $\mathcal{L}$.

Technically, we encode components uniformly as Abstract State Machines $\mathcal{M} = ((\mathtt{OP}_i)_{i \in I}, St, Init, Cr, \mathtt{Rec})$. These expose some operations $\mathtt{OP}_i$ as external interface, which have input and output parameters and preconditions. Operations are defined by abstract imperative programs that compute on an internal state $s : St$, with the usual constructs such as assignments, conditionals, loops, recursion, nondeterministic choice, and calls to submachines. Power cuts are specified by a crash predicate $Cr \subseteq St \times St$, subsequent recovery is implemented by the designated recovery operation $\mathtt{Rec}$. A run of an ASM starts in an initial state $s_0 : St$ with $Init(s_0)$ and repeatedly executes operations, that either terminate normally, or are interrupted in an intermediate state followed by a crash and execution of the recovery operation.

Correctness of a concrete ASM $\mathcal{C} = ((\mathtt{COP}_i)_{i \in I}, CSt, CInit, CCr, \mathtt{CRec})$ is defined not by giving a postconditions per operation, but instead in terms of another, more abstract ASM $\mathcal{A} = ((\mathtt{AOP}_i)_{i \in I}, ASt, AInit, ACr, \mathtt{ARec})$ that encodes the specification and requirements. Intuitively, $\mathcal{C}$ refines $\mathcal{A}$, if for each run of $\mathcal{C}$ there is a matching run of $\mathcal{A}$ with the same inputs and outputs. Formally, we follow the contract approach to refinement [31]. We prove refinement by forward simulation with a coupling relation $R \subseteq ASt \times CSt$ and commuting diagrams (we omit the standard proof obligations for each pair $\mathtt{COP}_i$ and $\mathtt{AOP}_i$).

On a semantic level, it is easy to integrate correctness of power cuts into the refinement approach with a small-step semantics for operations: a crashed call to a concrete operation and its recovery must be matched by a crashed call of the corresponding abstract operation and recovery. This would lead, in principle to a temporal proof obligation of the form $\Box\, crashsafe$ that must hold during the run of any $\mathtt{COP}$. Such a property would lead to a huge number of verification conditions and cannot be expressed in weakest-precondition/Hoare calculus. One can, however, express the recovery condition *in between completed operations* as a variant of the standard forward simulation condition prefixed with a crash

recovery:

$$R(as, cs) \wedge CCr(cs, cs')$$
$$\to \langle\!| \mathtt{CRec}(; cs') |\!\rangle\, (\, \exists as'.\ ACr(as, as') \wedge \langle \mathtt{ARec}(; as') \rangle\, R(as', cs')\,), \quad (1)$$

where $\langle\!| p |\!\rangle\, \varphi$ denotes the weakest precondition (total correctness) of the program p with respect to postcondition φ and $\langle p \rangle\, \varphi$ asserts the existence of some terminating execution of p satisfying φ in its final state.

Surprisingly, this property is sufficient, which can be derived on a purely semantic level given simple conditions about the concrete machine $\mathcal{C}$. This reduction exploits a close relationship between error handling and power cuts (see [21] for a similar idea): Intuitively, at the lowest level, each operation of the hardware has the possibility to fail without altering the flash memory. Conversely, all other state is in RAM and will be completely arbitrary after a crash (for a suitable definition of CCr). This means that each partial run has at least one completion that leaves the flash untouched, which implies that the crashed flash states are a subset of the final ones, reducing the verification burden to an entirely big-step setting (i.e., expressible with standard verification methodology).

This observation can be generalized to a state space of some intermediate machine that does not clearly separate flash and RAM data, which is important for flexibility in modeling. Formally, an operation $\mathtt{COP}_i$ of $\mathcal{C}$ is *crash-neutral*, if there is the possibility to postpone the effect of a crash to some final state of $\mathtt{COP}_i$, which leads to the additional proof obligation

crash-neutrality:

$$pre_{COP_i}(in, cs) \wedge CCr(cs, cs') \rightarrow \langle \mathtt{COP}_i(in; cs, out) \rangle \ CCr(cs, cs') \qquad (2)$$

For a state that is entirely in RAM, this condition is trivial, since CCr is not constrained then, i.e., admits arbitrary transitions. In practice this means that (2) must only be proved for abstract submachines $\mathcal{L}$ called by $\mathcal{C}$, which is typically easy. The formalization of this approach and the proofs are detailed in [11].

In the remainder of the paper, we use the following notational conventions: We write variables in *italic* and operations/functions/predicates in `typewriter` font. We frequently use partial functions/finite maps $f : A \nrightarrow B$. For key $a \in \mathrm{dom}(f)$ the value associated to it by f is written $f[a]$. Function override is denoted by $f[a \mapsto b]$. The assignment $f[a] := b$ abbreviates $f := f[a \mapsto b]$.

3   Formal Specification of the Journal and Index

This section presents the formal model of the journal, which defines the requirements for the work of this paper. It is based on our previous work [28]. The model reflects the limited access characteristics of flash memory. Operations presented here should be interpreted as atomic transitions, which captures the requirement of transactional behaviour to be implemented in Sect. 4. The model furthermore admits that the hardware may sporadically refuse to perform an operation. We present several invariants that can be expressed (and proved easily) at this level of abstraction and can be assumed later on for the verification of the refinement.

The abstract state is given by an unordered flash store fs and a list log of addresses that have been written to since the last commit (c.f. Fig. 3)

$$\textbf{spec var} \quad fs : Address \nrightarrow Node, \qquad log : List\langle Address \rangle.$$

The journal has an operation to read a node from flash, and operations to store groups of n nodes,[5] extending the *log*. All operations may fail nondeterministically without changing the state,[6] this can be observed with the returned error code *err* (recall that output parameters follow the semicolon). In case of success, the outputs $adr_{1...n}$ contain the addresses of the new nodes on flash, which are later stored in the index.

jnl_spec_get(adr; nd, err)

  { $nd := fs[adr]$, $err :=$ ESUCCESS }   or   { $err :=$ EFAIL }

jnl_spec_append$_n$($nd_1, \ldots, nd_n$; $adr_1, \ldots, adr_n$, err)

   { **choose** $adr_{1...n} \notin \mathbf{dom}(fs)$ distinct

    $fs := fs[adr_1 \mapsto nd_1] \cdots [adr_n \mapsto nd_n]$ $(\star)$

    $log := log + adr_1 + \cdots + adr_n$

    $err :=$ ESUCCESS }

  or { $err :=$ EFAIL }

We also need a formal model of the index (its implementation is out of scope of this paper, though). The state of the corresponding ASM maintains two maps

   spec var ri, $fi : Key \rightharpoonup Address$,

the R̲AM i̲ndex ri and the f̲lash i̲ndex fi. All operations, except commit and recovery which are explained later on, access the RAM index only. There are ASM operations to lookup, store, and remove mappings that directly refer to their algebraic counterparts, e.g.,

    idx_lookup(key; adr) { $adr := ri[key]$ }

    idx_store(key, adr)   { $ri[key] := adr$ }

    idx_remove(key)   { $ri := ri - key$ }

The system maintains several invariants, for example that the RAM index does not contain unallocated addresses; and that all addresses in the *log* are valid.

   invariant $\mathbf{ran}(ri) \subseteq \mathbf{dom}(fs)$ and $\{ adr \mid adr \in log \} \subseteq \mathbf{dom}(fs)$

Addresses $adr \notin \mathbf{ran}(ri)$ are obsolete and can be cleaned up by garbage collection (see Sect. 5). However, the index is accessible (efficiently) only by keys. Each node nd stores its respective key, denoted by $nd.key$, and thus one can equivalently check $fs[adr].key \notin \mathbf{dom}(ri)$. The induced invariant is

   invariant $\forall\ key \in ri.\ fs[ri[key]].key = key$ (3)

---

[5] A maximum group size of $n = 4$ nodes is sufficient for all operations of the FS core. Note that an entire write operation is already decomposed into fixed-size writes of individual segments by higher components.

[6] The failure case also witnesses the crash-neutral run wrt. (4) as required by (2).

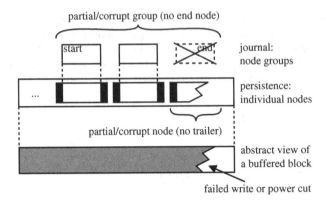

Fig. 4. Detecting partially written nodes and groups

The RAM index determines exactly, which part of the flash memory constitutes the observable file system state. However, in the event of a power cut the RAM state is lost. We model this by setting ri to an arbitrary value, without changing fs. Formally, the effect of a crash is specified by

$$Cr_{\mathrm{idx}}(ri, fi, ri', fi') \;\leftrightarrow\; fi = fi'$$
$$Cr_{\mathrm{jnl}}(fs, log, fs', log') \;\leftrightarrow\; fs = fs' \wedge log = log' \tag{4}$$

(where the overall effect is the conjunction of the two predicates). That the RAM index is truly redundant and can be recovered to its previous state after a power cut is expressed by

$$\textbf{invariant}\quad ri = \texttt{replay}(log, fi, fs), \tag{5}$$

where `replay` is part of the recovery operation `Rec` of the FS core. It traverses the log from oldest to newest and (re-)applies all missing operations to the outdated fi. As a consequence, the log must be computable by the implementation (see Fig. 10), even though it is not part of the actual concrete state.

The size of the log determines how long it takes to mount the file system initially. In order to keep the log reasonably small, a periodic commit writes the current index to flash and empties the log. This has to happen atomically, otherwise power cuts in between can lead to inconsistent states. Note that a commit trivially establishes the recovery invariant. Commit is modeled as follows:

$$\texttt{spec\_commit}()\ \{\ fi := ri,\ log := [\,]\ \}$$

4 Transactions in the Journal

The *transactional journal* layer introduces a structured view of the flash storage that takes the block structure of flash memory into account. It implements the

```
jnl_append₂(nd₁, nd₂; adr₁, adr₂, err)
  let size = size(nd₁) + size(nd₂)
  jnl_allocate(size; loghead, err)
  if err = ESUCCESS then
    persistence_add_node(loghead, gnode(nd₁, true, false); adr₁, err)
  if err = ESUCCESS then
    persistence_add_node(loghead, gnode(nd₂, false, true); adr₂, err)
  if err = ESUCCESS then
    persistence_flush(loghead, err)
  if err ≠ ESUCCESS then validhead := false
```

Fig. 5. Journal implementation to store two nodes on flash.

specification given in Sect. 3 by mapping fs to an array of blocks, each of which contains a list of nodes. The log is represented implicitly within the blocks: since blocks already give a sequential ordering for the contained nodes, it is sufficient to maintain a list of those blocks which constitute the nodes referred to by the abstract log. The main difficulty is that the journal needs to implement transactions of multiple nodes *atomically* wrt. hardware errors and power cuts, based on a (abstract specification of the) *persistence* layer that caches writes until a page boundary is reached.

In order to guarantee this atomicity, the journal groups nodes per operation. The whole group must have been written successfully in order to make a valid contribution to the observable file system state. Atomicity at the level of individual nodes is required as well, but for the sake of modularization this concept is not addressed in the journal but in the persistence layer. This approach permits the journal to treat its underlying storage as a simple sequence of nodes in contrast to a more complicated view.

Figure 4 puts the two layers in relation. A single erase block is shown at the bottom, the grey area denotes the part that has already been written to (omitting its partitioning into pages). Within the block the persistence layer stores the sequence of nodes, each of which is marked by a header and a trailer. A node group has a start/end marker at the first/last node. The ragged delimitations at the right in Fig. 4 indicate a failed write or power cut, accordingly the last node lacks its trailer, hence it is invalid and so is the entire group.

Transactional Journal. Appending $n = 2$ nodes to the transactional journal is then implemented as shown in Fig. 5 (the cases $n = 1, 3, 4$ are similar). The algorithm first selects a block number $loghead$ with sufficient remaining space to hold the new data.

$$\textbf{state var } loghead : \mathbb{N}, \quad validhead : \mathbb{B}$$

The current block can be reused if the last write did not fail, leaving partially written nodes at the end. So for example the erase block in Fig. 4 can not be reused.[7] We store in *validhead* whether the current block is still usable. Each node is then written individually wrapped in a group node

data type *GroupNode* = gnode(nd : *Node*, start? : $\mathbb{B}$, end? : $\mathbb{B}$),

with the additional start and end marker. The first flag indicates whether this node is the first one of a group, the second flag indicates whether it is the last one (c.f. Fig. 4). A singleton group has both flags set. Every call to the persistence layer can fail so the returned error code is checked after each step.

At the end of the operation, the corresponding block is flushed to ensure that all nodes have actually been written. The persistence layer has a write cache in order to improve efficiency—no guarantees are given about what has been written until a block is flushed. Note that the returned addresses adr_i are chosen by the persistence layer and are simply passed through.

Persistence Specification. The journal uses the persistence layer to write nodes. The specification of the persistence layer maintains the finite map *blocks* from block numbers to block content of type *GroupBlock*. Each block consists of a list of group nodes and additional data, that exposes some details of the persistence implementation in a controlled way in order to express preconditions and invariants precisely.

$$\textbf{spec var } blocks : \mathbb{N} \nrightarrow GroupBlock$$
$$\textbf{data type } GroupBlock = \texttt{gblock}(\texttt{nodes} : List\langle GroupNode\rangle, \qquad (6)$$
$$\texttt{addrs} : List\langle Address\rangle,$$
$$\texttt{flushindex} : \mathbb{N}, \texttt{rsize} : \mathbb{N})$$

Field addrs gives for each node in nodes the address where it is stored; rsize stores the total size of all nodes in a block that are still referenced by the in-RAM index. It is used to determine blocks suitable for garbage collection as explained in Sect. 5. Finally, the flushindex exposes, which part of the list nodes has been persisted; nodes nodes[i] at a position $i \geq$ flushindex are (conceptually) still cached in RAM and lost on a power cut. Flushing increases flushindex to the length of nodes.

The log itself is implicit in the final file system. It can be determined from the blocks that contain new nodes. For this purpose the persistence layer keeps their numbers in a list *logblocks*.

$$\textbf{spec var } logblocks : List\langle \mathbb{N}\rangle$$

Whenever the journal requests a fresh erase block to be used as part of the log, this block is recorded at the end of *logblocks*. Each such addition needs to be persisted to flash immediately in the implementation.

---

[7] We need to be able to read all nodes from the erase block in order to perform garbage collection, but detecting partially written nodes reliably *in between* completely written ones is not possible.

Verification. For the correspondence between *fs* and *log* on the one hand and *blocks* and *logblocks* on the other, unflushed nodes and partial groups need to be omitted. The abstraction considers *valid* nodes only, which are part of a proper group that has been flushed entirely. We write $blocks_\downarrow$ for the state *blocks* stripped of all invalid nodes (at the end of each erase block, c.f. Fig. 4) and corresponding addresses. The abstraction relation is formalized as

coupling $fs = \mathtt{abs\text{-}fs}(blocks_\downarrow)$ and $log = \mathtt{abs\text{-}log}(logblocks, blocks_\downarrow)$

where

$$\mathtt{abs\text{-}fs}(blocks)[adr] = nd \tag{7}$$
$$\text{iff } blocks[n].\mathtt{nodes}[i].\mathtt{nd} = nd \quad \text{and}$$
$$blocks[n].\mathtt{addrs}[i] = adr \quad \text{for some } n, i \text{ within bounds}$$

and $\mathtt{abs\text{-}log}$ collects the addresses of the blocks in *logblocks* recursively

$$\mathtt{abs\text{-}log}([\,], blocks) = [\,] \tag{8}$$
$$\mathtt{abs\text{-}log}(n + logblocks, blocks) = blocks[n].\mathtt{addrs} + \mathtt{abs\text{-}log}(logblocks, blocks)$$

The difficulty during the verification of $\mathtt{jnl\_append}_n$ is that assertions in intermediate states can not be expressed adequately in terms of $\mathtt{abs\text{-}fs}(blocks_\downarrow)$ and $\mathtt{abs\text{-}log}(logblocks, blocks_\downarrow)$. Both abstractions only reflect the changes *after* flushing the cache. Intermediate assertions therefore refer to $blocks_{\downarrow loghead}$, which removes all invalid nodes from all blocks except for the block *loghead*, where all the changes take place.

The other aspect crucial for the verification of $\mathtt{jnl\_append}_n$ is that if the journal head is valid, it is the last block in the log and it ends on a complete, flushed group, i.e., if *validhead* is true then **invariant**

$$loghead \in blocks \land logblocks \neq [\,] \land loghead = logblocks.\mathtt{last}$$
$$\land \; (blocks[loghead].\mathtt{nodes} \neq [\,] \rightarrow blocks[loghead].\mathtt{nodes.last.end?})$$
$$\land \; \#blocks[loghead].\mathtt{nodes} = blocks[loghead].\mathtt{flushindex}$$

also holds. Otherwise, it would be possible that a newly appended node completes a previously invalid node group.

5   Garbage Collection

The out-of-place updates of the transactional journal will necessarily accumulate a lot of obsolete data over time, i.e., data that is no longer referenced by the index. Garbage collection (GC) of the journal area remedies this problem by moving and compacting live data at the granularity of nodes. The GC procedure thus depends on and modifies the RAM index; furthermore, it is the only point where flash memory space is actually reclaimed.

The difficulties from a formal perspective are twofold: caching of writes of nodes is crucial for the effectiveness of garbage collection, but again considerably complicates the verification. Furthermore, choosing a block for garbage collection requires additional information and ties several layers closer together than already necessary, especially with respect to the recovery from power failures as explained in more detail in Sect. 7.

Specification. Again referring to the view in terms of fs and ri of the journal specification (Sect. 3), we can denote the central correctness property of the GC that no data is lost. Formally,

$$fs \circ ri = fs' \circ ri' \quad \text{and} \quad \text{dom}(ri) = \text{dom}(ri') \tag{9}$$

must hold for the primed state after the run of the GC, where $\_ \circ \_$ denotes function composition. The GC algorithm roughly corresponds to a number of transitions of the form

$$fs[adr'] := fs[ri[key]], \quad ri[key] := adr', \quad log := log + adr',$$

for some $key \in \text{dom}(ri)$ and adr' fresh in fs. The first assignment moves live data to a different location, the second assignment updates the index, and the third records the operation in the log. Subsequently, some addresses $adrs \cap \text{ran}(ri) = \emptyset$ can be deleted by

$$fs := fs \backslash adrs.$$

Implementation. In practice, a number of side conditions need to be satisfied, though. For example, a block that is part of the log cannot be collected until it is merged into the ordinary part of the journal during a commit, because it is needed for recovery (Sect. 7). Also, while the whole block is collected in one go, the corresponding index updates must be deferred: Due to caching, low-level write failures may not be detected immediately and only at the end (after flushing) it is clear whether the copying succeeded. The implementation of garbage collection is shown in Fig. 6. It first selects a block for garbage collection. Then the live nodes of the selected block are copied, which yields a list *keys* of affected keys and corresponding new addresses *dstadr* that are to be updated in the index. Finally, the now obsolete block is deallocated.

The heart of the garbage collection is the procedure `jnl_copy_block`. It reads all nodes *nds* and their addresses *srcadrs* from flash. In a loop, each node *nd* in *nds* is checked whether it is still in the index, i.e., if the key *nd*.key exists in the index and still maps to the node's address *srcadr*. Note that the index does not support queries by address, only by key, therefore each node has to store its own key, and by invariant (3) the keys match. If the node is not obsolete, we append a new copy to the journal and keep the index update $key \mapsto dstadr$ for later. At the end, we ensure that all nodes are persisted by flushing the block.

Verification. In the invariant (not shown) for the while loop in `jnl_copy_block`, it is necessary to state that *keys* and *dstadrs* collected so far correspond to the

```
jnl_garbage_collection()
  persistence_get_gc_block(; block)
  jnl_copy_block(block; keys, dstadrs, err)
  if err = ESUCCESS then   idx_update_all(keys, dstadrs; err)
  if err = ESUCCESS then   persistence_deallocate(block; err)


jnl_copy_block(block; keys, dstadrs, err)
  let srcadrs = [ ], nds = [ ]
    persistence_read_block(block; srcadrs, nds, err)
    while srcadrs ≠ [ ] ∧ err = ESUCCESS do {
      let srcadr = srcadrs.head, nd = nds.head.nd, exists, idxadr, dstadr in
        idx_lookup(nd.key; exists, idxadr, err)
        if err = ESUCCESS ∧ exists ∧ idxadr = srcadr then
          . . .      // if necessary move the log head and flush the old block
          if err = ESUCCESS then
            persistence_add_node(loghead, gnode(nd, true, true); dstadr, err)
            keys := keys + key, dstadrs := dstadrs + dstadr
            srcadrs := srcadrs.tail, nds := nds.tail
    }
    if err = ESUCCESS then   persistence_flush(loghead; err)
```

Fig. 6. Garbage collection procedures

nodes that are still referenced by the index. Furthermore, not all of the nodes written are actually persisted immediately, so in the actual abstraction only a prefix of the written nodes appears in *fs* and *log*. It is therefore necessary to reason about the abstraction "after" a flush to the current journal head. Additionally, there may not always be a current journal head, leading to several distinct cases in the invariant.

Choosing Blocks for GC. From the perspective of functional correctness it is sufficient to choose any block of the journal that is outside the log,[8] but we certainly want to ensure that garbage collection picks a reasonable one. The information necessary for a good choice is for each block how many bytes still belong to live data, encoded in the **rsize** field (Sect. 4).

Here we have an example of coupling between components: although stored within the persistence layer, **rsize** is updated alongside index operations, which ultimately determines what data (addresses) are referenced. In order to make the index aware of the *size* of nodes without the need to access them directly,

---

[8] Note that wear-leveling is performed by a lower layer and therefore is not limited by the choice of block of the garbage collection, i.e., blocks in the log can be moved by wear-leveling.

addresses carry the number of bytes the corresponding node occupies on flash. Addresses therefore are structured, they contain an erase block, a byte-offset in the block, and the size of the node stored:

$$\textbf{data type } \textit{Address} = @(\texttt{block} : \mathbb{N}, \texttt{offset} : \mathbb{N}, \texttt{size} : \mathbb{N})$$

If an index update replaces address *adr* stored under *key* with new *adr'*, the `rsize` field of the block *adr* belongs to is decreased by *adr*.`size`. Symmetrically, the field of *adr'*'s block is increased. For the quality of the garbage collection this information should match the one we could obtain (inefficiently) from the index. Therefore, we prove the **invariant**

$$blocks[n].\texttt{rsize} = \sum \{ adr.\texttt{size} \mid adr \in \texttt{ran}(ri), adr.\texttt{block} = n \} \qquad (10)$$

for all $n \in \texttt{dom}(blocks)$. The range operator yields the set of addresses in the index, we restrict to those addresses in block n and then sum up all their `size` fields. Note that invariant (10) is independent of the question of how many nodes are actually stored on flash in block n, i.e., it does not mention $blocks_\downarrow$ but only the size stored in addresses. This simplifies reasoning about changes to `rsize`.

6   Persistence: Atomic Commit and Write Buffering

The persistence layer encodes all data structures of the flash file system to bytes. It maintains the disk layout in order to decide which erase blocks are allocated for which purpose.

One challenge for the implementation and verification is again atomicity; this time in the form of the commit operation and writing of individual nodes. The second challenge is that free space management and the garbage collection (in the form of the `rsize` field) requires additional information stored per block. This information is kept in the Block Property Table (BPT) that is maintained in RAM and (in an outdated form) on flash, stored during the commit. As shown in Sect. 7, recovering the BPT after a power failure is quite delicate.

Disk Layout and Atomic Commit. The disk is partitioned into two parts:

superblock	BPT 1	BPT 2	logblocks 1	logblocks 2	main area: journal & index

The first part spans the superblock, a copy of the internal management data BPT from the last commit and the list of blocks allocated for the log (corresponding to *logblocks* in Sect. 4). For the BPT and log blocks, space for *two* versions is provisioned. The superblock references the "current" one to be read at startup time. The spare one is written during commit, a subsequent change of the superblock ensures atomic transition to the new state. Assuming the flash index is also written out-of-place by the index model, this already yields a correct implementation of the commit operation from Sect. 3.

The second part of the device consists of all erase blocks with group nodes, i.e., the blocks occupied by the journal, and erase blocks storing the on-flash index (not covered in this paper).

The Block Property Table (BPT) is an array with some data for each erase block of the main area:

state var *bpt* : *Array⟨BPTEntry⟩*

data type *BPTEntry* = bptentry(size : ℕ, rsize : ℕ, type : *BPTType*)

data type *BPTType* = FREE | GROUP_NODES | INDEX_NODES

The BPT is consulted to find a **FREE** block when a fresh one is requested by the journal layer. The **rsize** field corresponds to the abstract counterpart shown in (6). The **size** field stores how many bytes have been written to the block.

Fig. 7. Write buffer

Write Buffering. The main functionality required by the journal is appending a single (group-) node to a block. The implementation is shown in Fig. 8. It is based on a write buffer, which stores one flash page as a cache in RAM to aggregate non-aligned writes. Figure 7 visualizes how this cache is overlaid with the data on flash: the whole part marked in grey designates written bytes. Write buffers are allocated on demand and stored in the map *wbufs*.

state var *wbufs* : ℕ ↠ *WBuf*

data type *WBuf* = wbuf(off : ℕ, buf : *Array⟨Byte⟩*, nbytes : ℕ)

In order to create a write buffer the offset where we want to start writing data must be known, which is readily available in the BPT as **size**. Procedure **persistence_add_node** then writes a header containing the length of the encoded node, the node itself and a trailer. The block number, offset and size are assembled into the returned address *adr*. A partially written node is detected by a missing trailer. Flushing of a block (**persistence_flush**) requires a write of a padding node that spans the space until the next page boundary.

Verification. The abstraction relation between the specification and implementation of the persistence layer basically states that

- the current version of *logblocks* is stored on flash,
- the BPT from the last commit is stored on flash,
- all group nodes are stored in the main area and
- the **flushindex** of each block corresponds to the exact number of nodes that have been written to flash and are no longer held in the write buffer.

Difficult in terms of verification and specification is that the encoding of all nodes in one block is not functional, since the abstraction needs to filter out padding nodes and partially written nodes at the end of each block.

persistence_add_node($block, gnode; adr, err$)

  if $\neg$ wbuf_is_buffered($block$) then   wbuf_create($block, bpt[block]$.size)

  let buf = encode-group-node($gnode$)

    let buf_0 = encode-header(nodeheader($\#buf, false$))

    wbuf_write($block$, HEADER_SIZE, buf_0; err)

    if err = ESUCCESS then   wbuf_write($block, \#buf, buf; err$)

    if err = ESUCCESS then   wbuf_write($block$, HEADER_SIZE, trailer; err)

    if err = ESUCCESS then

      let $size = 2 \cdot$ HEADER_SIZE $+ \#buf$

        adr := @($block, bpt[block]$.size, $size$), $bpt[block]$.size $+= size$

    else $bpt[block]$.size = BLOCK_SIZE

Fig. 8. Writing a single group node

7   Power Cuts and Recovery

In this section we describe how the various models interact in the event of a power cut. It is modeled as assigning arbitrary values to all in-RAM data structures. The persistent storage is left unchanged. In bottom-up fashion we give each model a chance to recover to a consistent and desirable state via the recovery operation. The machine of the journal layer, for example, starts with the recovered state of the persistence layer.

In general we show recovery property (1) for each refinement, i.e., the power cut and subsequent recovery between abstract and concrete model match, in the sense that invariants and abstraction relations hold afterwards. The difficulty from a specification and verification perspective is that different parts of the state behave differently: Some parts are restored to the state directly before the power cut while other parts are restored to the state of the last commit. Some parts need to be fixed and do not resemble any previous state. Furthermore, several aspects of recovery from power cuts leak through abstractions, making it an inherently collaborative effort of several models.

By definition (4) the journal and persistence implementation together restore to the same state and return the list of addresses of the log for its replay (see invariant (5)). The implementation of the recovery operations is shown in Figs. 9 and 10 (error handling omitted for brevity). After the persistence layer has read the necessary data from flash and fixed the outdated BPT (which is the hard part, as explained below), the journal takes over to scan the erase blocks that form the log, removing invalid group nodes at the end of each block and concatenating all the addresses. Not incidentally, this corresponds exactly to the abstraction abs-log in (8).

The BPT read from flash needs to be adapted in two ways: The blocks that have been allocated for group nodes since the last commit (subset of those in the log) need to be marked as allocated. The blocks constituting the log at the persist_recover(; *bpt*, *logblocks*)

  read_superblock(; *superblock*)

  read_log(*superblock*; *logblocks*)

  read_bpt(*superblock*; *bpt*)

  fix_bpt(*logblocks*; *bpt*)

Fig. 9. Recovery of persistence

jnl_recover(*logblocks*; *log*)

  log := []

  while *logblocks* ≠ [] do

    persistence_read_blk(*logblocks*.head; *adrs*, *nds*)

    remove_nonend_nodes(; *adrs*, *nds*)

    log := *log* + *adrs*, *logblocks* := *logblocks*.tail

Fig. 10. Recovery of the log

time of the power cut must be considered non-writable: it cannot be determined how far exactly they have been written. Therefore, we treat those blocks as full and set their **size** field in the BPT accordingly.

Abstractly, after the recovery by the persistence implementation the journal implementation sees the following changes to the group blocks *blocks*:

1. the nodes that were not yet persisted (i.e., are above **flushindex**) vanish,
2. the **rsize** field is reverted to the value from the last commit,
3. previously garbage collected and deallocated group blocks reappear.

The first point is no problem, because the abstraction (7) in terms of *blocks*₁ upwards to the flash store *fs* only considers the persisted nodes anyway.

The reverted **rsize** has the consequence that the invariant (10) is violated if one considers the in-RAM index before the power cut. However, after a power cut, we read the index from the last commit, too. And the index and the **rsize** fields from the last commit obviously satisfied invariant (10) at the point of commit. This establishes the invariant right after the recovery of the persistence layer and reading of the on-flash index. Replaying the index afterwards then also updates the **rsize** fields correctly.

The reappearing blocks are problematic, because they may contain garbage data (it is unknown whether they have been erased on flash or not) and reallocation is precluded until they are deallocated once again. We store the blocks that have been deallocated since the last commit abstractly, exclude their contents in the abstractions **abs-log** and **abs-fs** (and disallow reading and writing), propagating this constraint towards the upper layers. After the replay of the index by upper layers the RAM index will no longer reference them, since this was the reason for their deallocation, and we can now safely remove these blocks.

8   Related Work

NASA's proposal [19] has prompted a large body of related work, covering many aspects of file systems in general and also specific to flash memory.

High-level specifications include the early work of Morgan and Sufrin [22] and mechanized models and proofs [1,14,15,17]; a recent model of POSIX which is very complete and detailed is presented in [24]. These efforts are orthogonal to this paper, see [13] for a detailed comparison to our development. Formalizations of flash memory below the models presented here include [5].

Two developments actually connect a high-level view to the pages and blocks of flash hardware [8,20]. In both cases, only file content is mapped, written, and garbage collected at the granularity of flash pages, at the expense of extra state that is kept in memory. An encoding of the directory/file structure and any other auxiliary data structures (such as the BPT, log and on-flash index) down to flash and caching of writes are not considered. Kang and Jackson [20] deals only with crashes during a write operation and intertwines the recovery strategy with the implementation of the write operation. Some Flash Translation Layers (FTLs) and [8,20] have a page-based allocation scheme assuming additional, overwritable bits in each page that track the allocation status. These are not always present or might be used entirely for error-correction codes [30]. We have to recover newly allocated blocks and deallocate reappearing blocks after a power cut. Furthermore, the models do not consider the restriction to sequential writes within an erase block. [8] reads all pages during mounting/recovery in order to rebuild the index.

Chen et al. [6] discuss different formalisms to express crash and recovery on a high level, and settle for a pre/post verification in the Hoare-logic style, augmented with a crash specification and a designated recovery operation attached to individual operations. Very nice follow up work [7] introduces Crash Hoare Logic in more detail and presents the verification of a small but complete file system called FSCQ targeting conventional magnetic drives. In comparison, their approach requires one to reason about intermediate states using a special logic, whereas we are able to reduce the proof effort on a semantic level.

Marić and Sprenger [21] consider a storage system with similar properties of that of a file system, but with a strong focus on redundancy.

9   Discussion and Conclusion

We have presented two central components for verified flash file systems, covering concepts not realistically addressed in previous work.

The work has been done in the context of the Flashix project and it is strongly connected to the design of the overall system. One observation is that it is non-trivial to find a good decomposition of the system. Since we have taken the existing implementation UBIFS as a blue-print, many concepts were already worked out properly, but isolating these from the verification point-of-view took quite some time—we estimate somewhat less than half a person-year in total for the models and proofs; the overall project effort is in the order of three to four person years. At least half can be attributed to errors and power cut safety. The specifications developed in this work specifically are in the order of 4 k lines of ASM code and algebraic definitions in addition to around 800 theorems.

The large gap in representation of system state (abstract tree down to bytes) leads to a deeply nested hierarchy of layers, see the full version of Fig. 1 in [26]. It is beneficial to be able to pinpoint the individual concepts as abstract models (i.e., ASMs) in their own respect: one can verify invariants on the abstract level, executable specifications were also useful during testing and validation.

However, a deep hierarchy has the issue that models become semantically entangled, which breaks modularity in a way that is *hard* to resolve, as noted before in e.g., [2]. Resilience against hardware errors and abrupt power cuts aggravates the problem of finding suitable, sufficiently abstract specifications. It is likewise not obvious, to what extent such effects should be masked within the implementation of a specific component.

Specification entanglement manifests for example in the `flushindex` and `rsize` fields in Sect. 4 and the extra size field in addresses. Garbage collection has issues on its own: it should be pointed out that upper layers in the software stack must be able to deal with it, namely, the file system core should be agnostic to GC (which is established in terms of its specification). Another issue are the reappearing blocks in Sect. 7 caused by the fact that some internal data structures are stored only during a commit. We think that this emphasizes that specifying systems well is at least as hard as the verification itself.

It is doubtful whether it would pay off to further refactor the design, as we found that even small changes tend to affect large parts of the verification, mainly due to hardware failures and power cuts. Of course, improving tool support for such refactoring is one way to mitigate this problem.

With previous work [13, 23, 28] we have now completed the design of a fully functional flash file system. All models and proofs are available online at [9]. The verification is almost done (missing: parts of the B^+ trees) and we're generating preliminary C code, which is in the order of 10 kLoC. An evaluation of the performance of the file system is currently under way.

Two important features that require further research are caching across POSIX operations and concurrency. Caching across operations is in principle supported by our implementation, but a suitable refinement theory still needs to be worked out. Internal concurrency for garbage collection and erasing of blocks reduces the latency of operations from the user's point-of-view. To support this eventually ($\diamond$), the semantics of our crash-refinement theory has been made compatible with the temporal logic RGITL [27] implemented by KIV.

Acknowledgement. We thank the anonymous reviewers for their detailed and helpful comments.

References

1. Arkoudas, K., Zee, K., Kuncak, V., Rinard, M.: Verifying a file system implementation. In: Davies, J., Schulte, W., Barnett, M. (eds.) ICFEM 2004. LNCS, vol. 3308, pp. 373–390. Springer, Heidelberg (2004)
2. Baumann, C., Beckert, B., Blasum, H., Bormer, T.: Lessons learned from Microkernel verification - specification is the new bottleneck. In: SSV, pp. 18–32 (2012)
3. Börger, E.: The ASM refinement method. Form. Asp. Comput. **15**(1–2), 237–257 (2003)
4. Börger, E., Stärk, R.F.: Abstract State Machines – A Method for High-Level System Design and Analysis. Springer, Berlin (2003)

5. Butterfield, A., Woodcock, J.: Formalising flash memory: first steps. In: IEEE International Conference on Engineering of Complex Computer Systems, pp. 251–260 (2007)
6. Chen, H., Ziegler, D., Chlipala, A., Kaashoek, M.F., Kohler, E., Zeldovich, N.: Specifying crash safety for storage systems. In: 15th Workshop on Hot Topics in Operating Systems (HotOS XV). USENIX Association (2015)
7. Chen, H., Ziegler, D., Chlipala, A., Zeldovich, N., Kaashoek, M.F.: Using crash hoare logic for certifying the FSCQ file system. In: Proceedings of SOSP. ACM (2015)
8. Damchoom, K.: An incremental refinement approach to a development of a flash-based file system in Event-B, Ph.D. thesis, University of Southampton (2010)
9. Ernst, G., Pfähler, J., Schellhorn, G.: Web presentation of the Flash Filesystem (2015). https://swt.informatik.uni-augsburg.de/swt/projects/flash.html
10. Ernst, G., Pfähler, J., Schellhorn, G., Haneberg, D., Reif, W.: KIV - overview and VerifyThis competition. Softw. Tools Technol. Transf. (STTT) 17(6), 677–694 (2015)
11. Ernst, G., Pfähler, J., Schellhorn, G., Reif, W.: Modular, crash-safe refinement for ASMs with submachines. Science of Computer Programming, ABZ special issue, 2015 (submitted) (2014)
12. Ernst, G., Schellhorn, G., Haneberg, D., Pfähler, J., Reif, W.: A formal model of a virtual filesystem switch. In: Proceedings of Software and Systems Modeling (SSV), EPTCS, pp. 33–45 (2012)
13. Ernst, G., Schellhorn, G., Haneberg, D., Pfähler, J., Reif, W.: Verification of a Virtual Filesystem Switch. In: Cohen, E., Rybalchenko, A. (eds.) VSTTE 2013. LNCS, vol. 8164, pp. 242–261. Springer, Heidelberg (2014)
14. Ferreira, M.A., Silva, S.S., Oliveira, J.N.: Verifying intel Flash File System core specification. In: Modelling and Analysis in VDM: Proceedings of the Fourth VDM/Overture Workshop, pp. 54–71, Technical report CS-TR-1099 (2008)
15. Freitas, L., Woodcock, J., Fu, Z.: POSIX file store in Z/Eves: an experiment in the verified software repository. Sci. Comput. Program. 74(4), 238–257 (2009)
16. Gleixner, T., Haverkamp, F., Bityutskiy, A.: UBI - Unsorted Block Images (2006). http://www.linux-mtd.infradead.org/doc/ubidesign/ubidesign.pdf
17. Hesselink, W.H., Lali, M.I.: Formalizing a hierarchical file system. Form. Asp. Comput. 24(1), 27–44 (2012)
18. Hunter, A.: A brief introduction to the design of UBIFS (2008). http://www.linux-mtd.infradead.org/doc/ubifs_whitepaper.pdf
19. Joshi, R., Holzmann, G.J.: A mini challenge: build a verifiable filesystem. Form. Asp. Comput. 19(2), 269–272 (2007)
20. Kang, E., Jackson, D.: Formal Modeling and Analysis of a Flash Filesystem in Alloy. In: Börger, E., Butler, M., Bowen, J.P., Boca, P. (eds.) ABZ 2008. LNCS, vol. 5238, pp. 294–308. Springer, Heidelberg (2008)
21. Marić, O., Sprenger, C.: Verification of a transactional memory manager under hardware failures and restarts. In: Jones, C., Pihlajasaari, P., Sun, J. (eds.) FM 2014. LNCS, vol. 8442, pp. 449–464. Springer, Heidelberg (2014)
22. Morgan, C., Sufrin, B.: Specification of the UNIX filing system. Specification Case Studies, pp. 91–140. Prentice Hall Ltd., Hertfordshire (1987)
23. Pfähler, J., Ernst, G., Schellhorn, G., Haneberg, D., Reif, W.: Formal specification of an erase block management layer for flash memory. In: Legay, A., Bertacco, V. (eds.) HVC 2013. LNCS, vol. 8244, pp. 214–229. Springer, Heidelberg (2013)

24. Ridge, T., Sheets, D., Tuerk, T., Giugliano, A., Madhavapeddy, A., Sewell, P.: SibylFS: formal specification and oracle-based testing for POSIX and real-world file systems. In: Proceedings of SOSP. ACM (2015)
25. Schellhorn, G.: Completeness of fair ASM refinement. Sci. Comput. Program. **76**(9), 756–773 (2009). Elsevier
26. Schellhorn, G., Ernst, G., Pfähler, J., Haneberg, D., Reif, W.: Development of a verified flash file system. In: Ait Ameur, Y., Schewe, K.-D. (eds.) ABZ 2014. LNCS, vol. 8477, pp. 9–24. Springer, Heidelberg (2014)
27. Schellhorn, G., Tofan, B., Ernst, G., Pfähler, J., Reif, W.: RGITL: a temporal logic framework for compositional reasoning about interleaved programs. Ann. Math. Artif. Intell. (AMAI) **71**, 1–44 (2014)
28. Schierl, A., Schellhorn, G., Haneberg, D., Reif, W.: Abstract specification of the UBIFS file system for flash memory. In: Cavalcanti, A., Dams, D.R. (eds.) FM 2009. LNCS, vol. 5850, pp. 190–206. Springer, Heidelberg (2009)
29. The Open Group: The Open Group Base Specifications Issue 7, IEEE Std 1003.1, 2008 Edition. http://www.unix.org/version3/online.html (login required)
30. UBI - Out-of-Band Data. http://www.linux-mtd.infradead.org/faq/ubi.html
31. Woodcock, J.C.P., Davies, J.: Using Z: Specification. Proof and Refinement. Prentice Hall International Series in Computer Science. Prentice Hall, New York (1996)

How to Avoid Proving
the Absence of Integer Overflows

Martin Clochard[1,2], Jean-Christophe Filliâtre[1,2(✉)], and Andrei Paskevich[1,2]

[1] Lab. de Recherche En Informatique, Univ. Paris-Sud, CNRS, Orsay 91405, France
[2] INRIA Saclay – Île-de-France, Orsay 91893, France
{martin.clochard,jean-christophe.filliatre,andrei}@lri.fr

Abstract. When proving safety of programs, we must show, in particular, the absence of integer overflows. Unfortunately, there are lots of situations where performing such a proof is extremely difficult, because the appropriate restrictions on function arguments are invasive and may be hard to infer. Yet, in certain cases, we can relax the desired property and only require the absence of overflow during the first n steps of execution, n being large enough for all practical purposes. It turns out that this relaxed property can be easily ensured for large classes of algorithms, so that only a minimal amount of proof is needed, if at all. The idea is to restrict the set of allowed arithmetic operations on the integer values in question, imposing a "speed limit" on their growth. For example, if we repeatedly increment a 64-bit integer, starting from zero, then we will need at least 2^{64} steps to reach an overflow; on current hardware, this takes several hundred years. When we do not expect any single execution of our program to run that long, we have effectively proved its safety against overflows of all variables with controlled growth speed. In this paper, we give a formal explanation of this approach, prove its soundness, and show how it is implemented in the context of deductive verification.

1 Introduction

Proving the safety of a program involves showing the absence of arithmetic overflows. By itself, an overflow does not crash the program, but it silently results in a meaningless value with, typically, fatal consequences in other places of the program. A famous example is described in Joshua Bloch's blog post *Nearly All Binary Searches and Mergesorts are Broken* [1]. It is related to the computation of the mean of two 32-bit array indices involved in these two algorithms in the Java standard library. When using large arrays, an arithmetic overflow may occur, possibly resulting in a negative array index and hence a program crash.

Today, most formal methods do tackle arithmetic overflows, *e.g.*, abstract interpretation [2], model checking [3], or deductive verification [4]. In deductive verification, for instance, one models machine integers as specific data types where operations are given suitable statically-verified preconditions to prevent overflows. In the case of binary search, it can be proved that the computation of the mid-point of low and high as low + (high - low)/2 does not overflow.

© Springer International Publishing Switzerland 2016
A. Gurfinkel and S.A. Seshia (Eds.): VSTTE 2015, LNCS 9593, pp. 94–109, 2016.
DOI: 10.1007/978-3-319-29613-5_6

Yet there are many situations where it is extremely difficult to prove the absence of arithmetic overflows. Perhaps the simplest example is that of a global counter that is incremented by one every time a fresh value is requested, for instance to generate labels or timestamps. Deductive verification, in principle, could accommodate the necessary bound pre-conditions; yet such bounds would invade specifications throughout the program, resulting in an impractical annotation/proof burden.

We may, however, observe, that to overflow this global counter— assuming it is stored as a 64-bit unsigned integer and starts from zero— we need to perform 2^{64} individual increment operations, plus all the work we do on each new value. Even if we perform one billion increment operations per second, it would take us more than 584 years to reach the limit. Unless we expect our program to have century-long runs, we can rest assured that this particular counter is, for all intents and purposes, safe from overflow. The crucial part of the argument is that the counter can only grow by one at a time: arbitrary additions, multiplications and so on are not allowed. In this paper, we propose a way to make this meta-argument formal, and we prove the soundness of our approach. We also demonstrate an implementation of this method in Why3 [5], a tool for deductive program verification.

We stress that this approach does not reduce the need in traditional methods (such as deductive verification, abstract interpretation, or model checking) for proving the absence of integer overflows, as they target different uses of integers. The idea is to use our technique in combination with other methods, within the same program. We give an example of such a combination in this paper.

The paper is organized as follows. Section 2 motivates our work with classes of programs where we want to avoid exhibiting bounds on integers to prove the absence of overflows. Section 3 introduces our solution, along with its proof of soundness. Section 4 describes our implementation in Why3 and illustrates it with a representative example. We conclude with a discussion.

2   Motivating Examples

We have already mentioned the example of a symbol generator (*gensym* for short): a program returning a fresh integer on each call. A gensym is trivially implemented with a global variable, as described in Program 1. (A more robust implementation would hide the global variable s, using for instance a static variable local to function GENSYM.)

Program 1. Symbol generator

```
1: s ← 0
2: function GENSYM
3:     s ← s + 1
4:     return s
5: end function
```

Suppose that we want to prove, in a usual way, that the increment operation in GENSYM does not overflow the counter. In the context of deductive verification, we have to put a bound pre-condition on GENSYM, requiring s to be strictly less than $2^{64} - 1$. In order to satisfy this precondition, we now have to constrain, in the same way, every user of GENSYM in our program. In cases where we call GENSYM inside a loop or a recursive function, new preconditions and invariants are needed in order to put a bound on the number of iterations or recursive calls. Essentially, we have to unroll the whole execution of our program and come up with sufficient bounds on its input in order to satisfy the bound pre-condition of GENSYM. At the very least, these added annotations will inflate the program specification and hamper verification. What is worse, inferring suitable bounds for the program input might be a computationally hard problem. However, if s is a 64-bit unsigned integer, and if we agree, as explained above, to content ourselves with the absence of overflows *during the first hundred years* of the program execution—suddenly, we have nothing to prove about GENSYM itself, and we only have to ensure that counter s is not modified in some dangerous way (say, doubled) elsewhere in the program.

A large class of examples, where one might want to apply this meta-argument, is that of programs computing the size of a data structure. Consider, for instance, a function computing the length of a linked list. It can be implemented either recursively (Program 2) or iteratively using a while loop (Program 3). In both cases, it amounts to incrementing the length by one for each list element. Just as in the previous case, if the result is stored in a 64-bit integer, it would take too much time to overflow it.

Program 2. Length of a list, recursive

```
1: function LENGTH(l)
2:     if l = null then return 0
3:     else return 1 + LENGTH(l.next)
4:     end if
5: end function
```

Program 3. Length of a list, iterative

```
1: function LENGTH(l)
2:     len ← 0
3:     while l ≠ null do
4:         len ← len + 1
5:         l ← l.next
6:     end while
7:     return len
8: end function
```

Another example in this category is Program 4 which computes the size of a binary tree, recursively. In this code, we compute the *sum* of the sizes of the two sub-trees, as returned by the recursive calls. Yet, in terms of computation,

---

Program 4. Size of a tree

```
1: function SIZE(t)
2:     if t = empty then return 0
3:     else return 1 + SIZE(t.left) + SIZE(t.right)
4:     end if
5: end function
```

---

this addition is equivalent to a sequence of increments by one. This equivalence is evident if we rewrite the program to accumulate the size in a global counter.

Data structures with sharing are a special case. Consider for instance the tree of depth h shown on the right. It has size $2^h - 1$. If, when computing its size, we employ memoization in order to exploit the sharing and speed up computation, our meta-argument does not hold anymore. In that case, the additions performed could overflow since results of previous computations are reused and thus accumulated several times in the result.

However, if memoization is not used, our approach applies even for trees with sharing. Indeed, if we call the SIZE function from Program 4 on a tree with sharing, it will simply not terminate in practice for a large value of h, say 100, even if we were able to build that tree in space and time $O(h)$. This shows that our meta-argument is really about *time* (in this case, the time spent in the traversal of the data structure) and not *space* (the space used to store the data structure).

Another class of programs for which our approach applies is that of data structures that store integers for internal management. An example is non-empty linked lists with destructive concatenation, as illustrated in Fig. 1. Each list contains its length and two pointers to its first and last elements. When performing the concatenation of lists a and b, the last element of a now points to the first element of b. The pointer to the last element of a is updated so that it now points to the last element of b. Finally, the length of list a is updated and list b is invalidated, by setting its pointers to *null*. The code is given in Program 5.

Just as in the previous program, the addition on line 3 is not dangerous. Indeed, the length of each list is limited by the time spent to build it. Since list b is invalidated when performing APPEND(a, b), we are moving the "time credits" earned by the construction of b into the updated length of a, without risking an overflow.

Program 5. Destructive Append on Linked Lists

```
1: procedure APPEND(a, b)
2:     assert a ≠ b ∧ a.first ≠ null ∧ b.first ≠ null
3:     a.size ← a.size + b.size
4:     a.last.next ← b.first
5:     a.last ← b.last
6:     b.first ← null
7:     b.last ← null
8: end procedure
```

Before:

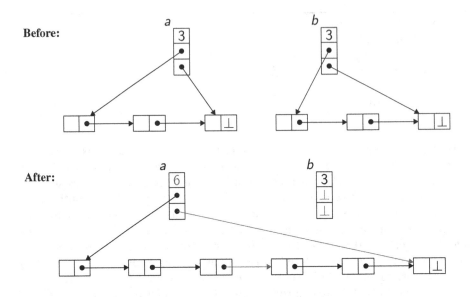

Fig. 1. Destructive append on linked lists.

Another example involving integers stored in a data structure is union-find with weighted union. A union-find structure implements equivalence classes with canonical representatives. It is a forest, where each node contains a pointer *link* to its father and an integer w, its weight, which is an upper bound of the length of a path from this node to a leaf. When performing the union of two classes represented by root nodes a and b, the weights are used to decide whether a is linked to b or, conversely, b is linked to a. When the weights are equal, we choose arbitrarily and we increment the weight of the root node by one. There is obviously no danger of arithmetic overflow here, since weights are only obtained by successive increments by one.

Program 6. Union-Find with Weighted Union

```
1: procedure UNION(a, b)
2:     if a ≠ b then
3:         if a.w < b.w then a.link ← b else b.link ← a end if
4:         if a.w = b.w then a.w ← a.w + 1 end if
5:     end if
6: end procedure
```

Another potential use case, which we do not consider in detail here, is that of de Bruijn indices [6], a technical solution to the implementation of binders in symbolic computation. A variable is represented as an integer, which counts the number of binders under which it appears. When performing substitutions, such integer must be updated, being either incremented or decremented. Such increments only occur one by one, hence are safe.

Program 7. Number of solutions to the N-queens problem

```
 1: function N-QUEENS(b)
 2:     if board b contains N queens then return 1
 3:     else
 4:         r ← 0
 5:         for any legal board b' obtained by adding a queen to board b do
 6:             r ← r + N-QUEENS(b')
 7:         end for
 8:         return r
 9:     end if
10: end function
```

Our final class of examples are combinatorics programs in which backtracking is used to enumerate all the solutions of a problem. Consider for instance the famous n-queens problem, where we count the number of ways to place n non-attacking queens on a $n \times n$ board. Program 7 contains pseudo-code for a function N-QUEENS that progressively adds queens to a board b until a solution is found. The numbers manipulated in this program are bounded by the number of solutions that have already been enumerated by the recursive calls.

What is important in this example is that we do not know any reasonable upper bounds on the value that we compute, so it would not be feasible to prove the absence of arithmetic overflow. Another, more useful, example in this category is the computation of Littlewood-Richardson coefficients [7].

3   A Solution

We propose the following method for verifying the safety against arithmetic overflows in programs like those enumerated in the previous section.

First of all, we identify, inside the program code, the integer values for which we do not want to (or realistically can not) exhibit bounds. For any such value, represented as an n-bit machine integer, we relax the safety property and seek to prove that overflow is impossible during the first 2^n execution steps (with respect to a reasonable operational semantics, where execution steps translate to a proportional number of processor cycles). We leave to the user the responsibility of verifying that the relaxed property is sufficient, that is, execution duration of this magnitude indeed exceeds all practical expectations. We believe that 64-bits integers fit perfectly our use case. On one hand, they are natively supported by modern general-purpose CPUs; on the other hand, we are not aware of any application where a single execution of a sequential program is expected to run long enough to be able to overflow a 64-bit integer with singular increment operations.

To ensure the relaxed safety property for the selected integer values, we restrict the operations available for manipulating these integers so as to prohibit arbitrary growth. Depending on the programming language and the verification methods, this restriction can be achieved in various ways. For example, we can introduce new data types for such "restricted integers" and let the type system verify that only the permitted operations are used on them. Of course, these integers are still compiled to native machine integers. This is the approach we show in this paper. Alternatively, one can work with a program where the native integer types are used indiscriminately, and use a static analysis procedure to detect the values for which the restrictions are respected. Notice that this static analysis is itself, in essence, some form of type inference.

Below, we describe two kinds of such restricted integers. The first are *Peano integers*, where only the increment operation is available to produce a number greater than those already reached. Using Peano integers, we can implement Programs 1 (symbol generator), 2 and 3 (length of a list), and 6 (union-find). The second class allows us to use addition as well, provided that we do not let the same number to be used more than once. To this end, we introduce *one-time integers*, where operations like addition invalidate their arguments. Using one-time integers, we can implement the remaining examples, namely Programs 4 (tree size), 5 (destructive append), and 7 (n-queens).

3.1   Peano Integers

Peano integers are introduced as a new data type *peano*. We provide a constant *zero* and a successor operation on that type:

$$zero : \ peano$$
$$succ(p : peano) : peano$$

Other operations on Peano integers are provided, such as the conversion into an arbitrary-precision integer

$$to\_int(p : peano) : \mathbb{Z}$$

or the construction of a Peano integer from an arbitrary integer x, provided it is no greater than a Peano integer p we have already built:

$$cap(x : \mathbb{Z}, \ p : peano) : peano$$

This is not an exhaustive list. For instance, it is safe to compare two Peano integers, to compute the minimum or the maximum of two of them, etc.

3.2   One-Time Integers

One-time integers are introduced as a new data type *onetime*. To account for the idea that one-time integers are used in a *linear way* or, equivalently, in a destructive way, each one-time integer carries a Boolean validity flag in addition to its value. The validity flag is mutable, and is changed from *true* to *false* when the one-time integer is invalidated. The value itself is immutable, and the allowed operations generate fresh one-time integers.

For one-time integers, we provide zero and successor functions:

$$fresh\_zero() : onetime$$
$$succ(p : onetime) : onetime$$

Contrary to Peano integers, *fresh_zero* is not a constant, since it must return a new one-time integer distinct from all others. Function *succ* is also different from the Peano version: it requires its argument to be valid, destroys its validity, and returns a new, valid one-time integer. One-time integers also feature a destructive addition:

$$add(x : onetime,\ y : onetime) : onetime$$

As function *succ*, function *add* requires valid arguments and destroys them. Additionally, it requires x and y to be *distinct* one-time integers, to prevent one from doubling the value of a one-time integer. Finally, one-time integers can be non-destructively turned into Peano integers:

$$to\_peano(x : onetime) : peano$$

Notice that we provide no operation to check the validity state of a one-time integer in a program; the validity flag is used for verification purposes only. Since the compiler ought to translate one-time integers to native machine integers, the validity of a given one-time integer cannot be available at the run time. For the same reason, we provide no operation to check whether two one-time integers are physically the same object.

3.3   Formalization

To prove the soundness of our approach, we consider a small While-like programming language with heap-allocated records. Figure 2 introduces the abstract syntax of this language, which distinguishes values v, expressions e, and statements s. Values are either Peano integers, memory addresses, Booleans, or arbitrary-precision integers. The set of addresses is assumed to be infinite. A one-time integer is represented as a record with two fields: a field otP containing its value, as a Peano integer; and a field otV containing its validity flag. As a consequence, operation *to_peano*, which turns a one-time integer into a Peano integer, is simply a field access. Access to the otV field, though, is forbidden, for the reasons explained above.

We equip our language with a small-step operational semantics. A heap Σ is a finite-domain partial mapping from address/field pairs to values. A program state is a triple (V, Σ, s), where V is a mapping from variables to values, Σ is a heap, and s is a statement representing the remaining execution. The operational semantics defines a one-step execution for expressions, written $V, \Sigma, e \rightarrow V, \Sigma', e'$, as well as a one-step execution for statements,

$$
\begin{aligned}
v ::= {}& \langle p \rangle && \text{Peano integer } (p \in \mathbb{N}) \\
\mid {}& a && \text{memory address} \\
\mid {}& \bot \mid \top && \text{Boolean value} \\
\mid {}& n && \text{arbitrary-precision integer } (n \in \mathbb{Z})
\end{aligned}
$$

$$
\begin{aligned}
e ::= {}& x && \text{variable} \\
\mid {}& v && \text{value} \\
\mid {}& succ(e) && \text{Peano/one-time successor} \\
\mid {}& fresh\_zero() && \text{fresh one-time integer} \\
\mid {}& add(e,e) && \text{one-time addition} \\
\mid {}& to\_int(e) && \text{conversion from Peano to arbitrary integers} \\
\mid {}& cap(e,e) && \text{conversion from integers to Peano (partial)} \\
\mid {}& \{f = e,\ldots,f = e\} && \text{record construction} \\
\mid {}& e.f && \text{field access} \\
\mid {}& \ldots && \text{Boolean connectives, operations on arbitrary integers, etc.}
\end{aligned}
$$

$$
\begin{aligned}
s ::= {}& skip && \text{skip} \\
\mid {}& x \leftarrow e && \text{variable assignment} \\
\mid {}& e.f \leftarrow e && \text{memory assignment} \\
\mid {}& s; s && \text{sequence} \\
\mid {}& \textbf{if } e \textbf{ then } s \textbf{ else } s && \text{conditional} \\
\mid {}& \textbf{while } e \textbf{ do } s \textbf{ done} && \text{loop}
\end{aligned}
$$

Fig. 2. Abstract syntax for a small programming language.

$V, \Sigma, s \rightarrow V', \Sigma', s'$. As usual, such relations are defined with head reductions (Figs. 3, 4 and 5) and reduction contexts (Fig. 6). Note that expressions do not modify the variable store V. Standard reduction rules for arbitrary-precision integers and Booleans are omitted, for the sake of brevity. It is worth pointing out that direct construction and mutation of one-time integers is not allowed; see rules ALLOC and MEM-ASSIGN.

$$
\text{VAR} \frac{}{V, \Sigma, x \rightarrow V, \Sigma, V(x)} \qquad
\text{FIELD} \frac{a.f \in \Sigma \qquad f \neq otV}{V, \Sigma, a.f \rightarrow V, \Sigma, \Sigma(a.f)}
$$

$$
\text{ALLOC} \frac{a \notin \Sigma \qquad \forall i.\, f_i \notin \{otP, otV\}}{V, \Sigma, \{f_1 = v_1, \ldots, f_n = v_n\} \rightarrow V, \Sigma[a.f_1 \leftarrow v_1, \ldots, a.f_n \leftarrow v_n], a}
$$

Fig. 3. Reduction rules for expressions.

Informally, the main theorem can be stated as follows: a program that contains no non-zero Peano constants will not cause any Peano/one-time integer to exceed n in its first n steps of execution. Formally, we first define a notion of bounded program states:

$$\text{SKIP}\frac{}{V,\Sigma,(\textsf{skip}\,;s)\ \to\ V,\Sigma,s} \qquad\qquad \text{ASSIGN}\frac{}{V,\Sigma,x\leftarrow v\ \to\ V[x\leftarrow v],\Sigma,\textsf{skip}}$$

$$\text{MEM-ASSIGN}\frac{a.f\in\Sigma \qquad f\notin\{otP,otV\}}{V,\Sigma,a.f\leftarrow v\ \to\ V,\Sigma[a.f\leftarrow v],\textsf{skip}}$$

$$\text{IF-TRUE}\frac{}{V,\Sigma,(\textsf{if }\top\textsf{ then }s\textsf{ else }s')\ \to\ V,\Sigma,s}$$

$$\text{IF-FALSE}\frac{}{V,\Sigma,(\textsf{if }\bot\textsf{ then }s\textsf{ else }s')\ \to\ V,\Sigma,s'}$$

$$\text{WHILE}\frac{}{V,\Sigma,(\textsf{while }e\textsf{ do }s\textsf{ done})\ \to\ V,\Sigma,(\textsf{if }e\textsf{ then }s;\textsf{while }e\textsf{ do }s\textsf{ done else }skip)}$$

Fig. 4. Reduction rules for statements.

$$\text{PEANO-SUCC}\frac{}{V,\Sigma,succ(\langle p\rangle)\ \to\ V,\Sigma,\langle p+1\rangle}$$

$$\text{ONE-TIME-SUCC}\frac{\Sigma(a)=\{otP=\langle p\rangle,otV=\top\}\qquad a'\notin\Sigma}{V,\Sigma,succ(a)\ \to\ V,\Sigma[a.otV\leftarrow\bot,a'.otP\leftarrow\langle p+1\rangle,a'.otV\leftarrow\top],a'}$$

$$\text{FRESH\_ZERO}\frac{a\notin\Sigma}{V,\Sigma,fresh\_zero()\ \to\ V,\Sigma[a.otP\leftarrow\langle 0\rangle,a.otV\leftarrow\top],a}$$

$$\text{TO\_INT}\frac{}{V,\Sigma,to\_int(\langle n\rangle)\ \to\ V,\Sigma,n} \qquad \text{CAP}\frac{0\le n\le m}{V,\Sigma,cap(n,\langle m\rangle)\ \to\ V,\Sigma,\langle n\rangle}$$

$$\text{ADD}\frac{\Sigma(a_1)=\{otP=\langle n\rangle,otV=\top\}\quad \Sigma(a_2)=\{otP=\langle m\rangle,otV=\top\}\quad a_1\neq a_2\quad a_3\notin\Sigma}{V,\Sigma,add(a_1,a_2)\ \to\ V,\Sigma[a_1.otV\leftarrow\bot,a_2.otV\leftarrow\bot,a_3.otP\leftarrow\langle n+m\rangle,a_3.otV\leftarrow\top],a_3}$$

Fig. 5. Reduction rules for operations.

$$
\begin{aligned}
C_e ::=\ &\square \mid succ(C_e)\\
&\mid add(C_e,e)\mid add(e,C_e)\\
&\mid int(C_e)\\
&\mid cap(C_e,e)\mid cap(e,C_e)\\
&\mid \{f=e,...,f=C_e,...,f=e\}\\
&\mid C_e.f\\
&\mid ...\quad\text{(other usual reduction contexts, for Boolean connectives/etc.)}
\end{aligned}
$$

$$
\begin{aligned}
C_s ::=\ &\square\mid x\leftarrow C_e\\
&\mid C_e.f\leftarrow e\mid e.f\leftarrow C_e\\
&\mid C_s;s\\
&\mid \textsf{if }C_e\textsf{ then }s\textsf{ else }s\\
&\mid \textsf{while }C_e\textsf{ do }s\textsf{ done}
\end{aligned}
$$

Fig. 6. Reduction contexts.

Definition 1. *A state* (V, Σ, s) *is n-bounded if:*

- *Any Peano integer occurring anywhere in the state, including constants in the program s, is no greater than n;*
- *The sum of all valid one-time integers allocated in Σ is no greater than n.*

Then we can state the main result. It uses the notion of 0-bounded state to capture the idea that all Peano integers are zeros at the start of a program.

Theorem 1. *Let (V, Σ, s) be a 0-bounded state. Then, for any state (V', Σ', s') reachable after n steps of execution, (V', Σ', s') is n-bounded.*

Proof. First, we generalize the claim: if (V, Σ, s) is m-bounded (with $m \geq 0$), then for any state (V', Σ', s') reachable after n steps of execution, (V', Σ', s') is $(m + n)$-bounded. By a straightforward induction on the number of steps, we reduce to the case of a single step of execution. Then we proceed by case analysis on the head reduction rule:

- PEANO-SUCC: as the Peano integer is bounded by m, its successor is bounded by $m + 1$. Other parts of the state do not change, so the resulting state is indeed $(m + 1)$-bounded.
- ONE-TIME-SUCC: Similar to the rule PEANO-SUCC, except that the sum of valid one-time integers also changes. However, it increases by exactly one, so the resulting state is indeed $(m + 1)$-bounded.
- FRESH_ZERO: the newly introduced one-time integer is 0, so the total sum of valid one-time integers stays unchanged. As it is itself trivially m-bounded, the resulting state is m-bounded as well, hence $(m + 1)$-bounded.
- CAP: by hypothesis, it creates a Peano integer smaller than an existing one, thus respecting the bound.
- ADD: the total sum of valid integers stays unchanged and is therefore m-bounded. All we need to show is that the result of the addition is no greater than $m + 1$. Using the separation hypothesis, the result is no greater than the total sum of valid one-time integers in the initial state, hence no greater than m.
- MEM-ASSIGN: it does not introduce any new Peano nor one-time integer. Also, one-time integers are not modified by this rule, so the sum of valid one-time integers is still no greater than m.
- ALLOC: since this rule cannot be used to build a one-time integer, the resulting state is still m-bounded.
- other rules: As they do not introduce new Peano/one-time integers and do not change the memory, they preserve m-boundedness. $\square$

Note that in the proof above, the bound may only increase after successor operations. This yields the following corollary:

Corollary 1. *For any execution $(V, \Sigma, s) \to^\star (V', \Sigma', s')$, where (V, Σ, s) is a 0-bounded state, (V', Σ', s') is bounded by the number of successor steps in the execution (rules PEANO-SUCC and ONE-TIME-SUCC).*

4 Implementation in Why3

Why3 is a platform for deductive program verification. It provides a rich language, called WhyML, to write programs [5] and their logical specifications [8,9], and it relies on external theorem provers to discharge verification conditions. Why3 is based on first-order logic with rank-1 polymorphic types, algebraic data types, inductive predicates, and several other extensions. The programming language can be seen as an ML dialect, providing variant types, pattern matching, exceptions, and mutable data structures. In order to keep proof obligations reasonably easy to read and to debug, Why3 imposes static control of aliases: every l-value in a program must have a finite set of names and these names must be known at the time of generation of verification conditions.

Verified WhyML programs can be automatically translated to OCaml, producing executable correct-by-construction code. This procedure, called *code extraction*, is guided by *drivers*: configuration files which assign OCaml translation to symbols that have not been given definition in the WhyML program. During extraction, Why3 erases from the program so-called *ghost code* which serves to facilitate specification and verification and is guaranteed to not affect the observable program behaviour and its final result [10]. For example, a ghost function argument can be used to pass a witness of some existential pre-condition; a ghost record field may hold a pure logical "view" of the record's contents.

Here is how Peano and one-time integers are introduced in Why3.

```
type peano model { v: int }

type onetime model { peano: peano; mutable valid: bool }
```

Here, type `int` is that of mathematical, arbitrary-precision integers. Both types are introduced as *model types* whose structure is hidden from programs but can be accessed from specification annotations. By virtue of being model types, their values cannot be constructed in programs directly: the client code has to employ abstract functions. For instance, addition over Peano integers can be implemented via the basic abstract operation `cap` as follows:

```
val cap (x: int) (p: peano) : peano requires { 0 <= x <= p.v }
                                      ensures  { result.v = x }
```

```
let add (p q r: peano) : peano requires { 0 <= p.v + q.v <= r.v}
                                 ensures  { result.v = p.v + q.v }
  = cap (to_int p + to_int q) r
```

Notice that addition takes a third argument, serving as an upper bound for the result. For comparison, addition over one-time integers is specified as follows:

```
val add (o1 o2: onetime) : onetime writes { o1, o2 }
  requires { o1.valid ∧ o2.valid }
  ensures  { result.peano.v = o1.peano.v + o2.peano.v }
  ensures  { result.valid ∧ not o1.valid ∧ not o2.valid }
```

Notice that we do not need to add any separation pre-condition for the arguments of add: Why3 assumes it by default and checks separation whenever add is called.

To produce executable OCaml code, Why3 provides appropriate driver files that translate Peano and one-time integers directly to OCaml's native unboxed 63-bit integers on 64-bit architectures. For instance, Peano's operation add is translated into the OCaml function (fun p q _ → p + q). Notice that the translation does not contain any run-time safety assertion: the bound argument is simply ignored. Deductive verification of the initial WhyML program ensures, statically, that the precondition of add is satisfied in any possible execution.

Similarly, operation add for one-time integers is translated into OCaml native addition (+). It is worth pointing out that the validity flag appears nowhere in the extracted code. Indeed, once the safety of calls to operations over one-time integers has been established during the verification phase, the validity bit has no further influence on the program behaviour and can be eliminated.

Example. To illustrate the use of our approach, let us consider implementing Program 7 in Why3. Figure 7 shows a code where backtracking is implemented with recursive function count_bt_queens. Its argument solutions is a Peano counter, which is incremented each time we find a new solution (line 22). For the sake of brevity, we omit specification annotations.

This program uses two flavors of machine integers. Type int63 is used for array indexes and chessboard coordinates and we prove statically the safety of operations on this type. For example, at line 12, a proof obligation is generated to ensure that q can be incremented without overflow. This obligation is easily discharged, thanks to the loop condition. The other flavor is Peano integers, which we use to count the solutions; see the incrementation at line 22. No proof obligation is generated for this operation. This is fortunate, since we would not be able to prove it. Indeed, we do not have any *a priori* bound on the number of solutions, except the obviously too large $n!$-related ones. And any bound inferred automatically (*e.g.*, by abstract interpretation) would be even larger. Both types int63 and peano become OCaml type int in the extracted 64-bit code.

Caveats. It may seem that the bounds passed to functions cap and add for Peano integers should be ghost arguments, as they only serve the verification purposes and are ignored in the extracted OCaml code. Indeed, it is tempting to specify add as

```
val bad_add (p q: peano) (ghost r: peano) : peano
  requires { 0 <= p.v + q.v <= r.v }
  ensures { result.v = p.v + q.v }
```

and simplify the translation to "(+)". This, however, would compromise the safety of the Peano integers, because a client code could write a ghost loop, incrementing some ghost variable up to an arbitrarily big value, well beyond 2^{64}. This ghost loop incurs zero run-time expense, as it is erased during extraction. Yet the ghost variable can be used in a call to bad_add, giving a "false alibi" to an overflowing non-ghost integer. In future versions of Why3, we may work

```
1    exception Inconsistent
2
3    let check_is_consistent (board: array int63) (pos: int63)
4    = try
5        let q = ref (of_int 0) in
6        while !q < pos do
7          let bq   = board[!q]   in
8          let bpos = board[pos] in
9          if bq        = bpos      then raise Inconsistent;
10         if bq - bpos = pos - !q then raise Inconsistent;
11         if bpos - bq = pos - !q then raise Inconsistent;
12         q := !q + of_int 1
13       done;
14       True
15     with Inconsistent →
16       False
17     end
18
19   let rec count_bt_queens (solutions: ref peano)
20       (board: array int63) (n: int63) (pos: int63)
21   = if eq pos n then
22       solutions := Peano.succ !solutions
23     else
24       let i = ref (of_int 0) in
25       while !i < n do
26         board[pos] ← !i;
27         if check_is_consistent board pos then
28           count_bt_queens solutions board n (pos + of_int 1);
29         i := !i + of_int 1
30       done
31
32   let count_queens (board: array int63) (n: int63) : peano
33   = let solutions = ref (Peano.zero ()) in
34     count_bt_queens solutions board n (of_int 0);
35     !solutions
```

Fig. 7. N-queens in Why3.

around this problem by forbidding calls to succ in ghost code, making bad_add safe to use.

It should also be noted that we must not provide a function converting a peano value to a fixed-size machine integer. Just as in the previous case, as long as succ is admitted in ghost code, we can create an out-of-bounds ghost Peano value. Converting it to a 64-bit integer would lead to a contradiction (*i.e.*, a proof of false) in a reachable state of execution, compromising all subsequent verification conditions. Moreover, such conversion is dangerous even in the case where the offending value is not ghost. Indeed, while we may consider the states after 2^{64} steps as effectively unreachable (which justifies the contradiction), it is disturbing if the system validates the total functional correctness, termination included, of

```
let p = ackermann_with_peano 4 2  (* = 2^65536 - 3 *) in
let n = to_int64 p in
assert { n > max_int64 >= n }
```

without raising any red flags.

On the other hand, it is perfectly safe to provide variants of the cap function taking fixed-size integers as first argument. For programs that work with native integers, this avoids an unnecessary conversion to arbitrary-precision integers.

5   Conclusion

We have presented a method to avoid proving the absence of arithmetic overflows when we do not expect a single execution to run long enough to overflow a machine integer of a fixed width. To the best of our knowledge, this is the first practical approach to verifying safety of programs such as the ones listed in Sect. 2. Despite its sheer simplicity, we feel that it effectively addresses a real-life verification challenge.

Our technique consists in placing an upper bound on reachable integer values in a sequential program, as a function of the number of execution steps. To apply this technique safely, a number of conditions must be taken into account. The most obvious one is the ratio of the chosen integer size to the available processor speed. We believe that 64-bit integers are a good match for the modern hardware.

If the program is written in a compiled language, one also needs to be aware of compiler optimisations. If a compiler rewrites **for** $i = 1$ **to** 2^{32} **do** $s \leftarrow s + 1$ **end for** into $s \leftarrow s + 2^{32}$ then our meta-argument clearly does not hold anymore. In practice, this should not be a concern for reasonably written algorithms. We observe that most of the time, if not always, the use of function succ on Peano/one-time integers coincides with an allocation or a branching point in the program, and thus is not amenable to an aggressive optimization. To reduce doubt, one can instrument the succ operation with some kind of "barrier instruction" that the compiler is not allowed to optimize out.

Computation on multiple cores introduces some additional constraints. For example, it would be unsound to add one-time integers computed on different cores: the individual increments are not serialized in this case, and the addition should produce either an arbitrary-precision integer or a fixed-width integer with a run-time check.

The solution proposed in this paper is not readily applicable when we want to use short machine integers (of 8 bits or less). For example, when implementing balanced binary search trees with AVL [11], the height of the sub-tree is stored inside each node. The height of an AVL tree of n nodes does not exceed $1.44 \log_2(n)$. Thus 6 bits for the height would allow up to 2^{44} nodes and 8 bits for the height would allow up to 2^{177} nodes. The same argument applies to the union-find weights. One possible approach to this problem is to introduce a variation of one-time integers where the linear quantity (a subject to increments and destructive additions; for example, the size of a tree) is stored as a ghost field, and the desired logarithmic quantity (tree height) is stored as a non-ghost field linked to the linear quantity by a statically verified datatype invariant. Devising a suitable generic interface for this purpose is one future direction of this work.

It is tempting to apply our approach for physical limits other than time, such as available memory or energy. This is however not straightforward. It is not enough to impose a physical limit; we must also be able to verify, statically, that a particular integer value in the program grows "in lockstep" with the consumption of the resource. So far, we were not able to ensure such a property for any non-trivial use case.

Acknowledgments. We are grateful to Arthur Charguéraud for detailed and constructive comments regarding a first draft of this paper.

References

1. Bloch, J.: Nearly all binary searches and mergesorts are broken (2006). http://googleresearch.blogspot.com/2006/06/extra-extra-read-all-about-it-nearly.html
2. Blanchet, B., Cousot, P., Cousot, R., Feret, J., Mauborgne, L., Miné, A., Monniaux, D., Rival, X.: The Astrée static analyzer. http://www.astree.ens.fr/
3. Cordeiro, L., Fischer, B., Marques-Silva, J.: SMT-based bounded model checking for embedded ANSI-C software. In: Proceedings of the 2009 IEEE/ACM International Conference on Automated Software Engineering, ASE 2009, pp. 137–148. IEEE Computer Society, Washington, DC (2009)
4. Tuch, H., Klein, G., Norrish, M.: Types, bytes, and separation logic. In: Hofmann, M., Felleisen, M. (eds.) Proceedings of 34th ACM SIGPLAN-SIGACT Symposium on Principles of Programming Languages (POPL 2007), pp. 97–108, Nice, France, January 2007
5. Filliâtre, J.-C., Paskevich, A.: Why3 — where programs meet provers. In: Felleisen, M., Gardner, P. (eds.) ESOP 2013. LNCS, vol. 7792, pp. 125–128. Springer, Heidelberg (2013)
6. de Bruijn, N.G.: Lambda calculus with nameless dummies, a tool for automatic formula manipulation, with application to the Church-Rosser theorem. Proc. K. Ned. Akad. **75**(5), 380–392 (1972)
7. Littlewood, D., Richardson, A.: Group characters and algebra. In: Philosophical Transactions of the Royal Society of London: Mathematical and Physical Sciences. Harrison & Sons, London (1934)
8. Bobot, F., Filliâtre, J.C., Marché, C., Paskevich, A.: Why3: shepherd your herd of provers. In: Boogie 2011: First International Workshop on Intermediate Verification Languages, pp. 53–64, Wrocław, Poland, August 2011
9. Filliâtre, J.-C.: One logic to use them all. In: Bonacina, M.P. (ed.) CADE 2013. LNCS, vol. 7898, pp. 1–20. Springer, Heidelberg (2013)
10. Filliâtre, J.-C., Gondelman, L., Paskevich, A.: The spirit of ghost code. In: Biere, A., Bloem, R. (eds.) CAV 2014. LNCS, vol. 8559, pp. 1–16. Springer, Heidelberg (2014)
11. Adel'son-Vel'skiĭ, G.M., Landis, E.M.: An algorithm for the organization of information. Sov. Math.-Dokl. **3**(5), 1259–1263 (1962)

Machine-Checked Proofs
for Realizability Checking Algorithms

Andreas Katis[1]([✉]), Andrew Gacek[2], and Michael W. Whalen[1]

[1] Department of Computer Science and Engineering,
University of Minnesota, 200 Union Street, Minneapolis, MN 55455, USA
katis001@umn.edu, whalen@cs.umn.edu
[2] Rockwell Collins Advanced Technology Center, 400 Collins Road NE,
Cedar Rapids, IA 52498, USA
andrew.gacek@gmail.com

Abstract. *Virtual integration* techniques focus on building architectural models of systems that can be analyzed early in the design cycle to try to lower cost, reduce risk, and improve quality of complex embedded systems. Given appropriate architectural descriptions, assume/guarantee contracts, and compositional reasoning rules, these techniques can be used to prove important safety properties about the architecture prior to system construction. For these proofs to be meaningful, each leaf-level component contract must be *realizable*; i.e., it is possible to construct a component such that for any input allowed by the contract assumptions, there is some output value that the component can produce that satisfies the contract guarantees.

We have recently proposed (in [1]) a contract-based realizability checking algorithm for assume/guarantee contracts over infinite theories supported by SMT solvers such as linear integer/real arithmetic and uninterpreted functions. In that work, we used an SMT solver and an algorithm similar to k-induction to establish the realizability of a contract, and justified our approach via a hand proof. Given the central importance of realizability to our virtual integration approach, we wanted additional confidence that our approach was sound. This paper describes a complete formalization of the approach in the Coq proof and specification language. During formalization, we found several small mistakes and missing assumptions in our reasoning. Although these did not compromise the correctness of the algorithm used in the checking tools, they point to the value of machine-checked formalization. In addition, we believe this is the first machine-checked formalization for a realizability algorithm.

1 Introduction

An ongoing effort at Rockwell Collins and The University of Minnesota has explored algorithms and tools for compositional proofs of correctness. The idea is to support hierarchical design and analysis of complex system architectures

© Springer International Publishing Switzerland 2016
A. Gurfinkel and S.A. Seshia (Eds.): VSTTE 2015, LNCS 9593, pp. 110–123, 2016.
DOI: 10.1007/978-3-319-29613-5_7

and co-evolution of requirements and architectures at multiple levels of abstraction [2]. We have created the AGREE reasoning framework [3] to support compositional assume/guarantee contract reasoning over system architectural models written in AADL.

The soundness of the compositional argument requires that each leaf-level component contract is *realizable*; i.e., it is possible to construct a component such that for any input allowed by the contract assumptions, there is some output value that the component can produce that satisfies the contract guarantees. Unfortunately, without engineering support it is all too easy to write contracts of leaf-level components that can't be realized. When applying our tools in both industrial and classroom settings, this issue has led to incorrect compositional "proofs" of systems; in fact the goal of producing a compositional proof can lead to engineers modifying component-level requirements such that they are no longer possible to implement. In order to make our approach reasonable for practicing engineers, tool support must be provided for checking realizability.

The notion of realizability has been well-studied for many years [4–9], both for component synthesis and checking correctness of propositional temporal logic requirements. Checking realizability for contracts involving theories, on the other hand, is still an open problem. In recent work [1], we described a new approach for checking realizability of contracts as a Satisfiability Modulo Theories (SMT) problem and demonstrated its usefulness on several examples. Our approach is similar to k-induction [10] over quantified formulas. In that work, we provided hand-proofs for several aspects of two algorithms related to the soundness of the approach with respect to both proofs and counterexamples.

Unfortunately, hand proofs of complex systems often contain errors. Given the criticality of realizability checking to our tool chain and the soundness of our computational proofs, we would like a higher level of assurance than hand proofs can provide. In this paper, we provide a formalization of machine-checked proofs of correctness that ensure that the proposed realizability algorithms will perform as expected, using the Coq proof assistant.[1] The facilities in Coq, notably mixed use of induction and co-induction, make the construction of the proofs relatively straightforward. This approach illustrates how interactive theorem proving and SMT solving can be used together in a profitable way. Interactive theorem proving is used for describing the soundness of the checking algorithm (described in this paper). The algorithm is then implemented using a SMT solver, which can automatically solve complex verification instances.

The main contribution of this paper is, therefore, the first machine-checked formalization (to our knowledge) of a realizability checking algorithm. This is an important problem for both compositional verification involving virtual integration and component synthesis. In addition, the formalization process exposed errors regarding our initial definitions, including necessary assumptions to one of the main theorems to be proved and an error in the definition of realizability itself. While these errors did not ultimately impact the correctness of the algorithm, they underscore the importance of machine-checked proof.

---

[1] The Coq file is available at https://github.com/andrewkatis/Coq/blob/master/realizability/Realizability.v.

In Sect. 2 we provide information on the Coq proof assistant. Section 3 contains the necessary informal background towards understanding our realizability checking approach. Sections 4.1 and 4.2 describe the definitions and theorems that were used both for defining realizability and the algorithms. In Sect. 5 we provide details on the algorithm's implementation. Finally, in Sect. 6 we discuss our experience from the process of defining realizability and the various changes that were made along the way, and we report our conclusions in Sect. 7.

2   The Coq Proof Assistant

Coq[2] is an interactive tool used to formalize mathematical expressions and algorithms, and prove theorems regarding their correctness and functionality [11]. The tool was a result of the work on the calculus of constructions [12]. Its uses in the context of computer science vary, such as being a tool to represent the structure of a programming language and its characteristics, as well as to prove the correctness of underlying procedures in compilers. Compared to other mainstream interactive theorem provers, Coq is a tool that provides support on several aspects, such as the use of dependent types, as opposed to the Isabelle theorem prover [13], and proof by reflection, which is not supported by the PVS proof assistant [14]. A particularly essential feature is the tool's support for inductive and coinductive definitions. Definitions using the *Inductive* type in Coq represent a least fixpoint of the corresponding type and are always accompanied by an induction principle, which is implicitly used to progress through a proof by applying induction on the definition. *CoInductive* definitions, on the other hand, represent a greatest fixpoint to their type. They describe a set containing every finite or infinite instance of that type, and their proofs are essentially infinite processes, built in a one-step fashion and requiring the existence of a guard condition that needs to hold for them to remain well-formed. Coinductive definitions allow a natural expression of infinite traces, which are central to our formalization of realizability, and are tedious to prove with hand-written proofs.

3   Realizability Checking

In [1] we presented our approach to the problem of realizability checking, introducing an algorithm involving the use of theories, a concept that, to the best of our knowledge, has yet to be examined. The realizability checks are defined over *assume-guarantee contracts*. Informally, *assumptions* describe the expectations of the component on its environment, usually in terms of component inputs. The *guarantees* describe the properties that will hold with respect to component outputs given that the assumptions are met. A contract *holds* on an infinite trace if either the assumption is violated or the guarantee holds throughout the trace.

To illustrate, consider a system with a single integer input *in* and output *out* and a contract consisting of no assumptions and two guarantees: $out = 2 * in$ and

---

[2] The Coq Proof Assistant is available at https://coq.inria.fr/.

$out \geq 0$. This contract is not realizable. At issue is the behavior of the system if $in < 0$. In this case, the output of the system must both be positive and equal to $2 * in$, which is not possible. While this example is trivial, it can be very difficult to determine whether a contract involving dozens or hundreds of assumptions and guarantees is realizable. In [1], we describe two large-scale compositional reasoning examples (one medical device and one flight control system) that contained unrealizable leaf-level contracts that were previously unknown that were detected by our tools.

Informally, a *realizable contract* is one for which there exists a *transition system* that correctly and completely implements the contract. By "correctly" we mean that the transition system always produces outputs that satisfy the guarantees as long as the assumptions have always been met, and by "completely" we mean that the transition system never deadlocks on an input, so long as the assumptions have always been met. We will make these definitions precise in the next section.

This definition, while providing the proper theoretical basis for realizability, is not actually useful for constructing our checking algorithm. At issue is that our current algorithm provides no way to construct this 'witness' transition system (doing so would solve the general problem of program synthesis over contracts with theories, which we are currently researching). We therefore propose an alternative definition, according to which a contract is realizable if there exists a *viable path* consisting of *viable states*. A viable state is one where, for any inputs that satisfy the assumptions, there are outputs that satisfy the guarantees and lead to another viable state. This alternative definition requires that the contract be able to start in a viable state.

To derive checking algorithms from first principles, we first demonstrate that the two definitions (transition systems and viability) are equivalent. We can then use the viable definition as the basis of an algorithm for realizability checking. This algorithm consists of a *base check*, which ensures that there exists a finitely viable state for paths of length at least n, and an *extend check* to show that all the valid paths can be further extended in response to any input. Unfortunately, the complexity of the base check does not allow for an SMT solver to handle it efficiently. Because of this, we propose a simplified version of the algorithm including a base check that ensures the extendability of every valid path consisting of viable states. This check is only guaranteed sound with regard to 'realizable' results, that is, it may generate "false positives" in which the tool declares a contract unrealizable when in fact it can be realized. In early experiments, however, the tool results have been accurate.

4   Formalization in Coq

In the next two subsections, we will describe the formalization and proofs of these ideas in Coq. Section 4.1 will describe the definitions of realizability, while Sect. 4.2 will describe the algorithms for realizability checking and their proofs of adequacy with respect to the definitions. To provide a graphical overview of the

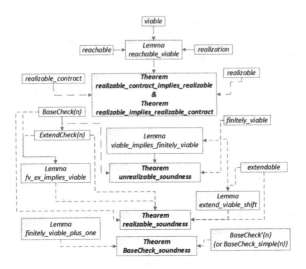

Fig. 1. Proof graph

proof process, Fig. 1 describes the connections between the various definitions, lemmas, and theorems in our work.

4.1 Definitions

The types *state* and *inputs* are used to represent a state, and a given set of inputs. We use Coq's *Prop* definition to describe the logical propositions regarding the component's *transition system* through a set I of *initial* states and the *transition* relation T between two states and a set of inputs. Finally, the contract is defined by its *assumption* and *guarantee*, with the latter being implicitly referenced by a pair of initial and transitional guarantees (*iguarantee* and *tguarantee*). The corresponding definitions in Coq are shown below. Note that we do not expect that a contract would be defined over all variables in the transition system – rather its outputs – but we do not make any distinction between internal state variables and outputs in the formalism. This way, we can use state variables to, in some cases, simplify statements of guarantees.

- Inductive *inputs* : Type :=
  input : *id* → *nat* → *inputs*.
- Inductive *state* : Type :=
  st : *id* → *nat* → *state*.
- Definition *initial* := *state* → Prop.
- Definition *transition* := *state* → *inputs* → *state* → Prop.
- Definition *iguarantee* := *state* → Prop.

- **Definition** $tguarantee := state \rightarrow inputs \rightarrow state \rightarrow$ **Prop**.
- **Definition** $assumption := state \rightarrow inputs \rightarrow$ **Prop**.

A state s is *reachable* with respect to the given assumptions if there exists a path from an initial state to s, while each transition in the path is satisfying the assumptions. Given a contract $(A, (G_I, G_T))$, a transition system (I, T) is its *realization* if the following four conditions hold:

1. $\forall s.\ I(s) \Rightarrow G_I(s)$
2. $\forall s, i, s'.\ reachable_A(s) \wedge A(s, i) \wedge T(s, i, s') \Rightarrow G_T(s, i, s')$
3. $\exists s.\ I(s)$
4. $\forall s, i.\ reachable_A(s) \wedge A(s, i) \Rightarrow \exists s'.\ T(s, i, s')$

Finally, we define that a given contract is *realizable*, if the existence of a transition system, which is a realization of the contract, is proved. The formalized definitions in Coq for the *reachable* state, the *realization* of a contract and whether it is *realizable* follow.

- **Inductive** *reachable* $(s : state)$ $(I : initial)$ $(T : transition)$ $(A : assumption)$
  : **Prop** :=
    rch :
      $((I\ s) \vee$
      $((\exists\ (s' : state)\ (inp : inputs),$
        $(reachable\ s'\ I\ T\ A) \wedge (A\ s'\ inp) \wedge (T\ s'\ inp\ s))) \rightarrow$
      $reachable\ s\ I\ T\ A)$.

- **Inductive** *realization* $(I : initial)$ $(T : transition)$ $(A : assumption)$ $(G_I :$
  $iguarantee)$ $(G_T : tguarantee)$: **Prop** :=
    $real$: $((\forall\ (s : state), (I\ s) \rightarrow (G_I\ s)) \wedge$
      $(\forall\ (s\ s' : state)\ (inp : inputs),$
      $((reachable\ s\ I\ T\ A) \wedge (A\ s\ inp) \wedge (T\ s\ inp\ s')) \rightarrow G_T\ s\ inp\ s') \wedge$
      $(\exists\ (s : state), I\ s) \wedge$
      $(\forall\ (s : state)\ (inp : inputs), (reachable\ s\ I\ T\ A \wedge (A\ s\ inp)) \rightarrow$
        $(\exists\ (s' : state), T\ s\ inp\ s'))) \rightarrow$
      $realization\ I\ T\ A\ G_I\ G_T$.

- **Inductive** *realizable_contract* $(A : assumption)$ $(G_I : iguarantee)$ $(G_T : tguar$-
  $antee)$: **Prop** :=
    rc : $(\exists\ (I : initial)\ (T : transition), realization\ I\ T\ A\ G_I\ G_T) \rightarrow$
      $realizable\_contract\ A\ G_I\ G_T$.

While the definitions of *realization* and *realizable_contract* are quite straightforward, they cannot be used directly to construct an actual realizability checking algorithm. Therefore, we proposed the notion of a state being *viable* with respect to a contract, meaning that the transition system continues to be a realization of the contract, while we are at such a state. In other words, a state is *viable* $(viable(s))$ if the transitional guarantee G_T infinitely holds, given valid inputs. Using the definition of *viable*, a contract is *realizable* if and only if $\exists s.\ G_I(s) \wedge viable(s)$.

- CoInductive *viable* $(s : state)$ $(A : assumption)$ $(G_I : iguarantee)$ $(G_T: tguarantee)$: Prop :=
  vbl : $(\forall (inp : inputs), (A\ s\ inp) \rightarrow$
    $(\exists (s' : state), G_T\ s\ inp\ s' \wedge viable\ s'\ A\ G_I\ G_T)) \rightarrow$
  $viable\ s\ A\ G_I\ G_T$.

- Inductive *realizable* $(A : assumption)$ $(G_I : iguarantee)$ $(G_T : tguarantee)$: Prop :=
  rl : $(\exists (s : state), G_I\ s \wedge viable\ s\ A\ G_I\ G_T) \rightarrow realizable\ A\ G_I\ G_T$.

Having a more useful definition for realizability, we need to prove the equivalence between the definitions of *realizable_contract* and *realizable*. The Coq definition of the theorem was split into two separate theorems, each for one of the two directions of the proof. Towards the two proofs, the auxiliary lemma that, given a realization, $\forall s.\ reachable_A(s) \Rightarrow viable(s)$ is necessary.

- Lemma *reachable_viable* : $\forall (s : state)$ $(I : initial)$ $(T : transition)$ $(A : assumption)$ $(G_I : iguarantee)$ $(G_T : tguarantee)$,
  $realization\ I\ T\ A\ G_I\ G_T \rightarrow reachable\ s\ I\ T\ A \rightarrow viable\ s\ A\ G_I\ G_T$.

The informal proof of the lemma relies initially on the unrolling of the *viable* definition, for a specific state s. Thus, we are left to prove that there exists another state s' that we can traverse into, in addition to being viable. The former can be proved directly from the conditions 2 and 4 of the definition of *realization*. For the latter, by the definition of *viable* on s' we need to show that s' is reachable. Given the definition of *reachable* though, we just need to prove that there exists another reachable state from which we can reach s', in one step. But we already know that s is such a state, and thus the lemma holds.

- Theorem *realizable_contract_implies_realizable* $(I : initial)$ $(T : transition)$:
  $\forall (A : assumption)$ $(G_I : iguarantee)$ $(G_T : tguarantee)$,
  $realizable\_contract\ A\ G_I\ G_T \rightarrow realizable\ A\ G_I\ G_T$.

- Theorem *realizable_implies_realizable_contract* $(I : initial)$ $(T : transition)$:
  $\forall (A : assumption)$ $(G_I : iguarantee)$ $(G_T : tguarantee)$,
  $realizable\ A\ G_I\ G_T \rightarrow realizable\_contract\ A\ G_I\ G_T$.

The first part of the theorem requires us to prove that there exists a viable state s for which the initial guarantee holds. Considering that we have a contract that is realizable under the *realizable_contract* definition, we have a transition system that is a realization of the contract, and thus from the third condition of the *realization* definition, there exists an initial state s' for which, using the first condition, the initial guarantee holds. Thus, we are left to prove that s' is viable. But, by proving that s' is reachable, we can use the *reachable_viable* lemma to show that s' is indeed viable.

The second direction requires a bit more effort. Assuming that we have a viable state s_0 with $G_I(s_0)$ being true, we define $I(s) = (s = s_0)$ and $T(s, inp, s') = G_T(s, inp, s') \wedge viable(s')$. Initially, we need to prove the *reachable_viable* lemma in this context, with the additional assumption that another viable state already exists (s_0 in this case). Having done so, we need to prove that there exists a transition system that is a realization of the given contract. Given the transition system that we defined earlier, we need to show that each of the four conditions hold. Since $I(s) = (s = s_0)$ and $G_I(s_0)$ hold, the proof for the first condition is trivial. Using the assumption that $T(s, inp, s') = G_T(s, inp, s') \land viable(s')$, we can also trivially prove the second condition, while the third condition is simply proved by reflexivity on the state s_0. Finally, for the fourth condition we need to prove that $\forall s, inp.\ reachable_A(s) \land A(s, inp) \Rightarrow \exists s'.\ G_T(s, inp, s') \land viable(s')$. By applying the *reachable_viable* lemma on the reachable state s in the assumptions, we show that s is also viable, if s_0 is viable, which is what we assumed in the first place. Thus, coming back into what we need to prove, and unrolling the definition of *viable* on s, we have that $\forall inp.\ A(s, inp) \Rightarrow \exists s'.\ G_T(s, inp, s') \land viable(s')$ which completes the proof.

4.2   Algorithms

In this section we provide a description of the formalization and proof of soundness of our realizability checking algorithms. Initially, we define an under-approximation of the definition of viability, for the finite case. Thus, a state is *finitely_viable* for n steps ($viable_n(s)$), if the transitional guarantee G_T holds for at least n steps, given valid inputs.

- **Inductive** *finitely_viable* : *nat* → *state* → *assumption* → *tguarantee* → **Prop** :=

    | *fvnil* : ∀ s A G_T, *finitely_viable* O s A G_T
    | *fv* : ∀ n s A G_T, *finitely_viable* n s A G_T →
         (∀ (inp : *inputs*), A s inp → ($\exists$ s', G_T s inp s')) →
         finitely_viable (S n) s A G_T.

    In addition to the *finitely_viable* definition, an under-approximation of viability is also used, called one-step extension. Therefore, a valid path leading to a state s is *extendable* after n steps, if any path from s, of length at least n, can be further extended given a valid input.

- **Inductive** *extendable* : *nat* → *state* → *assumption* → *tguarantee* → **Prop** :=
    | *exnil* : ∀ (s : *state*) (A : *assumption*) (G_T : *tguarantee*),
         (∀ (inp : *inputs*), A s inp → $\exists$ (s' : *state*), G_T s inp s') →
         extendable O s A G_T
    | *ex* : ∀ n s A G_T,
         (∀ inp s', A s inp ∧ G_T s inp s' ∧ *extendable* n s' A G_T) →
         extendable (S n) s A G_T.

An Exact Algorithm for Realizability Checking. The algorithm that we propose for realizability checking consists of two checks. The $BaseCheck(n)$

procedure ensures that $\exists s.\ G_I(s) \wedge viable_n(s)$, while $ExtendCheck(n)$ makes sure that the given state from $BaseCheck$ is extendable for any n.

- **Definition** $BaseCheck\ (n : nat)\ (A : assumption)\ (G_I : iguarantee)\ (G_T : tguarantee) :=$
  $\exists\ (s : state),\ (G_I\ s \wedge finitely\_viable\ n\ s\ A\ G_T).$

  Definition $ExtendCheck\ (n : nat)\ (A : assumption)\ (G_T : tguarantee) :=$
  $\forall\ s\ A\ G_T,\ extendable\ n\ s\ A\ G_T.$

Using the $BaseCheck(n)$ and $ExtendCheck(n)$, the algorithm determines the realizability of the given contract, using the following procedure.

> **for** $n = 0$ to ∞ **do**
>   **if not** $BaseCheck(n)$ **then**
>   **return** "unrealizable"
>   **else if** $ExtendCheck(n)$ **then**
>   **return** "realizable"
>   **end if**
> **end for**

Using the definitions of $BaseCheck$ and $ExtendCheck$, we proved the algorithm's soundness, both for the 'unrealizable' and 'realizable' case. The main idea behind the proof of soundness for the 'unrealizable' result is to prove the contrapositive, that is, given a realizable contract, there exists a natural number x for which $BaseCheck(x)$ holds. Unfolding the definition of $BaseCheck(x)$, we need to show that $\exists s.\ G_I(s) \wedge viable_x(s)$. Knowing that our assumption $realizable\_contract\ A\ G_I\ G_T$ is equivalent to the $realizable$ definition, provides us with a state s', for which $G_I(s') \wedge viable(s')$ holds. Here, we need an additional lemma, according to which $\forall s, n.\ viable(s) \Rightarrow viable_n(s)$ (stated as $viable\_implies\_finitely\_viable$ below). Thus, using the lemma on $viable(s')$ with $n = x$, we get that $viable_x(s')$, thus completing the proof.

- **Lemma** $viable\_implies\_finitely\_viable : \forall\ s\ A\ G_I\ G_T\ n,$
  $viable\ s\ A\ G_I\ G_T \rightarrow finitely\_viable\ n\ s\ A\ G_T.$

- **Theorem** $unrealizable\_soundness : \forall\ (I : initial)\ (T : transition)\ (A : assumption)\ (G_I : iguarantee)\ (G_T : tguarantee),$
  $(\exists\ n,\ \neg BaseCheck\ n\ A\ G_I\ G_T) \rightarrow \neg\ realizable\_contract\ A\ G_I\ G_T.$

For the soundness of the 'realizable' result, we first need to prove two lemmas. Initially, $extend\_viable\_shift$, shows the way that $Extend_n(s)$ can be used to shift $viable_n(s)$ forward. The proof for this lemma is done by using induction on n. The base case is proved trivially, by unfolding the definitions of $extendable$ and $finitely\_viable$ in the assumptions. For the inductive case, we assume that the same state s is extendable and finitely viable for paths of length $n + 1$, and try to prove that there exists a finitely viable state s' for paths of length $n + 1$, to which we can traverse from s, with the contract guarantees still holding after the transition. By considering that s is extendable for paths of length $n + 1$, we can use it as that potentially existing state in the proof, requiring that we can transition from s to itself, with the transitional guarantees staying true, and s being finitely viable for paths of length $n + 1$. The former is true through the definition of *extendable*, while the second is an already given assumption by the inductive step.

- Lemma *extend_viable_shift* : $\forall$ $(s : state)$ $(n : nat)$ $(inp : inputs)$ $(A : assumption)$ $(G_I : iguarantee)$ $(G_T : tguarantee)$,
  $(extendable\ n\ s\ A\ G_T \wedge finitely\_viable\ n\ s\ A\ G_T \wedge A\ s\ inp) \rightarrow$
  $(\exists\ s',\ G_T\ s\ inp\ s' \wedge finitely\_viable\ n\ s'\ A\ G_T)$.

- Lemma *fv_ex_implies_viable* : $\forall$ $(s : state)$ $(n : nat)$ $(A : assumption)$ $G_I\ G_T$,
  $(finitely\_viable\ n\ s\ A\ G_T \wedge ExtendCheck\ n\ A\ G_T) \rightarrow viable\ s\ A\ G_I\ G_T$.

- Theorem *realizable_soundness* : $\forall$ $(I : initial)$ $(T : transition)$ $A\ G_I\ G_T$,
  $(\exists\ n,\ (BaseCheck\ n\ A\ G_I\ G_T \wedge ExtendCheck\ n\ A\ G_T)) \rightarrow$
  $realizable\_contract\ A\ G_I\ G_T$.

To prove the theorem, we try to prove the equivalent for the *realizable* definition instead. The existence of a state for which the initial guarantees hold is derived from the assumption that *BaseCheck* holds for a finitely viable state, while the proof that the same state is also viable comes from the use of the *fv_ex_implies_viable* lemma, which is proved through the use of *extend_viable_shift*.

An Approximate Algorithm for Realizability Checking. Following the definition of our approach, we noticed the problematic nature of $BaseCheck(n)$ having $2n$ quantifier alternations, which cannot be handled efficiently by an SMT solver. To that end, we proposed a simplified version of the $BaseCheck(n)$ procedure, called $BaseCheck'(n)$, stated as *BaseCheck_simple* below.

- Definition *BaseCheck_simple* $(n : nat)$ $(A : assumption)$ $(G_I : iguarantee)$ $(G_T : tguarantee) := \forall\ s,\ (G_I\ s) \rightarrow extendable\ n\ s\ A\ G_T$.

- Lemma *finitely_viable_plus_one* : $\forall$ $s\ n\ A\ (gi : iguarantee)$ $(G_T : tguarantee)$ $(inp : inputs)$,
  $(extendable\ n\ s\ A\ G_T \wedge finitely\_viable\ n\ s\ A\ G_T) \rightarrow$
  $finitely\_viable\ (S\ n)\ s\ A\ G_T$.

- Theorem *BaseCheck_soundness* : $\forall$ $n\ A\ (G_I : iguarantee)$ $(G_T : tguarantee)$ $(i : inputs)$,
  $((\exists\ s,\ G_I\ s) \wedge (\forall\ k,\ (k \leq n) \rightarrow BaseCheck\_simple\ k\ A\ G_I\ G_T)) \rightarrow$
  $BaseCheck\ n\ A\ G_I\ G_T$.

The simplified $BaseCheck'(n)$, while being an easier instance for an SMT solver, is not sound for the 'unrealizable' case, falsely reporting some realizable contracts to not be so. Nevertheless, we proved the modified algorithm's soundness for the 'realizable' result, with the use of an auxiliary lemma.

The lemma, *finitely_viable_plus_one* simply refers to the fact that an extendable and finitely viable state s, for a given number of steps n, is also finitely viable for $n + 1$ steps. The proof is done by induction on n. The base case is trivially proved, by the definition of *finitely_viable*, and the assumption that s is extendable. For the inductive case, we use the inductive hypothesis, which leaves us to prove the assumptions on a specific state s. The extendability is trivially shown since we already know that s is extendable for paths of length $n + 1$, with the same idea being applied to prove that s is finitely viable for n.

Finally, the proof of soundness for the 'realizable' result of the $BaseCheck'(n)$ procedure is done by using induction on n. The base case is trivially true, using the fact that all paths of zero length are finitely viable. The inductive step then requires us to prove that $BaseCheck(n + 1)$ holds. In order to do so, we need to construct the inductive hypothesis' assumption, as a separate assumption to the theorem's scope. By applying the inductive hypothesis to the newly created assumption, we have that $BaseCheck(n)$ holds. By unrolling the definition of $BaseCheck(n)$ and applying the lemma *finitely_viable_plus_one* on the extracted state, say x, we finally prove that x is extendable through the definition of $BaseCheck'(n)$, completing the proof at the same time.

Figure 1 provides a simplified proof graph of all the necessary definitions and partially, for graph simplicity purposes, the way that they are used towards proving the lemmas and theorems stated in this paper.

5   Implementation

The algorithm is now an optional feature, namely JRealizability in JKind [15], a Java implementation of the KIND 2 model checker,[3] and supports models expressed using the Lustre language [16], which are a result of AGREE's translation process of contracts written in AADL. A typical process for checking models in the above environment starts from providing the corresponding Lustre program to JKind, which JRealizability uses to find a number n, $n \geq 0$, such that both $BaseCheck'(n)$ and $ExtendCheck(n)$ hold. Specifically, the model's variables and contract are being translated in the SMT-LIB2 format, followed by the construction of each check's corresponding query for the current value of n, in its negated form. The resulting SMT-LIB2 file is provided as input to the Z3 SMT solver [17], which attempts to answer the given query. In the case that the negated formula is unsatisfiable, JRealizability returns a 'realizable' result. On the other hand, a satisfiable query implies that the model is unrealizable. Consequently, the tool requests a model, i.e. an instance of the contract's variables that reflects Z3's result, and proceeds to construct a counterexample that describes the exact cause of the contract's unrealizability. Finally, in those cases where the quantified query is too difficult for Z3 to solve, an 'unknown' result is reported, both by Z3 and JRealizability.

The implementation was used in [1] to verify the correctness of contracts in terms of realizability in three different case studies. The performance was very

---

[3] You can download the KIND model checker at http://kind2-mc.github.io/kind2/.

good for the concrete results, with the tool exceeding its predefined timeout value for the 'unknown' ones. False positive results ($BaseCheck'(n)$) were not found during this process, as every unrealizable contract was manually proved to be a result of conflicts in the provided assumptions or guarantees. A final remark is the fact that the most critical case studies already had an implementation that was supposed to work correctly. As such, the discovery of unrealizable contracts in these systems eventually required a total revision of the formalized requirements defined for each system, thus hindering the development process.

6   Discussion

While our work on realizability is based on simple definitions, formalizing them and refining the algorithms in Coq was non-trivial. Proving the lemmas and theorems using Coq helped us discover minor errors in our informal statements. For example, our proof of the one-way soundness theorem for the simplified *BaseCheck* in [1] lacks the necessary assumption that there exists a state for which the initial guarantees hold. Another example is that we forgot to include initial states in our definition of reachable states in the informal proof. The use of a mechanized theorem prover exposed some missing knowledge in the informal text, and helped us provide a more precise version of the theorem. Although these errors in the hand proofs did not lead to problems with our implementation, Coq improved both our theorems and proofs, and provided a very high level of assurance that our algorithm is correct.

7   Conclusion

The work in this paper was particularly important towards verifying our approach and learning more about the actual functionality of the algorithm. Interactive theorem provers like Coq provide the necessary support to define the notions and assertions while being able to effectively prove theorems in a far more convenient and reassuring way, in contrast to hand-written, informal proofs, especially when it comes down to tracking formulas containing alternating quantifiers. Furthermore, the procedure of proving the theorems in an interactive way with a tool allowed us to refine our definitions. Additionally, the time that was required was minimal when compared to the process of considering the informal proofs and writing down our requirements in English. The most important outcome was the proof of correctness of our approach that enabled us to provide a complementary set of definitions and proofs, easily processed by an experienced Coq user.

To conclude, there is substantial additional work that could be performed in terms of fleshing out the formalisms used in the proofs for our particular implementation. For example, we could define the structure and types of inputs and outputs, and describe how transition systems are realized in the AGREE tool suite. However, the work that has been performed shows the soundness of the proof system and our algorithms with respect to proofs of realizability, allowing us to proceed with very high confidence as to the correctness of our approach.

Acknowledgments. This work was funded by DARPA and AFRL under contract 4504789784 (Secure Mathematically-Assured Composition of Control Models), and by NASA under contract NNA13AA21C (Compositional Verification of Flight Critical Systems), and by NSF under grant CNS-1035715 (Assuring the safety, security, and reliability of medical device cyber physical systems).

References

1. Gacek, A., Katis, A., Whalen, M.W., Backes, J., Cofer, D.: Towards realizability checking of contracts using theories. In: Havelund, K., Holzmann, G., Joshi, R. (eds.) NFM 2015. LNCS, vol. 9058, pp. 173–187. Springer, Heidelberg (2015)
2. Whalen, M.W., Gacek, A., Cofer, D., Murugesan, A., Heimdahl, M.P., Rayadurgam, S.: Your what is my how: iteration and hierarchy in system design. IEEE Softw. **30**(2), 54–60 (2013)
3. Cofer, D., Gacek, A., Miller, S., Whalen, M.W., LaValley, B., Sha, L.: Compositional verification of architectural models. In: Person, S., Goodloe, A.E. (eds.) NFM 2012. LNCS, vol. 7226, pp. 126–140. Springer, Heidelberg (2012)
4. Pnueli, A., Rosner, R.: On the synthesis of a reactive module. In: Proceedings of the 16th ACM SIGPLAN-SIGACT Symposium on Principles of Programming Languages (POPL 1889), pp. 179–190 (1989)
5. Bohy, A., Bruyère, V., Filiot, E., Jin, N., Raskin, J.-F.: Acacia+, a tool for LTL synthesis. In: Madhusudan, P., Seshia, S.A. (eds.) CAV 2012. LNCS, vol. 7358, pp. 652–657. Springer, Heidelberg (2012)
6. Hamza, J., Jobstmann, B., Kuncak, V.: Synthesis for regular specifications over unbounded domains. In: Proceedings of the Conference on Formal Methods in Computer-Aided Design, pp. 101–109 (2010)
7. Chatterjee, K., Henzinger, T.A.: Assume-guarantee synthesis. In: Grumberg, O., Huth, M. (eds.) TACAS 2007. LNCS, vol. 4424, pp. 261–275. Springer, Heidelberg (2007)
8. Gunter, C.A., Gunter, E.L., Jackson, M., Zave, P.: A reference model for requirements and specifications. IEEE Softw. **17**(3), 37–43 (2000)
9. Patcas, L.M., Lawford, M., Maibaum, T.: From system requirements to software requirements in the four-variable model. In: Automated Verification of Critical Systems (AVOCS) 2013. Citeseer (2014)
10. Sheeran, M., Singh, S., Stålmarck, G.: Checking safety properties using induction and a SAT-solver. In: Johnson, S.D., Hunt Jr., W.A. (eds.) FMCAD 2000. LNCS, vol. 1954, pp. 108–125. Springer, Heidelberg (2000)
11. The Coq Development Team, The Coq Proof Assistant Reference Manual, 8th edn. INRIA (2012–2014)
12. Coquand, T., Huet, G.: Constructions: a higher order proof system for mechanizing mathematics. In: Buchberger, B. (ed.) EUROCAL 1985. LNCS, vol. 203, pp. 151–184. Springer, Heidelberg (1985)
13. Paulson, L.C.: The foundation of a generic theorem prover. J. Autom. Reasoning **5**(3), 363–397 (1989)

14. Owre, S., Rushby, J.M., Shankar, N.: PVS: a prototype verification system. In: Kapur, D. (ed.) CADE 2011. LNCS (LNAI), vol. 607, pp. 748–752. Springer, Heidelberg (1992). http://www.csl.sri.com/papers/cade92-pvs/
15. Gacek, A.: JKind - a Java implementation of the KIND model checker (2014). https://github.com/agacek/jkind
16. Halbwachs, N., Caspi, P., Raymond, P., Pilaud, D.: The synchronous data flow programming language lustre. Proc. IEEE **79**(9), 1305–1320 (1991)
17. de Moura, L., Bjørner, N.S.: Z3: an efficient SMT solver. In: Ramakrishnan, C.R., Rehof, J. (eds.) TACAS 2008. LNCS, vol. 4963, pp. 337–340. Springer, Heidelberg (2008)

Dynamic Frames Based Verification Method for Concurrent Java Programs

Wojciech Mostowski[1,2]([envelope])

[1] Formal Methods and Tools, University of Twente, Enschede, The Netherlands
[2] Center for Research on Embedded Systems,
Halmstad University, Halmstad, Sweden
wojciech.mostowski@hh.se

Abstract. In this paper we discuss a verification method for concurrent Java programs based on the concept of dynamic frames. We build on our earlier work that proposes a new, symbolic permission system for concurrent reasoning and we provide the following new contributions. First, we describe our approach for proving program specifications to be self-framed with respect to permissions, which is a necessary condition to maintain soundness in concurrent reasoning. Second, we show how we use predicates to provide modular and reusable specifications for program synchronisation points, like locks or forked threads. Our work primarily targets the KeY verification system with its specification language JML* and symbolic execution proving method. Hence, we also give the current status of the work on implementation and we discuss some examples that are verifiable with KeY.

1 Introduction

Permission-based verification of concurrent programs relies on specifications in an appropriate formalism enriched with permission annotations [1]. These annotations specify the read or write access rights to memory locations of the program to be verified. The verification is *thread local* and, when successful, shows the absence of race conditions in the verified program as well as some functional properties to hold. Many verification formalisms for permission-based reasoning are built on Separation Logic [2] or equivalent Implicit Dynamic Frames [3,4].

In the context of the VerCors project[1] [5], which is concerned with verification of concurrent data structures, we propose an approach to permission-based verification built on top of the more fundamental Dynamic Frames [6] verification method. We base our work on the Java Dynamic Logic [7] and its implementation in the KeY verifier[2] [8]. KeY is a symbolic execution-based interactive verification system for Java programs annotated with JML [9]. In addition to our automated

---

This work is supported by ERC grant 258405 for the VerCors project and by the Swedish Knowledge Foundation grant for the AUTO-CAAS project.

[1] http://fmt.cs.utwente.nl/research/projects/VerCors/.
[2] http://www.key-project.org/.

A. Gurfinkel and S.A. Seshia (Eds.): VSTTE 2015, LNCS 9593, pp. 124–141, 2016.
DOI: 10.1007/978-3-319-29613-5_8

VerCors toolset [10], KeY is meant to provide interactive verification capabilities in the VerCors project for more involved Java programs.

In our earlier work we developed a symbolic permission system that remedies some of the problems we identified with fractional permissions [11] and we also provided a base line for verification of concurrent Java programs in KeY based on Dynamic Frames and explicit use of two memory heaps in the verification logic and the specification language [12]. In this paper we extend this earlier work and describe our method for showing self-framing of specification with respect to permissions, and we discuss the use of JML model methods [13] for modular specification and verification of concurrent Java programs that make use of API methods that involve synchronisation. Throughout the paper, we relate our approach to the existing ones.

The rest of this paper is organised as follows. Section 2 recapitulates our symbolic permission system, and briefly explains verification of Java programs with Dynamic Frames as implemented in the KeY verifier. Sections 3 to 5 present the main contributions of the paper. Section 6 concludes the paper, discusses the current state of the implementation and future work.

2 Background

2.1 Symbolic Permissions

In an earlier paper [11] we proposed a symbolic permission system for concurrent reasoning as an alternative to classical fractional style permissions. Symbolic permissions address some of the issues we identified with fractional permissions, like inflexibility to handle complex synchronisation scenarios. Here we only give a brief description of the main idea behind symbolic permissions and we refer the reader to [11] for full account, including formal definitions and mechanically proved consistency properties.

A single symbolic permission p refers to one heap memory location of the program to be verified. From the point of view of the currently running thread, permission p maintains information about which other threads possibly hold access to the memory location and which threads are the permission's *originators*, i.e., threads that the permission should be returned to during synchronisation. As in Java, threads are identified by their corresponding object references and the currently running thread is uniquely identified by ct. On the top level, the permission expression assigned to p consists of a list of permission *slices*, and each slice defines one piece of ownership of the permission. Such a slice is again a list that holds the history of owners (threads) of this slice, with the current owner at the head of the list, and the tail containing previous owners that this slice is owed to (originators of the slice). Permission p grants read access to thread t when there is at least one slice in p that is owned by t, while the write access requires all of the slices in p to be owned by t. In principle, no empty permissions (with no slices) or empty slices (with no owners) are allowed and the defined permission operations guarantee this property.

For example, after acquiring a simple read lock the running thread might hold a permission of the form $[[ct, l], [l]]$ to some memory location, where l is the lock that provides read access to the threads that acquire it.[3] This permission contains two slices. The first slice $[ct, l]$ belongs to the current thread and consequently grants it a read permission while upon lock release it will be returned to the lock l, the originator of this slice. The second slice belongs to lock l only and allows further acquirings of the lock by other threads. When the current thread releases the lock the complete permission becomes $[[l], [l]]$ which is semantically equivalent to $[[l]]$ (and can become so) meaning that the lock holds the full access to the associated memory location.

With symbolic permissions, the core difference compared to fractional style permissions is how permission transfers are specified. In our approach we state *what kind of transfer* is applied to a permission rather than saying *how much* of the permission is transferred. Using functional style expressions, we specify how a permission is changed with respect to its previous value upon a synchronisation point. For our lock example, when acquiring the lock, the specification would say $p = transferPermPart(l, ct, p')$. It states that the old permission p' becomes permission p after splitting one (any) slice that belongs to l and transferring the ownership of one of the newly created slices to ct. That is, if $p' = [[l]]$ it becomes p in two steps, first it becomes $[[l], [l]]$ and then $[[ct, l], [l]]$. For a write lock, by using another transfer function $transferPermAll$, no splitting of the permission would be applied and p would become $[[ct, l]]$, temporarily giving ct full access right to the associated resource.

Such functional style specifications are particularly suitable for dynamic frames with explicit heaps as we explain in the next section. However, in many situations it is not possible to operate on concrete permissions expressions that explicitly state all the threads that share the permission. In fact, in the example above the read lock would be passing the permission to other threads unknown to ct and it cannot be assumed that the slices we specified are the only ones that comprise the permission at any point in time. To cover situations like this, abstraction of the permission is necessary and possible, as we show later in Sect. 5. In particular, instead of spelling out concrete permission expressions, one simply uses *readPerm* or *writePerm* predicates that establish if a permission is sufficient to grant a read or write access, respectively, to a given thread.

2.2 Dynamic Frames in JML* Specifications

In Dynamic Frames specifications [6] memory locations are first class citizens, typically stored in ghost or model variables typed as location sets, which in turn are used to specify method frames or frame dependency relations, and mechanisms are provided that allow to specify dynamic changes of these frames (typically called memory footprints). In the KeY verification system, dynamic frames are added to the Java Modelling Language (JML) [9], a behavioural specification language for Java, to form a KeY-specific version of JML called JML* [7].

---

[3] Although locks are actually not threads, classifying them as such allows us to suitably generalise the symbolic permission approach.

```
public interface List {                  public class ArrayList implements
  //@ instance model \locset                 ↪ List {
    ↪ footprint;                         private Object[] contents;
  //@ accessible footprint :             private int size;
    ↪ footprint;                         //@ represents footprint = size,
                                            ↪ contents, contents[*];
  //@ ensures \result == size();
  //@ accessible footprint;              public int size() {
  public /*@ pure @*/ int size();        return size;
                                         }
  //@ ensures size()==\old(size())
    ↪ + 1;                               public void add(Object o) {
  //@ assignable footprint;                contents[size++] = o;
  public void add(Object o);             }
}                                        }
```

Lst. 1. Java program annotated with JML*

Listing 1 shows a simple example of a Java program specified with dynamic frames, purposely underspecified for clarity. It implements a simple array list based on an interface specification, which abstractly specifies a memory footprint that the implementations will be working with through declaring a model variable of a primitive type \locset . This footprint is made concrete in the implementing class with the **represents** clause that puts all the concrete locations used by the **ArrayList** class into the **footprint** model field. This model field is in turn used in two frame specifications. Firstly, the **assignable** clause of method **add** states that these are the locations that may change when **add** is called. Secondly, through the **accessible** clause, the **size** method specifies that its result only depends on the locations contained in the footprint. Such specifications are commonly used to prove *independence* of pure expressions; If an expression is to be evaluated on two different heaps and it can be proved that the two heaps differ only on locations disjoint with the ones in the **accessible** clause, then it can be concluded that the two expressions are equal. This in turn enables abstract reasoning about expressions.

Note that in dynamic frames there is no implicit framing as found in approaches based on Separation Logic [2] or Implicit Dynamic Frames [4], hence the **assignable** and **accessible** clauses have to be stated explicitly. In particular, we also have to explicitly specify that the footprint is self-framed. However, there is no obligation to use model (or ghost) fields as in our example, it is also possible to state the locations explicitly in the corresponding clauses. In this case the approach is equivalent to well known static frames [14].

To prove a JML* annotated programs correct in KeY, the specifications are translated to the Java Dynamic Logic (JDL) in which the memory heap is modelled with an explicit program variable using the *theory of arrays* [7]. This program variable, simply called **heap**, is used in translating Java and JML* expressions to JDL and generating suitable proof obligations over this variable to show the correctness of method framing. For example, an object field access o.f is typically translated to *select*(heap, o, f) which reads the contents of the heap variable at the location mapped by o and f. Further, a part of the formula that establishes correct framing of a method usually reads:

$$\forall_{o: Object, f: Field} \ (o, f) \in frame \lor o.f@\text{heap} = o.f@\text{heapAtPre} \tag{1}$$

where (i) *frame* is the methods frame, either concrete or abstract (in the latter case it can be concretely instantiated when the concrete instance of the object involved is known), (ii) @ is a shorthand notation for the *select* function, and (iii) heapAtPre is a snapshot of the heap taken before the method was called (which is also used to translate JML* \old expressions). The actual Java programs are embedded in and treated with Dynamic Logic $[p]\phi$ and $\langle p \rangle \phi$ modalities for partial and total correctness, respectively, where p is a program and ϕ is a correctness formula. Modalities are actually in most part a orthogonal issue to the subject of this paper, however, what is important is that during correctness proofs programs in modalities are evaluated on a statement by statement basis using symbolic execution. During this evaluation the program heap is modified accordingly by updating the heap variable. For example, an object field assignment o.f = v; results in a modification of the heap variable expressed by *store*(heap, o, f, v), which gives a newly modified heap.

2.3   JML* Model Methods

Model methods [13] are specification only methods that extend the notion of model fields to fully fledged abstract predicates. When abstract, they do not have any method body, when instantiated (typically in a subclass), they contain a single return statement that gives the predicate its definition. Model methods are strictly pure, which means that they are not allowed to modify any of the heaps. The accessible clause attached to the method specifies memory locations that the method at most depends on, this is used to reason about their (in-)equality upon state changes (see Sect. 4). Finally, a model method can have a specification of its own, which essentially serves as a lemma mechanism for predicates to state additional properties. Model methods are particularly suitable to specify linked data structures [15], in this paper we use them to provide modular specification of Java API synchronisation points. In Sect. 5 we give an example of the use of model methods for this.

3   Dynamic Frames with Permissions

The above described verification methodology works very well in a sequential setting. For the permission-based concurrent setting an appropriate extension is needed. Because the heap is a first class citizen in JDL, the extension is actually rather straightforward. The base heap stores the values of the memory locations that the program operates on, adding a second heap that stores our symbolic permissions in parallel to the values is in essence sufficient. Adding this *permission heap* means adding a second heap variable, which we simply call **permissions**, and extending the verification mechanisms of Java Dynamic Logic from one heap to two heaps. In fact, one can use more than two heaps in JDL easily, as long as the number of heaps is fixed, all mechanisms that work with the single **heap** variable extend naturally to multiple heaps [12].

For example, for proving the framing property (1) above, stemming from the **assignable** clauses, now two quantifiers, over the two heaps, are needed. The core semantics of the permission heap, i.e., granting of access permissions to heap locations, is encoded in the rules for heap location reading and assignment, these rules now operate on our two heaps. As before, the regular heap is read and modified to store the values of corresponding memory locations as briefly explained at the end of the previous section. In addition, each time a memory location is read from or stored onto this heap, the access right is checked on the permission heap. The permission heap is read at the corresponding location and the resulting permission value is checked accordingly to establish that the current thread has the respective permission.

More concretely, when a location writing statement `o.f = v;` is symbolically executed, the value mapped to `o.f` on the heap is updated with $store(\texttt{heap}, \texttt{o}, \texttt{f}, \texttt{v})$ as before, but first the permission p is read from the permission heap with $select(\texttt{permission}, \texttt{o}, \texttt{f})$ and p is checked to be a write permission for the current thread, i.e., as explained in Sect. 2 all slices in p have to belong to the current thread object ct. Reading of locations from the heap is analogous, only the permission is checked to be a read permission instead. In both cases, the permission values stored on the permission heap are only read, but in two cases writing of permission values can also occur. First, when objects are created and permissions are initialised to full permissions for the current thread, i.e., when object o is created, for all fields **f** of this object a new full permission is stored on the permission heap with $store(\texttt{permissions}, \texttt{o}, \texttt{f}, [[ct]])$. Second, permissions are changed, and hence written on the permission heap, when they are subjected to permission transfers upon synchronisation points, in which case the current permission is first read from the permission heap and a modified one is then written back. For example, when a permission for location `o.f` is transferred from the lock l to the current thread as explained in Sect. 2, the permission heap becomes $store(\texttt{permissions}, \texttt{o}, \texttt{f}, transferPermPart(l, ct, select(\texttt{permissions}, \texttt{o}, \texttt{f})))$.

For writing suitable user level specifications this extension of JDL to use two heaps has to be lifted to JML*. Following the explicit heap variable approach of JDL, we allow for the same explicit reference of the heap variables in JML* and provide operators to access permissions on the second heap and evaluate them. The following is a short example that illustrates this:

```
//@ requires \writePerm(\perm(this.o));
//@ ensures this.o == p;
//@ assignable<heap> this.o;
//@ assignable<permissions> \nothing;
public void set(Object p) { this.o = p; }
```

First, we allow to explicitly state the heap variable that the `assignable` clause refers to (and similarly for the `accessible` clauses). This allows us to decouple the two heaps in the specifications. In the example, we state that the value of the `this.o` field is changed by pointing the `assignable` clause to the main `heap` variable, however, on the `permissions` heap the frame is empty, because the permission to the field o does not change when the `set` method is executed, it is only read to check the (write) access to the field `this.o`.

Furthermore, we provide operators to access the permission heap in the pre- and postconditions, and to evaluate the permission values. In the example, we use the `\perm` operator to access the `this.o` location on the permission heap. Thus, `\perm` is somewhat analogous to the `\old` operator, which redirects access from the current heap to the heap before the method was called. In our specifications the combination of the two operators is also possible, `\old(\perm(·))` reads the value of the permission before the method was called. Then, `\writePerm` is a predicate that abstracts checking the permission to be a write permission for the current thread, an analogous predicate for checking the permission to be a read one is called `\readPerm` . Finally, operations `\transferPerm` and `\returnPerm` to modify permissions upon synchronisation points are also available. Typically, when this happens the corresponding location is also listed in the `assignable` clause for the permission heap, concrete examples of that are provided in Sect. 5.

4   Proof Obligations for Self-Framing

The above is sufficient to relate heap locations with their permissions and to perform basic permission-aware reasoning in the dynamic frames approach, i.e., permissions can be specified and are checked when locations are accessed in the verified program. However, permissions have also consequences for the specifications themselves, in terms of which specifications are actually sound and how they should be applied in modular reasoning. Namely, specifications themselves have to be self-framed with respect to permissions, i.e., specifications are only allowed to reference heap locations they have at least a read permission to. Locations with no permission can be modified by other threads that potentially hold a complete write permission, hence nothing can be said about them. The mechanism of applying method specifications in modular reasoning is also affected, i.e., when a permission to some memory location is lost, so should be the information about its current value on the heap. Unlike in Separation Logic (-like) approaches [4], in dynamic frames self-framing of expressions (even without permissions) is not given and has to be shown explicitly. In particular, explicit `assignable` clauses are required (not necessary in SL) and proof obligations have to be generated, like (1) above, to prove them correct.

In permission-based reasoning each thread is verified (on a per-method basis) in isolation under the assumption that it is the currently executing thread. The reasoning itself is very similar to the one for sequential programs, with the addition that if permission annotations are verified to be consistent for each thread then the threads are guaranteed to be non-interfering. In such a verification context, it is sufficient to abstract the permissions to be simply read, write, or no permission for the current thread, also when talking about soundness of specifications themselves. Hence, the actual permission system (symbolic or fractions-based) is irrelevant. What is relevant is how the memory and permissions are referred to in the logic, in our case through explicit heap variables.

4.1   Examples of Sound and Unsound Specifications

Suppose we have the following very simple method specified with JML*:

```
//@ requires \writePerm(\perm(this.f));
//@ ensures this.f == v;
//@ assignable<heap> this.f;
//@ assignable<permissions> \nothing;
void setF(int v) { this.f = v; }
```

This specification is sound with respect to permission annotations. The preconditions establishes at least a read permission (here a full write one) for this.f, the permission is not changed by this method, hence the postcondition can freely specify the value of this.f. However, if we change the scenario slightly to become:

```
//@ requires \writePerm(\perm(this.f));
//@ ensures this.f == v;
//@ assignable<heap> this.f;
//@ assignable<permissions> this.f;
void setFandUnlock(int v) { this.f = v; l.unlock(); }
```

then referencing this.f in the postcondition is no longer sound. Knowing that the unlock method modifies the permission to this.f we also have to put this location in the assignable permissions of setFandUnlock and consequently we cannot establish any permission to this.f in the postcondition. To fix this, if the unlock method leaves a read permission with the current thread then we can specify it:

```
//@ ensures \readPerm(\perm(this.f));
//@ ensures this.f == v;
```

Or, if no permission to this.f is left after unlock the postcondition over the value of this.f has to be removed altogether, and the specification becomes:

```
//@ requires \writePerm(\perm(this.f));
//@ assignable<heap> this.f;
//@ assignable<permissions> this.f;
```

On top of that, when client code that calls setFandUnlock is verified, it is mandatory to loose all information about this.f after the call.[4] However, it is

---

[4] This problem is common in permission-based approaches and makes reasoning about functional behaviour of concurrent programs difficult. Solutions exist to enable to keep certain information about temporarily inaccessible locations [16], however, they are beyond the scope of this paper, here we concentrate on the basic soundness of dynamic frames enriched with permissions.

sound to leave this location in the assignable clause for the base heap, and in fact necessary. The presence of this location in the assignable clause actually causes erasure of information about this location from the current verification context upon a `setFandUnlock` method call, because no postcondition can be specified that would give the new value of this location. In other verification systems the mechanism of erasing information is typically called *havocing* [17], in the Java Dynamic Logic it is called *anonymisation*, and incidentally it also gives us the base for showing that specifications are self-framed with respect to permissions in JDL. We show how this is done for the preconditions in their basic form. With small technical alternations, the method scales correspondingly to other specification constructs, like postconditions, `measured_by` termination clauses, or model methods with their specifications (see Sect. 5).

4.2   Anonymisation

Locations on the heap are anonymised with the $anon(\text{heap1}, locs, \text{heap2})$ function that returns a new heap with the locations not appearing in *locs* copied from `heap1` and otherwise the locations are copied from `heap2`. For example, to anonymise locations `o.f` and `o.g` on the base heap one typically creates a new heap with $anon(\text{heap}, \{(o, f), (o, g)\}, \text{anonHeap})$, where `anonHeap` is a fresh unspecified heap. Such an operation is applied to the current heap during modular verification, when a method call is dispatched using its specification, in which case *locs* are the locations defined in the assignable clause.

This function can also be used in an *inverse* way, i.e., all locations outside of a certain set *locs* can be anonymised with $anon(\text{heap}, allLocs \setminus locs, \text{anonHeap})$. Now all locations in *locs* keep their values in the resulting heap with respect to the input `heap`, while all other locations are left undefined. This mechanism is commonly used in JDL to show data independence of expressions, in particular, to prove the `accessible` clauses of read-only methods. Suppose a method `getVal()` is specified with an `accessible` clause to only depend on `o.f`. To prove that this is indeed so, the following JDL proof obligation has to be discharged:

$$\text{getVal}() = \{\text{heap} := anon(\text{heap}, allLocs \setminus \{(o, f)\}, \text{anonHeap})\}\text{getVal}() \quad (2)$$

The meaning of the right hand side of this equality is that `getVal` should be evaluated in a state with modified heap where all locations not in the set of locations *locs* are anonymised. Proving this equality means that changing the values of locations outside of the set *locs* *cannot* influence the valuation of `getVal` and indeed it depends at most on the values of locations in *locs*. In KeY, such a proof obligation is generated by default for every *state observing symbol* [7,13] with an accessible clause, in particular, for all read-only methods.

4.3   Proof Obligations for Self-Framing

To prove correct framing of specifications with respect to permissions a similar mechanism is used. The expression is simply our specification, e.g., a complete expression **pre** representing the method's precondition. However, there is no **accessible** clause to give the set of dependency locations of the expression, so we have to "extract" it from the expression instead. To this end, we introduce a fresh location set logic variable *readLocs* and we indirectly specify which locations it contains. Namely, locations that we can show at least a read permission for under the assumption that the expression **pre** itself holds. The complete proof obligation to show self-framing then reads:

$$\mathtt{pre} \wedge \forall_{o:Object,f:Field} \left(readPerm(o.f@\mathtt{permissions}) \to (o,f) \in readLocs \right) \\ \to \mathtt{pre} = \{\mathtt{heap} := anon(\mathtt{heap}, allLocs \setminus readLocs, \mathtt{anonHeap})\}\mathtt{pre} \quad (3)$$

For a postcondition this construction has small additional complexity, which stems from the fact that the read permission might be specified in the postcondition itself, or, if the permission is not modified by the method, it might be kept from the precondition. To account for this, additional base and permission heap operations are required to "find" the permission in the method specification. Due to space restrictions, we do not quote the formula here, however, the main principle is exactly the same as in (3).

Proof obligation (3) shows that every location referenced on the base heap is accompanied by at least a read access on the permission heap. As explained above, we also have to show that all locations that the method may loose permissions to, i.e., locations for which at least a read permission cannot be established, are included in the assignable clause for the base heap. For this, the following formula has to be proved:

$$\mathtt{post} \to \forall_{o:Object,f:Field} \left((o,f) \in permMod \\ \to readPerm(o.f@\mathtt{permissions}) \vee (o,f) \in heapMod \right) \quad (4)$$

where *permMod* and *heapMod* are locations listed in the assignable clauses for the permission and base heap, respectively. Note, that (a) it is not necessary to add locations to the base assignable clause for which the method did not have permissions for in the first place, only for the ones that are lost, (b) locations for which there is no permission can nevertheless remain in the base assignable clause without breaking the soundness. Locations without an initial permission (point (a)) cannot be used in method's specification or code. Hence, any information (or lack thereof) about such locations can remain in the verification context. For point (b) it is a simple case of over-approximation where the verification context will loose more information about locations than necessary.

4.4 Discussion

Enforcing the lost permission locations to be explicit in the assignable clause of the base heap puts unnecessary burden on the specifier. In (4) we name these locations directly and simply check that they are in the assignable clause. What is equivalently sound, but more practical, is to instead add these locations dynamically to the anonymisation set when the method contract is applied during a proof, in which case (4) does not have to be proved. In fact, this approach can be pushed even more to completely deduce assignable (and accessible) clauses from permission specifications. This exactly is the methodology used in Implicit Dynamic Frames (IDF) [4], where frames are inferred from permissions. A specified read permission implies that the corresponding location is in the accessible clause, and a specified write location puts the location in the assignable clause. The resulting reasoning system has the look-and-feel of permission-based Separation Logic [18,19]. It is also possible to achieve full IDF-style framing in our framework, however, we have chosen not to do so (yet) for two reasons. First, our explicit approach enables high specification and verification precision, in particular, explicit framing avoids frame over-approximation. For example, a write permission in the specification does not necessarily imply that the method assigns the corresponding location, in fact, it can still be a read-only method, in which case it can be used in specifications. For us, the query or mutator status of a method is indicated by the accessible, resp. assignable, clause independent of the permissions. Second, keeping the base and permission heaps explicit with separate framing enables decoupling permission-based reasoning from the classical sequential dynamic frames one while using the same specifications for both. To change from permission-based to sequential reasoning the permission heap is simply omitted during proof obligation generation, and our implementation in KeY provides a simple mechanism to do that.

5   Modular Specifications for Synchronisers

The most intricate part of permission-based reasoning are permission transfers that occur upon synchronisation points between threads, e.g., acquiring and releasing of locks, thread forking and joining, etc. In approaches based on quantitative permissions the modelling of the synchronisation involve the use of so-called resource (or monitor) invariants [20]. Such an invariant is essentially a quantitative amount of resource permissions that is passed to and from the current thread upon synchronisation. For example, in Chalice [3] every object can be used as a lock (as in Java), and when an object is locked all permissions from the object's resource invariant are transferred to the currently running thread. Using Java and JML would-be syntax, to use a shared counter one would specify and use it as follows:

```
class Counter {
  int val; /*@ monitor Perm(val, 1); @*/
}

class Client {
  void inc(Counter c) {
    synchronized(c) { c.val++; }
  }
}
```

Here, in the scope of the synchronized block the method inc temporarily holds the permission to c.val specified in the monitor of the Counter class.

To make this method more modular and flexible one typically uses predicates to embed a set of permissions in one formula and use it as a single resource invariant. This way, concrete permissions are hidden behind the predicate and are only unfolded when required during verification. Such a predicate can be also passed between different classes. In particular, this is used when complex API synchronisation methods are considered [21]. API based synchronisation brings the challenge that several different use scenarios are possible for each mechanism (for locks, e.g., there are read locks, write locks, reentrant locks, etc.) and that they cannot be considered as primitive language constructs with a fixed notion of a resource invariant as above. Instead, their semantics is given with a generic API specification, which is external to the concrete use case. By passing a suitably defined resource predicate one makes such a generic specification concrete [22].

However, we cannot use resource invariants in our approach in the same way, because we specify permission *transformations* instead of permission *amounts*. Instead, we use a two stage mechanism. First, similarly to resource invariants, we give a formula that describes the state of permissions for the given synchroniser. But here, this specification contains a compound description of the symbolic permissions for both the state when the synchroniser is *engaged* and when it is not, both of which are described with the reference to the current thread and the synchroniser itself. Second, we make a connection between this state description and the methods that change the state, i.e., the actual synchronisation calls, like `lock` and `unlock`. We explain our method based on a simple example of a write lock used to protect a single counter variable, as above.

The abbreviated listing of our lock specification and sample client is given in Listing 2. We compacted it for presentation, in particular we skipped all but one framing specifications to concentrate on the modular specification of the lock behaviour with respect to permissions. The full example that can be loaded and proved with KeY is available in the current development version of the system.[5] The specification of a lock is delegated to a separate interface `LockSpec` that serves as a template and provides signatures of all predicates that clients have to instantiate. The lock itself, specified in the `Lock` interface, "receives" this specification through a binding of its ghost field `spec` (l. 19). Then, the client code in the `Counter` class instantiates the specification and passes it to the lock object by specifying the binding in the invariant (l. 31).[6]

To enable modularity, our predicates are specified with JML* model methods [13] briefly introduced in Sect. 2. The `state` predicate (l. 4) describes the state of the permissions in the locked and unlocked state. In the client (ls. 35–36) the lock is specified to protect the `val` field of the `Counter` object. In the unlocked state the permission to `val` is a single slice belonging to the lock – `[[ lock ]]`. When locked, the permission is also a single slice, but temporarily

---

[5] Available at http://www.key-project.org/download/.

[6] This is not the most elegant way of passing specifications (predicates) around classes in JML*, however, a working one and currently the only one that the KeY implementation allows. In the future we plan to provide proper ghost and model parameters to classes and methods in the style of [22].

```
   public interface LockSpec {
2    //@ model \locset fpPerm();
     /*@ accessible<permissions> fpPerm(); ...
4          model boolean state(boolean locked); @*/
     /*@ accessible ...;
6          model boolean status(boolean locked); @*/

8    //@ model two_state boolean lockTr();
     //@ model two_state boolean unlockTr();
10
     /*@ ensures \result;
12         model final two_state boolean consistent() { return
             (\old(state(false)) && \old(status(false)) && lockTr() ==>
14            (state(true) && status(true))) &&
             (\old(state(true)) && \old(status(true)) && unlockTr() ==>
16            (state(false) && status(false)))); } @*/ }

18 public interface Lock {
     //@ public instance ghost LockSpec spec;
20
     //@ requires spec.status(false);
22   //@ ensures spec.status(true) && spec.lockTr();
     public void lock();
24
     //@ requires spec.status(true);
26   //@ ensures spec.status(false) && spec.unlockTr();
     public void unlock(); }
28
   public class Counter implements LockSpec {
30   private int val;
     private Lock lock; //@ invariant lock.spec == this && ...;
32
     /*@ model \locset fpPerm() { return \singleton(val); } @*/
34
     /*@ model boolean state(boolean locked) { return \perm(val) ==
36        locked ? [[ \ct, lock ]] : [[ lock ]]; } @*/
     /*@ model boolean status(boolean locked) { return locked ?
38        \writePerm(\perm(val)) : !\readPerm(\perm(val)); } @*/

40   /*@ model two_state boolean lockTr() { return \perm(val) ==
        \transferPermAll(lock, \ct, \old(\perm(val))); } @*/
42   /*@ model two_state boolean unlockTr() { return \perm(val) ==
        \returnPerm(\ct, lock, \old(\perm(val))); } @*/
44
     //@ requires status(false);
46   //@ ensures status(false);
     public void inc() { lock.lock(); val++; lock.unlock(); } }
```

Lst. 2. Modular specification for a lock in JML*.

belonging to the current thread that acquired the lock and owing the slice to the lock – [[\ct, lock]] . The status predicate (l. 6) serves two purposes. First, it represents the binary state of actually holding the lock at any given point. Second, it provides an abstracted view of the permission to the protected resource, here the val field. By knowing the status the client can also deduce the actual access permission to the resource without having to evaluate the concrete symbolic permission expression kept in the lock state. Our client code (ls. 37–38) specifies that in the locked state it holds a complete write permission to val, while in the unlocked state it holds no permission at all. Note that in this case these two are not the binary opposites of each other, hence the need for the locked parameter in status. The predicates lockTr and unlockTr (ls. 8 and 9) describe the permission change upon lock acquiring and releasing, respectively. They are two_state predicates, because they describe the state of permissions before and after the corresponding lock calls. Such two-state predicates can be used in an appropriate context, i.e., the method postcondition (e.g., l. 22). Upon locking (l. 41) all permission slices to val are transferred from the lock to the currently running thread (denoted with \ct). Upon unlocking (l. 43) all slices for val are returned from the current thread to the lock object.

Finally, the consistent predicate (ls. 11–16) binds the specification structure together. It establishes the relationship between the concrete and abstract view of permission for the lock, and that the two transfers correctly change the state of the lock. This predicate is defined directly in LockSpec – all clients instantiating this specification have to show this predicate to hold (its postcondition in l. 11 states so) to prove that their concrete lock specifications are consistent.

Following the same methodology we can develop similar generic specifications for other synchronisation triggering methods of the Java API, and in particular modular specification for asynchronous method calls invoked through the start() and join() methods of the Thread class [23]. In each such case a generic specification that would cover the typical usage scenarios is possible. Our Lock specification is not fully generic in this respect, in particular it does not cover Java re-entrant locks, but it can be extended to resemble the ones we developed before for Separation Logic [22] that cover all kinds of Java lock flavours. However, there will always be scenarios that would not fall within such a generic scheme. In particular, our version [11] of the motivating example from [24] that uses a primitive lock combined with a counter variable to effectively implement a semaphore-like read-write lock cannot be put in the frame of our Lock specification presented here without further extensions of this specification. Hence, we did not construct a complete generic specification solution for all API-based synchronisers, we only showed a methodology with a number of possible applications.

6   Conclusions

We presented an approach to the verification of concurrent Java programs based on Dynamic Frames extended with permissions. In particular, we showed how to treat the self-framing of specifications in Java Dynamic Logic and how to use JML* model methods to provide modular specifications for Java API synchronisation points.

6.1   Implementation Status

Our symbolic permission framework described in Sect. 2 is implemented in the current development version of the KeY verifier, and so is the extension from Sect. 3 that incorporates permissions into the JML* dynamic frames. Furthermore, model methods that we used for modular specification in Sect. 5 are also implemented in KeY [13], and in fact did not require any particular extensions to work with permissions, apart from accounting for one additional heap. What is not yet implemented, is the generation of the additional proof obligations and checks for self-framing with respect to permissions described in Sect. 4. This is work in progress and we expect this to be finished soon.

6.2   Further Examples

The current state of the implementation allows for all the examples that we discussed or referred to in this paper to be verified. Technically speaking, however, the tool is not yet fully sound, in the sense that possibly unsound specifications can be admitted by KeY. Nevertheless, we developed several more non-trivial examples and verified them with KeY, while checking specification framing by hand. In particular, the KeY distribution contains modularly specified and fully verifiable example of a multi-threaded plotter that we developed earlier using Separation Logic [5]. In this example four different threads manipulate two shared buffers to process and "draw" some input data passing the permissions to these buffers in a non-trivial way. Few other examples are available in the KeY distribution, in particular fully specified and verified read-write lock example from [24] we mentioned above, and the examples from this and earlier paper on symbolic permissions are included in the development version of the KeY system.

6.3   Related Work

To the best of our knowledge, our method so far is the only one that uses Dynamic Frames in the explicit form with permissions [1] and in this paper we have shown the necessary extensions and modifications to the Java Dynamic Logic used in the KeY verifier to build a fully functional verification system for this combination. The existing approaches to (fractional) permission-based reasoning with functional tools are based on Separation Logic (SL) [2] or Implicit Dynamic Frames (IDF) [4], e.g., our own VerCors toolset [5,19], VeriFast [25], Silicon [26], or Chalice [3].

Compared to these existing approaches, ours is based on symbolic permissions we developed earlier to allow for more flexibility in permission flow specifications.

Furthermore, we are more explicit in terms of exhibiting the underlying logic mechanism to the specifier, e.g., by allowing to refer to heaps directly in explicit JML* frame specifications. In comparison, e.g., in IDF memory and permission frames are calculated on the fly from pre- and postconditions. We stated two reasons for considering our explicit approach advantageous, namely very precise specifications and reasoning, as well as the possibility to decouple reasoning about functional and permission properties.

6.4   Future Work

Approaches based on SL and IDF have been shown to be practically equivalent [4]. On the verification end, the problems are translated to FOL formulas to be proved by an appropriate verifier, e.g., an SMT solver. In this respect our method is no different, symbolic execution of permission annotated program leads to pure FOL problems which are then discharged with FOL reasoning. However, our specification methodology is more explicit and closely related to the actual reasoning logic, in our case Java Dynamic Logic implemented in the KeY verifier. In this respect, for future work we also consider a translation from permission-based SL to Java Dynamic Logic with permissions making it an intermediate verification language, similarly to Silicon [26]. This translation would be a mixture of ideas presented in this paper and in [27] where a bridge between SL and Dafny – also based on dynamic frames – is described. Otherwise, we are finishing the implementation and working on more examples for our approach.

References

1. Boyland, J.: Checking interference with fractional permissions. In: Cousot, R. (ed.) SAS 2003. LNCS, vol. 2694, pp. 55–72. Springer, Heidelberg (2003)
2. Reynolds, J.C.: Separation logic: a logic for shared mutable data structures. In: 17th IEEE Symposium on Logic in Computer Science, pp. 55–74. IEEE Computer Society (2002)
3. Leino, K.R.M., Müller, P., Smans, J.: Verification of concurrent programs with Chalice. In: Aldini, A., Barthe, G., Gorrieri, R. (eds.) FOSAD 2007/2008/2009. LNCS, vol. 5705, pp. 195–222. Springer, Heidelberg (2009)
4. Parkinson, M.J., Summers, A.J.: The relationship between separation logic and implicit dynamic frames. In: Barthe, G. (ed.) ESOP 2011. LNCS, vol. 6602, pp. 439–458. Springer, Heidelberg (2011)
5. Amighi, A., Blom, S., Darabi, S., Huisman, M., Mostowski, W., Zaharieva-Stojanovski, M.: Verification of concurrent systems with VerCors. In: Bernardo, M., Damiani, F., Hähnle, R., Johnsen, E.B., Schaefer, I. (eds.) SFM 2014. LNCS, vol. 8483, pp. 172–216. Springer, Heidelberg (2014)
6. Kassios, I.T.: Dynamic frames: support for framing, dependencies and sharing without restrictions. In: Misra, J., Nipkow, T., Sekerinski, E. (eds.) FM 2006. LNCS, vol. 4085, pp. 268–283. Springer, Heidelberg (2006)
7. Schmitt, P.H., Ulbrich, M., Weiß, B.: Dynamic frames in Java dynamic logic. In: Beckert, B., Marché, C. (eds.) FoVeOOS 2010. LNCS, vol. 6528, pp. 138–152. Springer, Heidelberg (2011)

8. Ahrendt, W., Beckert, B., Bruns, D., Bubel, R., Gladisch, C., Grebing, S., Hähnle, R., Hentschel, M., Herda, M., Klebanov, V., Mostowski, W., Scheben, C., Schmitt, P.H., Ulbrich, M.: The KeY platform for verification and analysis of Java programs. In: Giannakopoulou, D., Kroening, D. (eds.) VSTTE 2014. LNCS, vol. 8471, pp. 55–71. Springer, Heidelberg (2014)

9. Leavens, G.T., Baker, A.L., Ruby, C.: Preliminary design of JML: a behavioral interface specification language for Java. SIGSOFT **31**(3), 1–38 (2006)

10. Blom, S., Huisman, M.: The VerCors tool for verification of concurrent programs. In: Jones, C., Pihlajasaari, P., Sun, J. (eds.) FM 2014. LNCS, vol. 8442, pp. 127–131. Springer, Heidelberg (2014)

11. Huisman, M., Mostowski, W.: A symbolic approach to permission accounting for concurrent reasoning. In: 14th International Symposium on Parallel and Distributed Computing (ISPDC 2015), pp. 165–174. IEEE Computer Society (2015)

12. Mostowski, W.: A case study in formal verification using multiple explicit heaps. In: Beyer, D., Boreale, M. (eds.) FMOODS/FORTE 2013. LNCS, vol. 7892, pp. 20–34. Springer, Heidelberg (2013)

13. Mostowski, W., Ulbrich, M.: Dynamic dispatch for method contracts through abstract predicates. In: 15th International Conference on MODULARITY, pp. 109–116. ACM (2015)

14. Beckert, B., Schmitt, P.H.: Program verification using change information. In: Proceedings, Software Engineering and Formal Methods (SEFM) 2003, pp. 91–99. IEEE Press (2003)

15. Bruns, D., Mostowski, W., Ulbrich, M.: Implementation-level verification of algorithms with KeY. Softw. Tools Technol. Transf. **17**(6), 729–744 (2013)

16. Blom, S., Huisman, M., Zaharieva-Stojanovski, M.: History-based verification of functional behaviour of concurrent programs. In: Calinescu, R., Rumpe, B. (eds.) SEFM 2015. LNCS, vol. 9276, pp. 84–98. Springer, Heidelberg (2015)

17. Leino, K.R.M.: Dafny: an automatic program verifier for functional correctness. In: Clarke, E.M., Voronkov, A. (eds.) LPAR-16 2010. LNCS, vol. 6355, pp. 348–370. Springer, Heidelberg (2010)

18. Bornat, R., Calcagno, C., O'Hearn, P., Parkinson, M.: Permission accounting in separation logic. In: Palsberg, J., Abadi, M. (eds.) Principles of Programming Languages, pp. 259–270. ACM (2005)

19. Amighi, A., Haack, C., Huisman, M., Hurlin, C.: Permission-based separation logic for multithreaded Java programs. Logical Methods Comput. Sci. **11**, 1–66 (2015)

20. O'Hearn, P.W.: Resources, concurrency and local reasoning. Theor. Comput. Sci. **375**(1–3), 271–307 (2007)

21. Blom, S., Huisman, M., Kiniry, J.: How do developers use APIs? A case study in concurrency. In: International Conference on Engineering of Complex Computer Systems, pp. 212–221. IEEE Computer Society (2013)

22. Amighi, A., Blom, S., Huisman, M., Mostowski, W., Zaharieva-Stojanovski, M.: Formal specifications for Java's synchronisation classes. In: Lafuente, A.L., Tuosto, E. (eds.) 22nd Euromicro International Conference on Parallel, Distributed, and Network-Based Processing, pp. 725–733. IEEE Computer Society (2014)

23. Haack, C., Hurlin, C.: Separation logic contracts for a Java-like language with fork/join. In: Meseguer, J., Roşu, G. (eds.) AMAST 2008. LNCS, vol. 5140, pp. 199–215. Springer, Heidelberg (2008)

24. Boyland, J., Müller, P., Schwerhoff, M., Summers, A.J.: Constraint semantics for abstract read permissions. In: Formal Techniques for Java-Like Programs (FTfJP). ACM (2014)

25. Jacobs, B., Smans, J., Philippaerts, P., Vogels, F., Penninckx, W., Piessens, F.: VeriFast: a powerful, sound, predictable, fast verifier for C and Java. In: Bobaru, M., Havelund, K., Holzmann, G.J., Joshi, R. (eds.) NFM 2011. LNCS, vol. 6617, pp. 41–55. Springer, Heidelberg (2011)
26. Juhasz, U., Kassios, I.T., Müller, P., Novacek, M., Schwerhoff, M., Summers, A.J.: Viper: a verification infrastructure for permission-based reasoning. Technical report, ETH Zürich (2014)
27. Bao, Y., Leavens, G.T., Ernst, G.: Translating separation logic into dynamic frames using fine-grained region logic. Technical report CS-TR-13-02a, Computer Science, University of Central Florida, March 2014

A Simpler Reduction Theorem for x86-TSO

Jonas Oberhauser[✉]

Saarland University, Saarbrücken, Germany
`jonas@wjpserver.cs.uni-saarland.de`

Abstract. The memory model of x86-TSO allows code to run in weakly synchronous fashion, resulting in a smaller memory bottleneck but also possibly causing inconsistent memory effects. Cohen and Schirmer [5] described an efficient software discipline which provably provides sequential consistency. The contribution of this paper is threefold:

- We extend the Cohen-Schirmer discipline to handle non-triangular races as defined by Owens [10], for which the Cohen-Schirmer discipline introduces unnecessary fences.
- We describe the discipline in terms of C11 data races and atomic accesses, and conclude that the behaviour of data-race-free programs is unchanged when executed on x86-TSO if no atomic load is issued by a thread whose store buffer contains an atomic store.
- We give a considerably simpler proof of this fact.

Keywords: Store buffer reduction · Order reduction · Relaxed memory · Sequential consistency · Consistency points · Compiler optimization · Verification

1 Introduction

When arguing about parallel programs, it is convenient to assume sequential consistency, i.e., that all steps occur in a global order that respects the local program order. Guaranteeing such a strong memory model in hardware requires synchronization overhead, which is why most modern hardware offers a more relaxed hardware model.

In order to allow a programmer to gain access to a strong memory model, the hardware may offer slow synchronization primitives (e.g., `mfence` on x86). The question then becomes one of using the synchronization primitives as economically as possible.

The relaxed memory model known as x86-TSO [12] is obtained by adding store buffers to a sequentially consistent memory (as in the relatively common processor family of x86/AMD64). These local FIFO buffers act as a bridge between the processor and the shared memory, buffering writes while the shared memory is used by other processors (and thus reducing bottlenecks in parallel processors). While buffered writes are made visible to the local processor by forwarding, they are not visible to other processors, leading to sequentially inconsistent behaviour.

© Springer International Publishing Switzerland 2016
A. Gurfinkel and S.A. Seshia (Eds.): VSTTE 2015, LNCS 9593, pp. 142–164, 2016.
DOI: 10.1007/978-3-319-29613-5_9

For this architecture, Cohen and Schirmer [5] developed a generic software discipline that provably guarantees sequential consistency while using relatively little synchronization. Furthermore, one can assume sequentially consistent memory when verifying that a program adheres to the discipline, meaning that traditional verification tools such as VCC [4] are fit for verifying this property.

The discipline marks memory accesses as volatile (shared) or non-volatile (local) based on dynamic ownership. Volatile writes have to be separated from later volatile reads on the same thread by a store buffer flush.

In this paper, we establish that the ownership state precisely defines the data races that are possible on each variable, and that exactly the memory accesses that race must be volatile. Therefore, atomic accesses in C11 and volatile accesses in the Cohen-Schirmer discipline are the same. From this observation one can easily conclude that the Cohen-Schirmer discipline can be expressed in terms of data races rather than ownership, which simplifies the model and brings us closer to languages like C11. In the remainder of the paper we will thus adopt the language of C11 and speak of data races and atomic accesses.

Furthermore, we consider non-triangular races, which are races of the form

$$\texttt{x.store() ; ... ; x.load() || x.store()}.$$

Owens [10] established that in such cases no fence is required between the atomic store and the atomic load, whereas the original Cohen-Schirmer discipline inserts a fence. Combining Owens' results and the Cohen-Schirmer discipline gives a new discipline: atomic writes have to be separated from subsequent atomic reads *to a different address* by a store buffer flush. In this paper, we give a short proof that the behaviour of programs obeying this new discipline is unchanged when executed under x86-TSO, thus strengthening the results of both Owens' and Cohen-Schirmer. The main motivation behind finding a short proof is the fact that modern multi-core processors use complex inter processor interrupt mechanisms, which are not considered by current store buffer reduction proofs. We hope that this simple proof can be extended to such machines easily.

1.1 Proof Overview

Like Cohen and Schirmer, we use two operational semantics in our proofs: one for the store buffer machine where write instructions are buffered, and one for a sequentially consistent abstract machine where write instructions immediately become visible to all processors. We consider now a program which obeys the software discipline while running on the abstract machine, and run it on the store buffer machine. We say that this execution is sequentially consistent if it simulates some execution of the program on the abstract machine. That is the case if there is a (possibly different) order of processor steps such that

1. The original and the new order cause the same local traces when using the store buffer machine, and
2. when executing the program in parallel on the store buffer machine and the abstract machine, using the new order of processor steps, the resulting executions are equal.

We do so using two techniques. First we show that if a processor uses a variable locally, this variable is not accessed by another processor until both processors synchronize via shared variables. We call this lemma the *Privacy Theorem*.

During an arbitrary execution, store buffers may contain conflicting atomic writes, and atomic reads to such a location may be served out of execution order. We consider instead executions in which the whole store buffer content is committed after each atomic write (including the atomic write itself). Effectively, atomic writes immediately become visible to all processors, and only non-atomic writes may be buffered. We thus call such executions *local store buffer* executions. In such executions, reads to local locations are correct due to the correctness of the forwarding mechanism, and reads to shared locations are always served from the shared memory, which is kept in sync with the abstract machine. Sequential consistency for such executions is therefore easy to show.

Finally we show that arbitrary executions of programs that satisfy the software discipline can be easily reordered into local store buffer executions. Furthermore, our method does not reorder steps to infinity as long as all store buffer entries are eventually committed.

1.2 Structure of this Paper

We first define the abstract and store buffer models and give their semantics in Sect. 2. In that section we also define equivalence between store buffer computations, and a straightforward coupling relation between an abstract and a store buffer computation. In Sect. 3, we describe how processors synchronize and give the Privacy Theorem. We define local store buffer schedules in Sect. 4.1, which is a class of schedules for which the abstract and store buffer computations coincide. In Sect. 4.2, we then define a method of iteratively constructing equivalent schedules of which a finite growing prefix falls into that class Applying this method infinitely often yields an equivalent local store buffer schedule, and we thus complete the store buffer reduction proof in Sect. 4.3. We sketch the corresponding store buffer reduction theorem for machines with MMUs in Sect. 4.4.

Note that this paper only includes high-level proofs; for details, refer to the technical report [9].

2 Definitions

2.1 Preliminaries

Let S, A, and V be sets of processor states, shared memory addresses, and values, respectively. Let p be the number of processors, and we define $P = [1 : p]$ as the set of processors.

For read-modify-write instructions we consider a set Σ_{RMW} of update flavors, and for each update flavor $\sigma \in \Sigma_{\mathrm{RMW}}$ we consider a memory update function

$$\delta_\sigma : V \to V.$$

For example, one might model a compare-and-swap instruction by

$$(\text{cas}, cmpdata \in V, newdata \in V) \in \Sigma_{\text{RMW}}$$

with the update function

$$\delta_{(\text{cas}, cmpdata, newdata)}(v) = \begin{cases} newdata & cmpdata = v \\ v & \text{o.w.} \end{cases}$$

Furthermore, we assume a transition function for processor states,

$$\delta : S \times (V \cup \{\bot\}) \to S,$$

where the second parameter is the value read from memory for read instructions. For instructions that do not read from memory, we supply the place holder $\bot$.

2.2 Instructions

We consider the following instructions I, the semantics of which we will formalize later:

$$I ::= \text{READ}_{at \in \mathbb{B}} (a \in A) \mid \text{WRITE}_{at \in \mathbb{B}} (a \in A, v \in V) \mid \text{PROCESSOR}$$
$$\mid \text{RMW} (a \in A, \sigma \in \Sigma_{\text{RMW}}) \mid \text{FENCE}$$

The bit $at \in \mathbb{B}$ stands for atomic and is ghost code, i.e., part of the program annotation used to prove that the program obeys the software discipline.

For instructions $n \in I$ we define predicates $Read(n)$, $Write(n)$, $RMW(n)$, $Fence(n)$, and $Processor(n)$ with the obvious meaning. We can access the components of an instruction using dot notation, e.g., for a write instruction n we have

$$n.at \in \mathbb{B}, n.a \in A, n.v \in V.$$

We also define the following shorthands:

$$R(n) = Read(n) \lor RMW(n)$$
$$W(n) = Write(n) \lor RMW(n)$$
$$Flush(n) = RMW(n) \lor Fence(n)$$
$$At(n) = RMW(n) \lor (Read(n) \lor Write(n)) \land n.at = 1$$

Whenever a processor is stepped, it will execute one instruction $n \in I$ that only depends on its current processor state. In particular, instruction fetch and instruction execution are two separate steps in our model; if our theory is to be applied to a model where fetch and execute are a single cycle, one has to prove that code regions are not modified by other processors. Note that this is already a condition for most pipelined machines and typically does not introduce additional proof effort. We denote this instruction by

$$pi : S \to I.$$

2.3   Models

We consider two models, the *store buffer machine* and the sequentially consistent *abstract machine*. The components of store buffer and abstract configurations are laid down in the table below. For each processor $i \in P$, component ϕ_i keeps track of the current processor state of that processor. The shared memory m also exists in both configurations. Note that the abstract components d_i are *ghost* components used only to prove adherence to the software discipline.

Store Buffer Configuration	Abstract Configuration
$\phi_i \in S$	
The processor state of processor i.	
$m : A \to V$	
The shared memory.	
$sb_i \in \{n \in I \mid Write(n)\}^*$	$d_i \in A \cup \{\bot\}$
The list of write instructions buffered in the store buffer of processor i, ordered by age: the oldest instruction is at the front.	The software discipline requires us to keep track of atomic writes. While an atomic write might be in the store buffer, we say the store buffer is dirty and d_i is the address of the last such write, otherwise we say the store buffer is clean and $d_i = \bot$.

Store buffer machines use *forwarding* to ensure that reads never overtake writes of the same processor. We define the memory system with forwarding by recursively applying all buffered writes to the shared memory in order:

$$fw(m, \epsilon, a) = m(a), \quad fw(m, w \circ sb, a) = fw(\text{apply}(w, m), sb, a)$$

where apply applies (write) instructions n to a shared memory configuration m as follows:

$$\text{apply}(n, m, a) = \begin{cases} n.v & Write(n) \wedge n.a = a \\ \delta_{n.\sigma}(m(a)) & RMW(n) \wedge n.a = a \\ m(a) & \text{o.w.} \end{cases}$$

2.4   Store Buffer Semantics

We consider an arbitrary initial store buffer configuration c^0 with empty store buffers:

$$c^0.sb_i = \epsilon.$$

Starting from this configuration, we apply steps in a non-deterministic order given by a *schedule* (or stepping function)

$$s : \mathbb{N} \to P \cup \{\text{SB}_i \mid i \in P\}.$$

This may yield a parametrized sequence of configurations $(c[s]^t)$, which we will define recursively.

Assume now that $c[s]^t$ is already defined.

We first introduce the following notation:

$$X[s]^t = c[s]^t.X,$$

for components $X \in \{m\} \cup \bigcup_i \{sb_i, \phi_i\}$, and

$$m_i[s]^t(a) = fw(m[s]^t, sb_i[s]^t)(a),$$

$$ei[s](t) = \begin{cases} pi(\phi_i[s]^t) & s(t) = i \\ \mathrm{hd}(sb_i[s]^t) & s(t) = \mathrm{SB}_i, \end{cases}$$

$$rv[s](t) = \begin{cases} m_i[s]^t(ei[s](t).a) & s(t) = i \wedge R(ei[s](t)) \\ \bot & \text{o.w.}, \end{cases}$$

where ei stands for *executed instruction* and rv for the *read value*. We will use this notation later and omit the index s whenever we consider only a single stepping function.

Furthermore we overload the elementship for addresses and store buffers as follows:

$$a \in sb \iff \exists w \in sb.\, w.a = a$$

Note that the sequence can get stuck, e.g., if an empty store buffer is supposed to make a step. We call step t *well-formed* if and only if

- $s(t) = i$ and $Flush(ei(t))$ imply $sb_i^t = \epsilon$,
- and $s(t) = \mathrm{SB}_i$ implies $sb_i^t \neq \epsilon$.

If step t is not well-formed, we leave the behavior undefined. If step t is well-formed, we distinguish between two cases: either step t is a processor step, or a store buffer step.

Let $i = s(t)$. We define the components of the next configuration by analysis of $n = ei(t)$, using notation analogous to what we have introduced, and leave unspecified components unchanged.

$$\phi_i^{t+1} = \delta(\phi_i^t, rv(t))$$

$$m^{t+1} = \begin{cases} \mathrm{apply}(n, m^t) & RMW(n), \\ m^t & \text{o.w.}, \end{cases}$$

$$sb_i^{t+1} = \begin{cases} sb_i^t \circ n & Write(n) \\ sb_i^t & \text{o.w.} \end{cases}$$

Let now $\mathrm{SB}_i = s(t)$. Note that the store buffer is not empty. We will *commit* the oldest instruction in the store buffer to the shared memory, which is the instruction at the head:

$$m^{t+1} = \mathrm{apply}(\mathrm{hd}(sb_i^t), m^t),$$
$$sb_i^{t+1} = \mathrm{tl}(sb_i^t).$$

This fully defines the semantics of the store buffer machine.

In what follows we will only consider *well-formed* schedules, i.e., schedules in which each step is well-formed.

Global and Local Steps. Note that only few steps t depend on or modify shared state. In such a case we say that the step is *global* for the store buffer machine. Read-modify-writes and the commits of atomic writes are always global. Reads are only global if they can not use forwarding from an atomic write. Note that intuitively, non-atomic writes never need to forward to atomic reads: since non-atomic writes can not race with accesses of other processors, the existence of a non-atomic write to the same address in the store buffer implies that the read access does not race either, and thus can be marked non-atomic. Formally, we write $G(t)$ in the following cases:

- if $s(t) = i$ and $RMW(ei(t))$,
- if $s(t) = SB_i$ and $ei(t).at = 1$,
- or if $s(t) = i$ and $Read(ei(t))$ and $ei(t).at = 1$ and $\forall w \in sb_i^t. w.a = ei(t).a \rightarrow w.at = 0$.

We call the remaining steps *local* for the store buffer machine and write $L(t)$.

2.5   Abstract Machine Semantics

For a stepping function s we define an abstract computation $(a[s]^t)$, where store buffer steps are ignored and writes have their effect immediately. Note that this means that each (well-formed) schedule s defines an abstract computation $(a[s]^t)$ and a store buffer computation $(c[s]^t)$.

In order to avoid confusion with the store buffer computation, we denote components and functions with a bar:

$$\overline{X}[s]^t = a[s]^t.X,$$

$$\overline{ei}[s](t) = \begin{cases} pi(\overline{\phi}_i[s]^t) & s(t) = i \\ \bot & s(t) = SB_i. \end{cases}$$

$$\overline{rv}[s](t) = \begin{cases} \overline{m}[s]^t(\overline{ei}[s](t).a) & R(\overline{ei}[s](t)) \\ \bot & \text{o.w.} \end{cases}$$

Again, we omit the index s when possible.

The starting configuration $a[s]^0$ is nearly identical to the initial store buffer configuration:

$$\overline{\phi}_i[s]^0 = \phi_i[s]^0,$$
$$\overline{m}[s]^0 = m[s]^0,$$
$$\overline{d}_i[s]^0 = \bot.$$

We formalize the computation along the same lines as before. Let $i = s(t)$. We define the components of the next configuration by analysis of $n = \overline{ei}(t)$, and leave unspecified components unchanged.

$$\overline{\phi}_i^{t+1} = \delta(\overline{\phi}_i^t, \overline{rv}(t)),$$

$$\overline{m}^{t+1}(a) = \text{apply}(n, \overline{m}^t(n.a)),$$

$$\overline{d}_i^{t+1} = \begin{cases} n.a & Write(n) \wedge n.at \\ \perp & Flush(n) \\ \overline{d}_i^t & \text{o.w.} \end{cases}$$

Store buffer steps have no effect in the abstract model. That is if $s(t) = \text{SB}_i$, then $a^{t+1} = a^t$.

Effectful Writes. Note that sometimes, a read-modify-write behaves as a regular read. For example, a compare-and-swap that fails its test has no effect on the shared memory. The software discipline distinguishes between such read-modify-writes and those that actually modify the memory. We say step t executes an *effectful write* and write $\overline{EW}[s](t)$ if

$$Write(\overline{ei}[s](t)) \vee RMW(\overline{ei}[s](t)) \wedge \overline{m}[s]^{t+1} \neq \overline{m}[s]^t.$$

2.6 Safety

Abstract Safety. Schedule s is safe if for all t the following holds. Let $i \neq j$ be distinct processors making steps t and $t + 1$, and

$$n = \overline{ei}[s](t), n' = \overline{ei}[s](t+1)$$

be memory accesses to the same address such that one of the accesses is an effectful write. Then both accesses must be atomic:

$$\overline{EW}[s](t) \wedge (R(n') \vee W(n')) \wedge n.a = n'.a \rightarrow At(n) \wedge At(n').$$

Furthermore, atomic writes and later atomic reads *to a different address* on the same thread must be separated by a store buffer flush. Formally, if $s(t) = i$, $Read(\overline{ei}[s](t))$, and $\overline{ei}[s](t).at = 1$, then $\overline{d}_i[s]^t \in \{\perp, \overline{ei}[s](t).a\}$.

In this document, we argue only about programs where all schedules are safe. We call those programs *safe*.

Cohen-Schirmer Safety. We describe here a simplified version of the Cohen-Schirmer discipline, which does not consider all of the safety conditions. Since programs that satisfy all conditions also satisfy the conditions shown here, we can then show that all programs that obey the Cohen-Schirmer discipline are safe.

First, we introduce ownership states

$$O = \bigcup_{i \in P} \{O_{i,\text{L}}, O_{i,\text{S}}\} \cup \{\text{S}, \text{R}\}.$$

A tabular overview over the individual ownership is given below:

Table 1. Ownership States in the Cohen-Schirmer Discipline

Status	Speech	Readers	Writers
S	Shared	P	P
$O_{i,\text{S}}$	Owned	P	$\{i\}$
$O_{i,\text{L}}$	Locally Owned	$\{i\}$	$\{i\}$
R	Read-Only	P	$\emptyset$

Each address is assigned one of these states by means of an additional ghost component

$$c.\mathcal{O} : A \to O,$$

and we consider a partial ownership transfer function

$$\delta_{\mathcal{O}} : S \times (V \cup \bot) \times A \nrightarrow O,$$

which for some states, read results, and addresses defines a new ownership state for that address that is assumed when the state is left.

Let $s(t) = i$ and $n = \overline{ei}(t)$. Then the new component changes as follows:

$$\overline{\mathcal{O}}^{t+1}(a) = \begin{cases} \delta_{\mathcal{O}}(\overline{\phi}_i^t, \overline{rv}(t), a) & (\overline{\phi}_i^t, \overline{rv}(t), a) \in Dom(\delta_{\mathcal{O}}) \\ \overline{\mathcal{O}}^t & \text{o.w.} \end{cases}$$

Note that each ownership state O is associated with a set of processors that can read and a set of processors that can modify an address with that ownership state, as indicated in Table 1. We write $Readers(O)$ and $Writers(O)$ to denote those sets, and lift this definition to addresses in a configuration as follows:

$$\overline{Readers}[s]^t(a) = Readers(\overline{\mathcal{O}}[s]^t(a)),$$
$$\overline{Writers}[s]^t(a) = Writers(\overline{\mathcal{O}}[s]^t(a)).$$

Processors may only read or write to addresses according to these sets. Whenever other processors may access the same address, accesses need to be atomic. Formally, let $n = \overline{ei}(t)$ and $i = s(t)$. Then

1. if $R(n)$ then $i \in \overline{Readers}^t(n.a)$,
2. if $\overline{EW}(t)$ then $i \in \overline{Writers}^t(n.a)$,
3. if $R(n)$ and $\overline{Writers}^t(n.a) \not\subseteq \{i\}$, then $At(n)$,

4. if $W(n)$ and $\overline{Writers}^t(n.a) \cup \overline{Readers}^t(n.a) \not\subseteq \{i\}$, then $At(n)$.

Furthermore, whenever $s(t) = i$, $Read(\overline{ei}(t))$, and $At(\overline{ei}(t))$, then

$$\overline{d}_i^t = \bot.$$

We can now prove the result.

Lemma 1. *Programs that obey the Cohen-Schirmer discipline are safe.*

Proof. We obviously have that whenever $Read(\overline{ei}[s](t))$, and $\overline{ei}[s](t).at = 1$, then $\overline{d}_i[s]^t \in \{\bot, \overline{ei}[s](t).a\}$. It remains to be shown that races are marked as atomic.
Assume thus that $s(t) \neq s(t+1)$ and

$$n = \overline{ei}[s](t), n' = \overline{ei}[s](t+1)$$

are racing:

$$\overline{EW}[s](t) \wedge (R(n') \vee W(n')) \wedge n.a = n'.a.$$

Let

$$a = n.a = n'.a.$$

We can infer from Rule 2

$$s(t) \in \overline{Writers}[s]^t(a) \not\subseteq \{s(t+1)\}. \tag{1}$$

We now swap the order of $t, t+1$ in s and obtain

$$s'(t') = \begin{cases} s(t+1) & t' = t \\ s(t) & t' = t+1 \\ s(t') & \text{o.w.} \end{cases}$$

By straightforward induction one can show that the same state is reached at t, i.e., $a[s]^t = a[s']^t$, and we conclude

$$\overline{ei}[s'](t) = ei[s](t+1) = n',$$
$$\overline{\mathcal{O}}[s]^t(a) = \overline{\mathcal{O}}[s']^t(a). \tag{2}$$

and thus by Rule 1 or Rule 2

$$s(t+1) = s'(t) \in \overline{Readers}^t[s'](a) \cup \overline{Writers}^t[s'](a) \not\subseteq \{s(t)\}.$$

Thus we conclude with Eqs. 1 and 2

$$\overline{Writers}[s]^t(a) \cup \overline{Readers}[s]^t(a) \not\subseteq \{s(t)\},$$
$$\overline{Writers}[s']^t(a) \not\subseteq \{s'(t)\},$$

and thus from Rules 3 and 4

$$At(n) \wedge At(n').$$

□

Store Buffer Safety. Note that we have safety only for abstract computations, not for the store buffer computations. In particular, safety allows us to argue about instructions executed in the abstract computation. However, if for some schedule, the store buffer computation executes the same instructions as the abstract computation, these properties directly transfer down to the store buffer computation. This is the case if the store buffer computation and the abstract computation reach the same processor states after each step. We say a schedule s is *t-abstract* and write $s \in \text{ABS}_t$ if processor states agree until step t:

$$\forall t' \leq t, i.\, \phi_i[s]^{t'} = \overline{\phi}_i[s]^{t'}.$$

If this is the case for all steps, we say s is *abstract* and write $s \in \text{ABS}$:

$$\forall t', i.\, \phi_i[s]^{t'} = \overline{\phi}_i[s]^{t'}.$$

2.7   Equivalence

We say two schedules are *equivalent* if they have the same local traces in the store buffer computation, that is, the sequences of processor states coincide.

We define the instruction count $ic_X : \mathbb{N} \to \mathbb{N}$ as the function that counts how often unit X has been stepped so far:

$$ic_X(t) = \# \{t' < t \mid s(t') = X\}.$$

We say s is equivalent to s' and write $s \equiv s'$ if both of the following hold:

- reached processor states are equal:

$$ic_i[s](t) = ic_i[s'](t') \to \phi_i[s]^t = \phi_i[s']^{t'},$$

- and the same states are reached:

$$(\exists t.ic_i[s](t) = m) \iff (\exists t'.ic_i[s'](t') = m).$$

A similar definition can be found in [11]. One can easily show that this relation is an equivalence relation.

2.8   Reordering

We can reorder certain steps and maintain equivalence. The permutation of two consecutive steps t, $t+1$ is defined as follows:

$$s[t \leftrightarrow t + 1](t') = \begin{cases} s(t') & t' \notin \{t, t+1\} \\ s(t+1) & t' = t \\ s(t) & t' = t + 1. \end{cases}$$

Iterating the permutation of two steps allows us to move a step to the front or delay it. This gives rise to the following two definitions:

$$s[t \leftarrow t'] = \begin{cases} s & t' \leq t \\ s[t'-1 \leftrightarrow t'][t \leftarrow t'-1] & \text{o.w.} \end{cases}$$

$$s[t \rightarrow t'] = \begin{cases} s & t' \leq t \\ s[t \rightarrow t'-1][t'-1 \leftrightarrow t'] & \text{o.w.} \end{cases}$$

3   Synchronization

We say step t' *reads from* t if t is an effectful write which is not overwritten until t', which executes a read on the same address. Formally, we write $t \lhd t'$ in the following case:

$$\frac{t < t' \quad \overline{EW}[s](t) \quad R(\overline{ei}[s](t')) \quad \overline{ei}[s](t).a = \overline{ei}[s](t').a}{\forall t'' \in [t+1 : t'-1].\neg(\overline{EW}[s](t'') \wedge \overline{ei}[s](t'').a = \overline{ei}[s](t').a)} \over {t \lhd [s]t'}$$

We say step t is *directly synchronized* with step t' and write $t \blacktriangleright t'$ if t reads from t' and both steps are atomic; or they are both steps of the same processor:

$$\frac{t < t' \quad s(t) = s(t') = i}{t \blacktriangleright [s]t'}$$

$$\frac{t \lhd [s]t' \quad At(\overline{ei}[s](t)) \quad At(\overline{ei}[s](t'))}{t \blacktriangleright [s]t'}$$

If $t \blacktriangleright^* t'$, we say step t is *synchronized* with t'.

Note that this definition, which is similar to the definition of *synchronized-with* in the C11 standard, is also very close to the definition of *happened-before* of Lamport [7]; it only differs from the latter in that it considers only atomic accesses for synchronization between threads. We will give two theorems that are very similar in structure and together establish that synchronization and happened-before are equivalent. Let in the following paragraphs t, t' be two steps such that $t < t'$.

The first theorem we call the *Communication Theorem*, which states that information flows between two processors only by synchronization:

Theorem 1 (Communication).

$$t \lhd t'$$

implies

$$t \blacktriangleright^* t'.$$

The second theorem we call the *Privacy Theorem*, which states that asynchronous accesses to the same variable are not possible:

Theorem 2 (Privacy). *Let*

$$n = \overline{ei}(t), n' = \overline{ei}(t')$$

be the instructions executed in t and t', respectively. Then

$$\overline{EW}(t) \wedge (R(n') \vee W(n')) \wedge n.a = n'.a \wedge \neg(At(n) \wedge At(n'))$$

implies

$$t \blacktriangleright^* t'.$$

Both theorems are proven in the same way.

Proof. We first assume for the sake of contradiction that t is not synchronized with t'. In the case of the Communication Theorem, this implies that either n or n' is not atomic; in the case of the Privacy Theorem, we already know that n or n' is not atomic. Consider now the last step

$$m \in [t : t']$$

that is not synchronized with t'. Since it is the last such step and synchronization is transitive, it is also not synchronized with any

$$l \in [m{+}1 : t'].$$

We establish that m can be delayed until such l, without affecting other processors $i \neq s(m)$ or addresses a not changed by it:

$$\overline{\phi}_i[s]^{l+1} = \overline{\phi}_i[s[m \to l]]^l, \tag{3}$$

$$\overline{m}[s]^m(a) = \overline{m}[s]^{m+1}(a) \to \overline{m}[s]^{l+1}(a) = \overline{m}[s[m \to l]]^l(a) \tag{4}$$

Proof. Let the instructions executed in those steps be

$$n_{\mathrm{m}} = \overline{ei}[s](m), n_l = \overline{ei}[s](l),$$

and we only consider the only difficult case where

$$\overline{EW}[s](m), \, Read(n_l) \wedge n_l.at = 0, \, n_{\mathrm{m}}.a = n_l.a.$$

We recursively delay m to $l-1$. One easily shows that the two instructions n_{m}, n_l are now executed next to each other, and from safety we conclude

$$\neg\overline{EW}[s[m \to l{-}1]](l - 1).$$

This means that $n_{\mathrm{m}}.a$ must have been overwritten by some step $l' \in [m{+}1 : l{-}1]$. Since m is not synchronized with l' in s, l' must have executed a regular write. The same write was also executed by $l'-1$ in $s[m \to l{-}1]$ and we conclude

$$\overline{m}[s[m \to l]]^{l-1}(n_l.a) = \overline{m}[s[m \to l{-}1]]^{l-1}(n_l.a) = \overline{m}[s]^l(n_l.a).$$

At this point it is trivial that l in s and $l-1$ in $s[m \to l]$ have the same effect, and Claims 3 and 4 follow.   □

We repeatedly delay the last unsynchronized step in this way with $l = t'$ until

$$m = t.$$

Similarly to before we execute $n_m = n$ and $n_l = n'$ next to each other, and conclude from safety that n and n' are atomic. This contradicts what we established earlier.   □

While both theorems are very natural, we could not find them in the literature.

4   Sequential Consistency

4.1   Local Store Buffer Schedules

Recall that our goal is to, starting from an arbitrary schedule, construct an equivalent, abstract schedule. Consider now a schedule where each processor step that writes to the store buffer is immediately followed by the store buffer step that commits that instruction to the shared memory. Clearly writes immediately become visible to all processors, and the abstract and the store buffer computation trivially coincide.

Constructing such a schedule turns out to be difficult, and we instead construct a weaker schedule, where non-atomic writes can stay in the store buffer until the next atomic write of the same processor. In such a schedule, a processor with a non-empty store buffer did not perform an atomic write and is thus not synchronized with other processors.

Consequently, addresses modified by non-atomic writes in the store buffer of this processor are not accessed by other processors (this follows from the Privacy Theorem). We call such a schedule a local store buffer schedule, since at the beginning of processor steps only non-atomic writes are buffered (i.e., the buffers are used only for local stores).

We say s is a k-local store buffer schedule and write $s \in \mathrm{LSBS}_k$ if the k-prefix of s has the local store buffer property. Formally,

$$s \in \mathrm{LSBS}_k \iff \forall t < k.\, s(t) = i \to \forall j.\, w \in sb_j^t \to w.at = 0.$$

We have already hinted at the fact that all k-local store buffer schedules are k-abstract, but we will require a stronger property. In a perfect world, it would hold that if a k-local store buffer schedule is followed by local steps until $l \geq k$, it is also l-abstract. This is not true, since atomic writes constitute local steps if they use forwarding; therefore, the following serves as a counter example, where in the store buffer computation Threads 1 and 2 execute only local steps:

$$Thread1 : x.store(); Thread2 : x.store(); Thread1 : x.load(); \ldots$$

Note that Thread 1 reads from its own write in the store buffer computation, but from the write of Thread 2 in the abstract computation.

We solve this problem by eliminating all interleavings in the local portion, and thus between a store and a load only steps of the same processor are executed. For convenience, we require that after the local store buffer portion of the schedule, local steps are ordered by processor: processor $i + 1$ only makes steps when processor i has completed all of its steps. Formally, Let $S_k^l(i)$ be the number of steps of i and its store buffer in the interval $[k : l - 1]$:

$$S[s]_k^l(i) = \#\{t \in [k : l - 1] \mid s(t) \in \{i, \mathrm{SB}_i\}\},$$

and $\alpha_k^l(i), \omega_k^l(i)$ be the beginning and end of the interleaving-free block in which processor i is executing:

$$\alpha[s]_k^l(i) = k + \sum_{j<i} S[s]_k^l(j), \ \ \omega[s]_k^l(i) = \alpha[s]_k^l(i) + S[s]_k^l(i) - 1$$

Then s has a block structure from k to l and write $s \in \mathrm{BLOCK}_k^l$ if for all $i \in P$ and $t \in [k : l - 1]$

$$(s(t) \in \{i, \mathrm{SB}_i\} \iff t \in [\alpha[s]_k^l(i) : \omega[s]_k^l(i)]) \land L(t)$$

We are now interested in schedules s which combine three properties:

- they are a k-local store buffer schedule,
- store buffers are clean at k,
- they have a block structure from k to l.

We consider the steps $[0 : k-1]$ the *local store buffer part* and $[k : l-1]$ the *local part* of such a schedule.

We can show that such schedules are l-abstract.

Lemma 2 (Abstraction).

$$s \in \mathrm{LSBS}_k \land (\forall i.w \in sb_i^k \to w.at = 0) \land s \in \mathrm{BLOCK}_k^l \to s \in \mathrm{ABS}_l$$

Proof. We augment the claim by a memory invariant stating that as long as an address is modified by writes in a store buffer, forwarding from that store buffer produces the same result as the shared memory in the abstract computation:

$$meminv_i(t) = \forall a.(\forall j.a \in sb_j^t \to a \in sb_i^t) \to m_i^t(a) = \overline{m}^t(a).$$

In the local store buffer part, the invariant holds for all processors; in the local part only for processors that still make steps, i.e., $i \geq j$ such that $s(t) \in \{j, \mathrm{SB}_j\}$.

We prove the augmented theorem by induction over $t \leq l$. Note that for $t = 0$, store buffers are empty and the invariants hold. Furthermore, $s \in \mathrm{ABS}_0$ by definition of a^0.

For the inductive step, note that we have abstraction for all the steps before t and can thus use abstract arguments like Theorems 1 and 2.

We first prove that the next configuration is abstract, then we sketch a proof for the memory invariant.

$\phi_i^{t+1} = \overline{\phi}_i^{t+1}$: it suffices to show that processors read the same values in step t of the abstract and store buffer computation, i.e.,

$$rv(t) = \overline{rv}(t).$$

This is only difficult if $s(t) = i$ and $R(ei(t))$, and by the memory invariant we only need to show

$$\forall j.a \in sb_j^t \rightarrow a \in sb_i^t.$$

Assume thus that there is j and $w \in sb_j^t$ such that $w.a = a$ and which was executed at t_j:

$$ei(t_j) = w.$$

We assume for the sake of contradiction $i \neq j$ and consider only the difficult case where either t_j executed a non-atomic write or t executed a non-atomic read. In this case by the Privacy Theorem we have

$$t_j \blacktriangleright^* t.$$

Since $i \neq j$ there must be steps t_w, t_r, and processor i' such that

$$t_w \blacktriangleright t_r,\ t_j \leq t_w < t_r \leq t,\ j = s(t_w) \neq s(t_r) = i'.$$

In particular, t_w and t_r execute atomic accesses and

$$t_w \lhd t_r.$$

Since atomic writes that are executed before k flush the store buffer and

$$w \in sb_j^t,$$

we obtain

$$t_r > t_w \geq k.$$

Thus t_r is a local step. Since t_r is an atomic read there must be an atomic write $w' \in sb_{i'}^{t_r}$ to the same address

$$w'.a = ei(t_r).a$$

Note again that atomic writes are always committed immediately before k and thus w' must have been executed at $t' > k$:

$$ei(t') = w'.$$

Since s has a block structure from k to l this implies that

$$t_w < t' < t_r,$$

which contradicts

$$t_w \lhd t_r.$$

Sketch for $meminv_i(t+1)$**:** Note that conflicting writes can exist in store buffers only during the local part of the schedule: for non-atomic writes this is a consequence of the Privacy Theorem (Theorem 2), and atomic writes are only buffered during the local part.

Note also that atomic writes are not committed during the local part of the schedule.

Consequently, writes to an address are committed in the same order as they are issued, and at least in the local store buffer part forwarding and abstract memory agree. For the local part, writes of processors with a lower index may be overwritten, and thus the invariant may no longer hold for such processors. Recall that we do not claim the invariant for such processors, and note that for the other processors the invariant is maintained.   □

4.2   Finite Reordering

We now describe a method to reorder a k-local store buffer schedule into an equivalent $k+1$-local store buffer schedule. Note that all schedules are 0-local store buffer schedules, and iterating the method yields an equivalent k-local store buffer schedule for all k. The method also maintains a technical invariant, which is that an atomic write is allowed into a store buffer only if the next global step is the commit of that write. We call this invariant *regularity* and define

$$s \in \text{REG}_k \iff w \in sb_i^k \wedge w.at = 1 \to s(\min\{t > k \mid G(t)\}) = \text{SB}_i.$$

The method is as follows. Let $r \in \text{LSBS}_k \cap \text{REG}_k$ be a k-local store buffer schedule maintaining the technical invariant. Then we define $r' \in \text{LSBS}_{k+1} \cap \text{REG}_{k+1}$ (proof of the membership omitted) by the following case analysis:

Atomic Write in SB: Let there be $w \in sb_i[r]^k$ such that $At(w)$. In order to get a local store buffer schedule, we must schedule the store buffer of i next.

$$t = \min\{t \geq k \mid r(t) = \text{SB}_i\},$$
$$r' = r[k \leftarrow t].$$

Note that t might not be the commit of w, since the store buffer might still contain older non-atomic writes.

Atomic Write in the Next Step: Assume $r(k) = i$ and $Write(ei[r](k))$ such that $ei[r](k).at = 1$. Due to regularity we can only allow an atomic write to be issued if the next global step is the commit of that write. Furthermore, we do not change the order of global steps, and thus must potentially delay the issue of the atomic write.

We therefore look for the next global step t'

$$t' = \min\{t' \geq k \mid G[r](t')\},$$

which belongs to processor j such that $r(t') \in \{j, \text{SB}_j\}$.

We want to move the next step belonging to that processor to the front. Note that this next step is not necessarily a processor step; e.g., if the next processor step of j is a flush, and there is still a non-atomic write in the store buffer of j, we must commit the non-atomic write first.

We thus set

$$t = \min \{t \in [k : t'] \,|\, r(t) \in \{j, \mathrm{SB}_j\}\},$$
$$r' = r[k \leftarrow t].$$

Note that $j = i$ is possible and occurs when the next global step is the commit of the atomic write.

Otherwise: In all other cases the schedule r is already a $k{+}1$-regular $k{+}1$-local store buffer schedule and we can set

$$r' = r = r[k \leftarrow t]$$

with $t = k$.

4.3   In the Limit

Note that none of constructed schedules is an abstract schedule. However, a growing prefix which never changes during the reordering is abstract, and it is therefore easy to show that the limit of the constructed schedules - if it is well-formed - is abstract.

Let $r_k \in \mathrm{LSBS}_k$ be the k-th reordered schedule, starting from s, and

$$r(t) = r_{t+1}(t)$$

the limit of these schedules. Clearly r is well-formed and abstract, and it is also possible to show that it is equivalent to s:

Theorem 3 (Sequential Consistency).

$$r \in \mathrm{ABS} \wedge r \equiv s.$$

Proof. The proof has two difficult steps.

1. We have to show that r_{k+1} and r_k are equivalent. This is difficult because non-atomic accesses might conflict unless we can prove abstraction. We construct an intermediate schedule r' which is equivalent to r_k and has a block structure from k to t, by reordering steps $l \in [k : t{-}1]$ one by one in the obvious fashion: when we have constructed a block structure from k to l, we move step l to its correct position. This is safe due to the Abstraction Lemma (Lemma 2) and the fact that all involved steps are local, in particular non-atomic accesses use distinct addresses and local atomic accesses use the store buffer. Having constructed r', we can now argue that it is safe to move t to the front.

2. It is difficult to show that no steps are lost, i.e.,

$$(\exists t.ic_i[s](t) = m) \rightarrow (\exists t'.ic_i[r](t') = m).$$

To prove this, one observes that we only delay local steps. Note that we only delay in two cases: an atomic write in the store buffer, or an atomic write that is going to enter the store buffer. In each case, we do not delay further than the commit of that write. One thus considers the last step t'' where an atomic write, which was issued before step t, is committed. By a technical argument, one can show that t' exists and $t' \leq t''$.   □

4.4   Memory Management Units

We only sketch how to treat Memory Management Units (MMUs). Note first that MMUs behave like processors with no store buffers, except for the fact that they share certain parts of the processor state with their processors, in particular the Translation Lookaside Buffer and page table origin register. This has two consequences: certain actions of the processor that modify shared state bypass the store buffer, and steps of the processor sometimes are only enabled by steps of its MMU. Therefore, reordering of processor and MMU steps is only possible in one direction, i.e., reordering the MMU step to the front, and not across steps that modify shared state. In order to obtain sequential consistency in such a setting, we need to make sure that the store buffer is always empty before we modify shared data.

Proof. For the proof, we consider all steps of the MMU and all steps that modify shared state as global steps. Furthermore, synchronization can now also occur between MMU and processor by means of shared state. Otherwise, we use exactly the same reordering strategy and lemmas to prove sequential consistency.

The proof changes in only one important place: we need to show that processor steps stay enabled throughout our reordering. Note that global steps are never delayed in our reordering strategy. Consequently, MMU steps are only moved to the front, and processor steps stay enabled.   □

4.5   Related Work

We use a software discipline similar to that of Cohen and Schirmer [5] but which does not use ownership. This allows us to argue about programs written in modern languages such as C11, D, Java, C++11, where racing accesses have to be flagged by the programmer. On the other hand, one is usually also interested in verifying properties other than store buffer reduction, and ownership is a valuable technique for many properties, e.g., order reduction. In those cases one has to show, as we have done in Lemma 1, that ownership suffices to detect racing variables and add memory fences accordingly. Our model is also simplified w.r.t. the Cohen-Schirmer model, which has ghost components that record history information. This history information is then used in a complex coupling relation, which can only be upheld using 23 invariants. Proving that the invariants are maintained during each step is the bulk work of the Cohen-Schirmer proof. In our proof, we simplify the content of the store buffers by straightforward reordering of steps. This has two important consequences: we can substitute the complex coupling relation by a straightforward one, and the invariants become a simple consequence of the software discipline. Both facts reduce the size of the proof considerably. Note that the store buffer reduction presented in this paper is slightly more efficient than the one in Cohen-Schirmer. This is due to the fact that atomic reads do not require a flush if the last atomic write is to the same address. However, this fact considerably complicates the Abstraction Lemma and its proof in Sect. 4.1, and adds an additional proof step in verifying the soundness of the reordering in Sect. 4.3. For the lecture hall it is thus more convenient to consider a proof for store buffer reduction without this optimization; a simple proof can be found in the technical report. Furthermore, this additional optimization is rarely useful in practice.

Chen, Cohen, and Kovalev [3] extended the Cohen-Schirmer proof to consider memory management units (MMUs) and programs that modify their own page tables and translation lookaside buffers (e.g., by deleting outdated translations). Their proof is 70 pages long. A corresponding proof using the techniques from this paper is less than 30 pages long, and can be found in our technical report [9]. We are not aware of other results proving sequential consistency in the presence of memory management units, let alone inter processor interrupts.

Our discipline also borrows a technique from Owens [10] store buffer reduction discipline. His discipline, which is called triangular race freedom, is complete for (memory trace preserving) sequential consistency. The key aspect of his discipline is the consideration that writes never overtake reads to the same address, which we model with the dirty address. However, Owens (in the terminology of our paper) sets the dirty address even for non-atomic writes, which thus have to be separated from subsequent atomic reads by unnecessary fences.

There are many results that prove sequential consistency under more restrictive disciplines or different memory models. Notably, Sullivan et al. [6] provide a semantics for programs in absolutely relaxed memory machines, where visibility and execution orders of instructions must be explicitly stated by the programmer. The compiler is then assumed to add synchronization that enforces these visibility orders. Stating visibility explicitly adds a relatively small overhead to the code, with a typical ratio of annotation lines to code lines of 1:2. For comparison, annotating ownership and exclusion-invariants for the Cohen-Schirmer method typically requires four times as much annotation (2:1). In the same paper, Sullivan et al. also prove sequential consistency for a less efficient software discipline, where all atomic memory accesses are separated by synchronization primitives - a condition that might be necessary to gain sequential consistency in the extremely relaxed memory they consider. Interestingly, the Cohen-Schirmer discipline arises naturally from the notions of visibility and execution order. Note that in store buffer machines writes become visible in program order, reads are executed in program order, and a read followed by a write are executed in program order; a write followed by a read, however, are executed in program order only if separated by a store buffer flush or when to the same address. Consequently, for memory locations that are accessed by other processors, store buffer flushes need to be introduced between writes and later reads.

Bouajjani, Derevenetc, and Meyer [2] gave a discipline that is complete for (modification order preserving) sequential consistency. Theoretically speaking, our discipline is less efficient than their discipline. In practice there is little difference. A notable counterexample is the MCS lock [8] implemented in the Linux kernel, for which our discipline requires one fence in the `lock` function, which is not necessary for sequential consistency on TSO. On the other hand, the completeness comes at a cost: their discipline is considerably more complicated. In fact, Bouajjani et al. have proven that minimal fence insertion for their discipline is PSPACE complete; this remains so even if the set of racing statements is known. In contrast, a conservative fence insertion algorithm for our discipline simply keeps track of the dirty bit and is linear in the program size (if racing accesses are known).

Abdulla, Atig, and Ngo [1] considered a simple discipline similar to that of Owens, but which does not preserve the reads-from relation: reads may be served by different writes in the store buffer and corresponding abstract computations, as long as the same value is read. In particular, they prove that programs do not require a fence between a write and a read on the same thread as long as the value at the read address is not modified between the write and the read. We are not aware of any practical example where this is the case; if the value of the read address is not modified, it is usually known beforehand, and there is no need to perform the read in the first place. This is also reflected in their benchmarks, which show improvements in performance only in programs that execute reads which read values that are known at compile time.

Vafeiadis and Nardelli [14] prove that fences are only necessary if they separate atomic writes from reads or writes from atomic reads, and integrated their findings in a working compiler. Our discipline is more efficient and it would thus be of practical interest to implement it as a compiler optimization as well.

A different approach to sequential consistency is to change the hardware, e.g., by adding atomic bits to the instruction set and letting the hardware ensure sequential consistency. Singh et al. [13] propose such a processor, where an out-of-order store buffer is added for non-atomic writes. Atomic reads stall the execution until the store buffer is empty. They also suggest changes to operating systems which, for guest applications and in conjunction with the extended hardware, can dynamically deduct ownership by observing memory accesses using address translation. If an error is detected, e.g., an address that was previously thought to be owned by a thread turns out to be shared, store buffers are synchronized by inter processor interrupts. The correctness of this approach obviously relies on sequential consistency proofs in the presence of inter processor interrupts. While their approach is already highly performant, it uses a static ownership model and a conservative classification of accesses. Adding hardware support for an efficient software discipline like that of Cohen-Schirmer is an interesting research topic.

5   Conclusion and Future Work

In this paper we have described a short proof of store buffer reduction in simple processors, using the techniques of Sects. 3 and 4. A straightforward extension to processors with address translation, running code that may modify the page tables, is included in our technical report [9]. Work on extending the proof to processors with inter processor interrupts is in progress.

When arguing about multi-core operating systems, one also has to prove sequential consistency of the operating system code in the presence of malicious guests that do not run sequentially consistent code. While modern operating systems use some techniques for ensuring this property, we are not aware of any proofs that these techniques work.

There are possible modifications to our discipline which allow us to eliminate further fences. For example, a read of a thread that witnesses the most recent atomic store of another thread may set the dirty address to null. On the other hand, there are certain relaxations of TSO that are useful in practice, e.g., allowing multiple threads to use the same store buffer, which are compatible with our discipline, but not with such modifications. Both practical optimizations of the discipline and other relaxed memory models are interesting avenues of research.

Acknowledgments. The author would like to thank Viktor Vafeiadis and Steven Schäfer for helpful discussions. The author would also like to thank Parosh Aziz Abdulla, Mohamed Faouzi Atig and Tuan-Phong Ngo for providing access to their benchmarks. Finally, the author would like to thank the VSTTE reviewers for their valuable feedback.

References

1. Abdulla, P.A., Atig, M.F., Ngo, T.-P.: The best of both worlds: trading efficiency and optimality in fence insertion for TSO. In: Vitek, J. (ed.) ESOP 2015. LNCS, vol. 9032, pp. 308–332. Springer, Heidelberg (2015)
2. Bouajjani, A., Derevenetc, E., Meyer, R.: Checking and enforcing robustness against TSO. In: Felleisen, M., Gardner, P. (eds.) ESOP 2013. LNCS, vol. 7792, pp. 533–553. Springer, Heidelberg (2013)
3. Chen, G., Cohen, E., Kovalev, M.: Store buffer reduction with MMUs. In: Giannakopoulou, D., Kroening, D. (eds.) VSTTE 2014. LNCS, vol. 8471, pp. 117–132. Springer, Heidelberg (2014)
4. Cohen, E., Dahlweid, M., Hillebrand, M., Leinenbach, D., Moskal, M., Santen, T., Schulte, W., Tobies, S.: VCC: a practical system for verifying concurrent C. In: Berghofer, S., Nipkow, T., Urban, C., Wenzel, M. (eds.) TPHOLs 2009. LNCS, vol. 5674, pp. 23–42. Springer, Heidelberg (2009)
5. Cohen, E., Schirmer, B.: From total store order to sequential consistency: a practical reduction theorem. In: Kaufmann, M., Paulson, L.C. (eds.) ITP 2010. LNCS, vol. 6172, pp. 403–418. Springer, Heidelberg (2010)
6. Crary, K., Sullivan, M.J.: A calculus for relaxed memory. In: Proceedings of the 42nd Annual ACM SIGPLAN-SIGACT Symposium on Principles of Programming Languages, pp. 623–636. ACM (2015)

7. Lamport, L.: Time, clocks, and the ordering of events in a distributed system. Commun. ACM **21**(7), 558–565 (1978). http://doi.acm.org/10.1145/359545.359563

8. Mellor-Crummey, J.M., Scott, M.L.: Algorithms for scalable synchronization on shared-memory multiprocessors. ACM Trans. Comput. Syst. (TOCS) **9**(1), 21–65 (1991)

9. Oberhauser, J.: A simpler store buffer reduction theorem. Technical report, Saarland University (2015). http://www-wjp.cs.uni-saarland.de/publikationen/OberhauserSB.pdf

10. Owens, S.: Reasoning about the implementation of concurrency abstractions on x86-TSO. In: D'Hondt, T. (ed.) ECOOP 2010. LNCS, vol. 6183, pp. 478–503. Springer, Heidelberg (2010)

11. Paul, W.J., Baumann, C., Lutsyk, P., Schmaltz, S.: System Architecture as an Ordinary Engineering Discipline. Springer (in press)

12. Sindhu, P.S., Frailong, J.M., Cekleov, M.: Formal specification of memory models. In: Dubois, M., Thakkar, S. (eds.) Scalable Shared Memory Multiprocessors, pp. 25–41. Springer, New York (1992). http://dx.doi.org/10.1007/978-1-4615-3604-8_2

13. Singh, A., Narayanasamy, S., Marino, D., Millstein, T., Musuvathi, M.: End-to-end sequential consistency. ACM SIGARCH Comput. Archit. News **40**, 524–535 (2012). IEEE Computer Society

14. Vafeiadis, V., Zappa Nardelli, F.: Verifying fence elimination optimisations. In: Yahav, E. (ed.) Static Analysis. LNCS, vol. 6887, pp. 146–162. Springer, Heidelberg (2011)

Moving Around: Lipton's Reduction for TSO
(Regular Submission)

Ali Sezgin[1]([✉]) and Serdar Tasiran[2]

[1] University of Cambridge, Cambridge, UK
as2418@cam.ac.uk
[2] Koc University, Istanbul, Turkey
stasiran@ku.edu.tr

Abstract. We generalize Lipton's reduction theory, hitherto limited to SC, for TSO programs. We demonstrate the use of our theory by specifying the conditions under which a particular write is SC-like (i.e. placing a fence immediately after the write does not constrain the behavior of the overall program) and a library implementation can be safely used (i.e. compositionality). Our theory is complete: a program has only SC behaviors iff there is a proof that establishes that every write in the program is SC-like. We adapt the notion of program abstraction to TSO analysis via our theory. We define precisely what is meant by abstraction, and propose a methodology by which one can obtain via abstraction SC summaries of a program which may have non-SC behaviors. Finally, we show how checking whether a write instruction is SC-like can be mechanized. We describe a transformation in which the execution of each thread of the original program (under TSO) is simulated by the execution of two tightly coupled threads in the new program (under SC).

1 Introduction

Analysis of programs running under any memory model weaker than sequential consistency (SC) is challenging. Total-store ordering (TSO), popular due to its being used in the x86-family of processors, is no exception [23]. Unlike SC where updates are assumed to take effect instantaneously over all threads, updates in TSO are observably split into two: a locally visible update and an instantaneous remote update not necessarily simultaneous with the local update. This split is due to a thread local store buffer which an update has to go through before becoming visible by other threads. Operational models of TSO formalize this explicitly: local updates are inserted into the thread local queue; entries are removed from these queues asynchronously and non-deterministically with each removal updating a globally shared memory location.

Main questions about TSO program analysis have centered around determining the existence of non-SC behaviors, the minimal additional synchronization to remove those behaviors, and the verification of safety properties. Formalisms, with axiomatic or operational semantics, have not been the center of attention and mostly been relegated to being expressive enough to derive the desired results.

© Springer International Publishing Switzerland 2016
A. Gurfinkel and S.A. Seshia (Eds.): VSTTE 2015, LNCS 9593, pp. 165–182, 2016.
DOI: 10.1007/978-3-319-29613-5_10

In this paper, we make the formalism our primary concern in the analysis of programs running under TSO. We generalize Lipton's reduction theory [17], hitherto limited to SC, for TSO programs. In this theory, an execution is an interleaving of the instructions of each thread; two executions are equivalent if their end states are identical; an instruction i moves to the right of the concurrent instruction j if $e \cdot i \cdot j \cdot e'$ is equivalent to $e \cdot j \cdot i \cdot e'$ for any e, e'; an instruction is a right-mover if it moves to the right of every concurrent instruction (and similarly with left-movers). Once mover types of instructions are determined, sequential code of the form $R^* \cdot N \cdot L^*$ (right-mover and left-mover instructions enveloping a non-mover instruction) can be treated as atomic, i.e. executing in isolation. Clearly, such a reduction in granularity simplifies the overall analysis (e.g. [12, 16, 22]).

Our adaptation to TSO is based on a partially commutative trace semantics in which every write is split into a pair of actions, a write into buffer and its flush from the buffer. We demonstrate the use of our theory by specifying the conditions under which a particular write is SC-like (i.e. placing a fence immediately after the write does not constrain the behavior of the overall program) and a library implementation can be safely used (i.e. compositionality). Our theory is complete: a program has only SC behaviors iff there is a proof that establishes that every write in the program is SC-like.

One immediate benefit of adapting a well-established theory to a new domain is the potential applicability of old methods to the new domain. In this paper, we give one such instance. To verify safety properties of program P in SC, it is common practice to abstract P to a new program P' if proving that the latter is safe implies the safety of the former. Such abstractions, in the context of concurrent program verification, usually lead to less concurrent behavior, hence easier overall analysis (e.g. [12]). We apply the same idea to TSO analysis via our theory, define precisely what is meant by abstraction, and propose a methodology by which one can obtain via abstraction SC summaries of a program which may have non-SC behaviors.

Finally, we show how checking whether a write instruction is SC-like can be mechanized. We describe a transformation in which the execution of each thread of the original program (under TSO) is simulated by the execution of two tightly coupled threads in the new program (under SC). Of these two threads, one performs the accesses that are thread-locally visible and the other performs accesses that are visible to other threads. The asynchronous nature of buffer flushes is captured by a semaphore-like communication between the two threads: as one performs the locally visible write, it also enables the write that will be globally visible without forcing a particular instant at which the latter will be performed. In the remainder of this section, we informally summarize the highlights of the paper, mention related work and give the outline of the paper.

Reduction for TSO. Consider a code snippet from a program with three threads:

$\{C_{t1}\}$	$\{C_{u1}\}$	$\{C_{v1}\}$
$X := 1;$	$Y := 2;$	$p := X;$
	$r := X;$	$q := Y;$
$\{C_{t2}\}$	$\{C_{u2}\}$	$\{C_{v2}\}$

where C_* represent code segments which refer to neither X nor Y. In the specified segment, the thread on the left, t, writes 1 into shared variable X. The thread in the middle, u, writes 2 to shared variable Y and then reads the value of X into local variable r. Finally, the thread on the right, v, reads the values of X and Y into local variables p and q.

It is possible to observe $r = q = 0$ and $p = 1$ under TSO semantics which constitutes a non-SC behavior. For instance, the execution segment

$$\mathsf{W}^l_u(Y/2) \cdot \alpha \cdot \mathsf{W}^l_t(X/1) \cdot \beta \cdot \mathsf{W}^r_t(X/1) \cdot \gamma \cdot \mathsf{W}^r_u(Y/2)$$

where $\mathsf{W}^l_u(Y/2)$ represents the insertion of the write of Y by u into its store buffer and $\mathsf{W}^r_t(X/1)$ represents the flushing of the associated entry from the buffer and α, β, γ are sequences of actions. The read values are possible if u executes its read either in α or β and v executes its reads in γ.

In terms of reduction theory, we can equivalently claim that the given execution is non-SC by arguing that it is impossible to *move* the local write by u next to its remote write without changing the values read by threads u and v. In the sample execution given above, since the read of X by u is not in γ and it cannot be reordered with $\mathsf{W}^r_t(X/1)$ without changing its observed value, the local write $\mathsf{W}^l_u(Y/2)$ cannot move to the right of $\mathsf{W}^r_t(X/1)$ either. On the other hand, the remote write $\mathsf{W}^r_u(Y/2)$ cannot move to the left of every action in γ since it contains the read of Y executed by v whose observed value of 0 will not be consistent with TSO semantics when it is preceded by a memory update of Y with 2. Since a TSO execution has an equivalent SC execution only when all local and remote write actions can be put together without changing the read values, the above sequence is indeed non-SC.

SC-like Writes. The sample program has non-SC behavior, or following the notation introduced in [20], it contains a *triangular race*. Briefly, a triangular race occurs when one thread updates a location, continues with a sequence of reads the last of which is to a different location and conflicts with the write of a concurrent thread. It was shown in [20] that a program does not have triangular race, called a *TRF* program, iff it only has SC behaviors. Now, before attempting to turn the sample program into a TRF program, we observe that the local and remote write actions due to the write by t can always be put together, if for the moment we ignore the presence of C_{t1} and C_{t2}; i.e. if we assume that t executes only the write to X. This is because a local write action, which only updates the thread local state (changing buffer contents), moves to the right of every concurrent action without changing the overall behavior of the execution. The nice property of an SC-like write is that, as we show, one can pretend that there exists a fence immediately after it, simplifying program analysis under TSO semantics, without restricting the overall behavior of the program. In the remainder of the paper, we will use the term *atomic write* interchangeably with SC-like write.

Removing Triangular Race. For the sake of simplicity, assume that the value of q is not subsequently used by v; i.e. q is not read in C_{v2}. Then, we can obtain a new program by replacing the read of Y with $q := \star$, which intuitively can assign any value to q. The behaviors of this new program subsumes the behaviors of the original program because of additional non-determinism. The fact that Y is not read by v in the new program immediately allows us to prove that the previously non-atomic write to Y now is atomic. However, unlike the atomicity argument for the write of X by t, the write to Y is atomic because we can move $W_u^r(Y/2)$ to the left of $W_t^r(X/1)$, in turn because γ does not contain the conflicting read of Y. Here again we assumed that C_{v1} and C_{v2} do not exist which brings us to our next observation.

Compositionality. At this point we know that in the abstracted program, the write by t is atomic because its local action is a right-mover (abstraction does not affect its atomicity argument), and the write by u is atomic because its remote action is a left-mover. One of our results implies the write to X remains atomic if the first action in C_{t2} is a fence statement. Dually, the write to Y remains atomic if the last action in C_{v1} is a fence statement. Thus, analyzing write atomicity based on reduction allows us to make these distinctions in finding places for requiring fence statements.

Program Transformation and Mechanical Verification. Transforming TSO programs into equivalent SC programs usually entails embedding an array per thread, representing the local store buffer. Then, each write is inserted into this array and a non-deterministic loop, representing flushing of the contents of the store buffer, is placed between each statement of the original program. This encoding for us is not suitable because we want to explicitly check the mover types of local and remote writes. To that end, we make use of the fact that there is a bijection between buffer insertions and removals that respect thread local program order.

When we apply our transformation to the sample code above, the write to X by t will be transformed into two writes, one by t to a new local copy of X and one by t' (the *dual* thread of t) to X. An important requirement is that the local write by t always precede the remote write by t', and this we achieve by using a semaphore like structure per write statement, which is incremented by t and decremented by t'.

Once an equivalent SC program is obtained, any SC analysis tool can be used to reason about the program. In this paper, we are primarily interested in the mover types of local and remote write actions and propose one particular way of doing it.

To summarize, in this paper we:

- develop a formal reasoning framework for TSO programs based on reduction,

- obtain numerous theoretical results adding to the understanding of what separates TSO programs with triangular races from those without,

- introduce abstraction for TSO programs in order to obtain TRF programs from those that are not TRF,

- present a novel transformation from TSO programs to equivalent SC programs,

- propose a way to mechanically verify TRF.

Related Work. Program analysis under relaxed memory models has been a field of intense study, e.g. formalization of memory models [6,7,18,23], program logics for relaxed memory models [5,13,21,25] or verification techniques [2,8,10,11,19]. In this discussion of related work, we focus only on research about TSO program analysis.

Fundamental studies such as [8,20] have established necessary and sufficient conditions for a program running under TSO semantics to have only SC behaviors. In [20], the concept of *triangular race* is defined and it was proved that a program is triangular race free (TRF) iff it only has SC behaviors. In [8], the equivalent concept of *feasible attacks* which coincide with non-SC behavior is defined, and a fence insertion algorithm that would remove all feasible attacks of a given program is proposed. Most of the remaining previous work have tackled the problem of removing non-SC behavior. In [9], a SAT-solver based method to detect non-SC behavior which can be removed by adding synchronization via fences is proposed. In [10], building on the delay set analysis of [24], a cycle detection algorithm running under SC semantics is developed. This was subsequently extended to other relaxed memory models along with methods which introduce enough synchronization to remove any non-SC behavior [4]. The works of [1–3] are extensions of the cycle detection idea to the verification of concurrent software running on relaxed memory including TSO. In particular, a method to convert a given program running under TSO (and several others) to another program with equivalent behavior running under SC is proposed in [2]. The SC equivalent program then can be analyzed by any SC tool, whose analysis results apply to the original program. Finally, in [15] a proof system to verify programs running under TSO is developed.

Representing TSO via an operational semantics framework as we do in this paper has been already done in [8,9,15,20]. In particular, approaches presented in [8,15] are very similar to ours, splitting write events into local and remote actions. The similarity with [15] goes even further since they are concerned with decreasing the granularity of concurrency, which is the essential problematic of Lipton's reduction theory. In both [8,15], the notion of equivalent computations exists, either in the proofs [8] or in the proof rules [15]. However, neither considers a full generalization to mover types in their respective frameworks. Our theoretical framework presents an orthogonal contribution to theirs: rules in the proof system of [15] or the main results, such as the feasible attacker theorem, of [8], can be proved within our framework. In other words, we offer an alternative and complementary meta-theory to existing and future work on the analysis of programs running under TSO semantics.

The notion of an *SC specification* of a TSO program was presented in [14]. Unlike [14] which does not contain a method to obtain those specifications, in this paper we show how one can obtain SC summaries of TSO programs. Our method is a direct consequence of applying Lipton's reduction theory to TSO semantics and making use of existing work on the former, most notably that of [12]. Similar to [2], we present a behavior preserving program transformation algorithm from TSO to SC. Unlike [2] which uses auxiliary arrays and non-deterministic loops, we capture the asynchronous nature of buffer flushes by delegating them to auxiliary threads. This alternative transformation has the benefit of identifying each buffer flush with a unique instruction in the program, a feature impossible to achieve in transformations similar to the one given in [2]. It is this syntactic correspondence between instructions of the program and each buffer flush that enables us to formulate the mover analysis of instructions.

2   Formal Framework

Notation. Let $\mathbf{a}$ be a sequence over A. We will use indexed notation to refer to the elements in $\mathbf{a}$: $\mathbf{a}[i]$ is the ith action in $\mathbf{a}$. Similarly, we let $\mathbf{a}\langle i, j \rangle$ denote the segment of $\mathbf{a}$ from $\mathbf{a}[i]$ to $\mathbf{a}[j]$ with both ends inclusive. The length of $\mathbf{a}$ is written as $\mathsf{len}(\mathbf{a})$ and gives the number of symbols in $\mathbf{a}$. Let π be a permutation over $[1, \mathsf{len}(\mathbf{a})]$. We use $\pi(\mathbf{a})$ to denote the sequence $\mathbf{a}[\pi(1)] \ldots \mathbf{a}[\pi(\mathsf{len}(\mathbf{a}))]$. Two sequences $\mathbf{a}$ and $\mathbf{b}$ are *permutationally equivalent*, written $\mathbf{a} \sim_\pi \mathbf{b}$, if there is a permutation π with $\mathbf{a} = \pi(\mathbf{b})$.

We will consider three types of memory operations: *writes*, W, W^l, W^r; *reads*, R; *barriers*, B. The type W is for write instructions executing on SC, W^l and W^r are for write instructions executing on TSO, where the former is for the insertion of the write into the local buffer, and the latter for the flushing of the buffered write to memory. For any operation type A, $A_t(l/v)$ denotes that A is executed by thread t to location l with value v. For simplicity, we omit locked operations which can be modeled by the given actions. We will use the notation $Act_{O,thr,loc}$ to denote the subset of Act which contains all actions of type $O \subseteq \{\mathsf{W}, \mathsf{R}, \mathsf{W}^l, \mathsf{W}^r, \mathsf{B}\}$, by thread thr, and into location loc. When O is a singleton, we will ignore the braces. Omitting parameters denotes existential quantification; e.g. $Act_{-,t,-}$ is the set of all actions done by thread t. The projection of a sequence $\mathbf{e}$ over Act into $Act_{O,t,l}$, written as $\mathbf{e} \downarrow_{O,t,l}$, is the subsequence obtained by keeping only those actions in $Act_{O,t,l}$. For instance, $\mathbf{e} \downarrow_{\mathsf{R},t,-}$ is the subsequence of $\mathbf{e}$ consisting of all the read actions done by t.

2.1   TSO and SC Executions

In this section, we define correct TSO and SC executions, and define what we mean by an equivalent SC-execution to a given TSO-execution whenever the former exists.

TSO-executions. *TSO actions*, subset of Act, exclude only the first kind, $\mathsf{W}_t(x/v)$. A remote write $\mathsf{W}_t^r(x/v)$ *matches* the local write $\mathsf{W}_u^l(y/w)$ iff $t = u$, $x = y$ and $v = w$. Let $\mathbf{e}$ be a sequence of TSO actions. It is *matched* if for all t, $\mathbf{e} \downarrow_{\mathsf{W}^r,t,-} [i]$ matches $\mathbf{e} \downarrow_{\mathsf{W}^l,t,-} [i]$. A local write $\mathbf{e}[i]$ is *buffered at* j if it is matched by a remote write at position $l > j$. We will call a matched $\mathbf{e}$ *complete* if there are no buffered writes at $|\mathbf{e}|$. Unless stated otherwise, sequences of TSO actions are assumed to be complete.

A TSO-execution is a sequence $\mathbf{e}$ of TSO actions subject to well-formedness constraints:

- Local write actions occur before their matching remote write actions. Formally, if $e[i] = W_t^l(x/v)$ and $e[j] = W_t^r(x/v)$ are respectively the kth local and remote write actions by thread t, then $i < j$.

- The read values are consistent. Formally, if $e[j] = R_t(x/v)$, then either (i) $W_t^l(x/v)$ is the most recent buffered write at j by t to x, or (ii) no buffered write to x by t at j exists and $W_u^r(x/v)$ is the most recent remote write, or (iii) neither condition applies and v is the initial value.

- The barrier operations can only happen when the buffer is empty. Formally, if $e[j] = B_t$ and if $W_u^l(x/v)$ is buffered at j, then $t \neq u$.

Definition 1 (Synchronous, Buffer-free). *A local write* $e[i]$ *is* synchronous *if it is not buffered at* $i + 1$. *A complete TSO-execution* e *is called* buffer-free *if all of its local writes are synchronous.*

Synchronous local writes form the crux of the reduction we present in this paper. The following observations state that a thread t can perform a synchronous local write only when its buffer is empty.

Lemma 1. *Let the local write* $e[i] = W_t^l(x/v)$ *of a TSO-execution* e *be synchronous. Then* $e\langle 1, i+1\rangle \cdot B_t \cdot e\langle i+2, \text{len}(e)\rangle$ *is also a (well-formed) TSO-execution.*

Proof. This follows from the definition of well-formedness which requires local and remote writes of the same thread to be in the same order because that implies that no local write can be buffered by t at i.

Each TSO-execution e induces a partial order $<_e^{tso}$ over $\{e[i] \mid i \in [1, |e|]\}$ such that $a <_e^{tso} b$ if a occurs before b in e, $a, b \in Act_{-,t,-}$ and either (i) both a and b are remote write actions, or (ii) neither a nor b is a remote write action, or (iii) a is the ith local write by t and b is the ith remote write by t. We will make use of $<^{tso}$ in defining equivalence relations over TSO runs.

SC-executions. SC *actions*, subset of *Act*, include only the first two kinds of actions; i.e., $\{W_t(x/v)\} \cup \{R_t(x/v)\}$. SC-executions have to satisfy: if $s[i] = R_t(x/v)$, then either i) there is $j < i$ with $s[j] = W_u(x/v)$ and there are no write actions to x in $s\langle j + 1, i\rangle$, or ii) there is no write action in $s\langle 1, i\rangle$ and v is $\bot$.

Correspondence between TSO and SC. For a TSO-execution e, let $\ulcorner e \urcorner$ denote the sequence obtained by replacing all local write actions $W_t^l(x/v)$ with $W_t(x/v)$ and projecting that sequence to SC actions, W, R.

Let e be a complete TSO-execution. We define $SC(e)$ to be the set of all SC-executions s such that $\ulcorner e \downarrow_{-,t,-} \urcorner = s \downarrow_{-,t,-}$ and $e \downarrow_{W^r,-,-} [i] = W_t^r(x/v)$ iff $s \downarrow_{W,-,-} [i] = W_t(x/v)$. Informally, s belongs to $SC(e)$ if it is an SC-execution, respects the thread local ordering of read and local write actions, and preserves the order among the remote write actions in e. We have the following result following immediately from definitions.

Proposition 1. *For any buffer-free TSO-execution* **e**, $\ulcorner$**e**$\urcorner \in$ SC(**e**).

The proof follows from the fact that in a buffer-free TSO-execution, all reads are from the memory (only condition (ii) of TSO well-formedness for consistent read values applies). The desired SC-execution then can be obtained by simply replacing each (adjacent) pair of local and remote write actions by their image under $\ulcorner\urcorner$.

Equivalence ($\approx$) and partial order ($\sqsubseteq$) over TSO-executions. Two complete TSO-executions **e** and **f** are *equivalent*, written **e** $\approx$ **f**, if they are permutationally equivalent and they both induce the same partial order. Formally, **e** $\approx$ **f** if **e** $\sim_\pi$ **f** and $<_{\mathbf{e}}^{tso}=<_{\mathbf{f}}^{tso}$. Whenever no confusion is likely to arise, we will use π to denote one of the permutations between two equivalent TSO-executions establishing their equivalence.

Synchronous writes induce a partial order $\sqsubseteq$ on equivalent TSO-execution. A TSO-execution **f** is *tighter* than **e**, written **f** $\sqsubseteq$ **e** if **f** $\approx$ **e** and whenever **e**[i] is a synchronous local write, then so is **f**[$\pi(i)$]. In other words, **f** is tighter than an equivalent **e** if all synchronous writes of the latter are also synchronous in the former. Each TSO-execution thus induces a set of tighter executions. Let T(**e**) = {**f** | **f** $\sqsubseteq$ **e**}; that is, the set of all TSO-executions tighter than **e**.

Definition 2 (SC-like). *Let* **e** *be a TSO-execution. It is called* SC-like *if* T(**e**) *contains a buffer-free execution. Otherwise, it is called* TSO-specific.

The terms are not arbitrarily named as the following proposition shows.

Proposition 2. *A TSO-execution* **e** *is SC-like iff* T(**e**) $\cap$ SC(**e**) $\neq \emptyset$.

Intuitively, permutationally equivalent TSO-executions have identical observations about the state of the memory; i.e. the values returned by the reads are identical. A tighter execution is one which has at most as many buffered local writes as those of the less tight one. At the limit, all local writes are synchronous (no buffered writes), which makes the execution buffer-free. Thus, if an execution is equivalent to a buffer-free execution, then its behavior is identical to that of an SC-execution which is obtained by replacing all synchronous write actions with direct write actions.

2.2   Programming Language

We briefly introduce the programming language we use. A *method* $M = (N, C)$ consists of a *name* N and a *code* C. A name is simply a string. A code is a, possibly empty, sequence of statements (S) sequentially composed (;). Statements read from memory ($r := $ mem[e]), update the contents of a memory location (mem[e] $:= e'$), empty the store buffer (fence), assign a value to a register ($r := e$). To model control flow, we have the usual branching (if e then {e_1} else {e_2}) and looping (while(e) {}) statements. Additionally, we also use an explicit blocking statement (assume e), which blocks as long as e evaluates to *false*. Finally, the statement (assert e) is used to claim that e should hold whenever this statement can execute. The shared data space is mapped by mem[e], where e is an expression which evaluates to $\mathbb{N}$. As a syntactic sugar, we will use words in italic font with first letters capitalized to denote a location in shared memory, e.g. *Obj* will stand for some mem[i].

A *program* is a set of methods. Each statement of a program P is uniquely identified, captured by a labelling function Lab : Stmt(P) → L, where Stmt(P) denotes the set of statements in P and L is the (universal) *label* set.

The run of a program follows the conventional interpretations for each statement. The semantics we define is in a unified framework, applicable to both SC and TSO semantics. A program run is *TSO-compliant* if every memory update statement mem[e] := e' causes the TSO write actions W^l and W^r with the proper arguments, and every memory read returns the most recent value inserted into the thread local buffer or in the absence of such a slot in the buffer, the value currently held in memory. Similarly, a program run is *SC-compliant* if every memory update statement mem[e] := e' causes the (SC) write action W, and every memory read returns the value currently held in memory. Let $\mathbf{R}_{tso}(P)$ denote the set of all TSO-compliant runs of P. Similarly, let $\mathbf{R}_{sc}(P)$ denote the set of all SC-compliant runs of P.

Memory Traces. Let Mem($q, trans$) denote the memory action associated with executing the transition $trans$ from state q. For instance, Mem($q, RdB, t : r :=$) mem[e] gives the memory action $R_t(l/v)$, where, in state q, l is what e evaluates to, there is a buffered update to l in the local buffer and v is the value of the most recent buffered update to l. With an abuse in notation, we let Mem(r) denote the memory trace of a run r. The following result establishes the link between runs and executions.

Proposition 3. *Let r be a TSO (resp. SC) compliant run. Then* Mem(r) *is a TSO-execution (resp. SC-execution).*

3   Reduction for TSO

In this section, we explain how the reduction theory of Lipton can be used for TSO. Our goal is to present sufficient conditions for programs such that when a program satisfies these conditions the program is guaranteed to be unable to distinguish TSO semantics from SC semantics. In the following sections, we will show how we can extend it to programs which are TSO-specific.

A statement s is *left mover* (resp. *right mover*) if reordering s before (resp. after) any other statement that is concurrent with s does not change the behavior (all runs belonging to the same equivalence have the same behavior). In the classic definition of reduction, the equivalence relation requires that the two sequences be permutations of each other and that the end states are identical, which corresponds to ≈ in the TSO context. Our first result about movers follows immediately from definitions.

Lemma 2. *Let P be a program. All of its TSO runs are SC-like if all remote writes are left-movers in ≈. Dually, all of its TSO runs are SC-like if all local actions (i.e. ignoring remote writes) are right-movers in ≈.*

Proof. Take any run $r \in \mathbf{R}_{tso}(P)$. If all remote writes are left-movers in $\approx$, then there exists a run $r' \approx r$ such that all local writes are synchronous. Then by Definition 2, r is SC-like. A symmetric argument applies for the second case.

This result depends on a strong constraint, all updates being left-movers or all reads being right-movers, which is unlikely to be satisfied by many programs. In what follows we will provide a series of incrementally more general results. Fix a labelled program $P = \{m_1, \ldots, m_n\}$. Let σ be a partitioning of (the methods of) P. The σ-*partitioned runs* of $P[T]$ is the subset of $\mathbf{R}_{tso}(P[T])$ containing all and only those runs in which each t executes methods from the same partition.

Lemma 3. *Let P be a program and σ be a partitioning of P. If σ is such that in σ-partitioned runs of $P[T]$ for each partition, all remote write actions executed by all the methods in the partition are left-movers or all local actions executed by all the methods in the partition are right-movers, then σ-partitioned runs are SC-like.*

Call a subset of $\mathbf{R}_{tso}(P[T])$ *singular* if it contains all and only those runs in which each thread $t \in T$ runs at most one method; i.e. the INIT-transition is executed at most once by each t. Then the following is a particular instance of the previous result.

Corollary 1. *All singular TSO runs of $P[T]$ are SC-like if for each method m_i, either all of its local actions are right-movers in $\approx$ or all of its remote write actions are left-movers in $\approx$.*

We can specialize even further, obtaining the following, which is also implied by triangular-race freedom of [20].

Corollary 2. *Let P be such that each m_i either only updates the shared memory (no read actions) or only reads shared memory (no write actions). Then all singular TSO runs of $P[T]$ are SC-like.*

Write Atomicity. We will call a statement s in P *atomic* if for every run of P there is an $\approx$-equivalent run such that actions due to each execution of s are adjacent. In particular, a memory update statement ($s = \mathtt{mem}[i]:=e$) is atomic if in an $\approx$-equivalent run the two transitions caused by s are adjacent; i.e. the local write actions due to s are synchronous. The reason we introduce write atomicity should be clear: By Lemma 1, if one can prove that for any TSO run of program P there exists an equivalent run in which s is atomic, then we can safely transform s to $\mathtt{atomic\{s;fence\}}$. This substitution decreases the number of possible interleavings, which in turn simplifies the analysis of the program. Indeed, the latter is a step towards the ultimate goal of analyzing the whole program under SC semantics. For the following fix an update statement s and let s^{loc} and s^{rem} denote its local and remote write actions.

Lemma 4. *If in any TSO run in which s^{loc} is executed by some thread t, all statements executed by t up to the occurrence of s^{loc} are atomic and s^{rem} is left-mover in $\approx$, then s is atomic.*

Observe that we have to require all the statements executed by t preceding s^{loc} be atomic. To understand why we need this (sufficiency) condition, consider the following run:

$$\alpha \cdot s^{loc} \cdot \beta_1 \cdot \mathsf{W}^r_t(x/v) \cdot \beta_2 \cdot s^{rem}$$

If the remote write action $\mathsf{W}^r_t(x/v)$, whose matching local action must precede s^{loc}, cannot move to the left of every action in β_1, then even though s^{rem} itself is a left-mover, there is not an equivalent run in which s^{loc} and s^{rem} are adjacent because of the presence of $\mathsf{W}^r_t(x/v)$ in between the two.

However, the above argument leads to the following special instance which incidentally gives an insight about how fence statements can lead to SC-like programs.

Corollary 3. *If in any TSO run in which s^{loc} is executed by thread t, there exists a fence action executed by t preceding s^{loc}, no other local write actions by t occur between the two actions and s^{rem} is left-mover, then s is atomic.*

Essentially, the antecedent of the Corollary 3 implies the absence of $\mathsf{W}^r_t(x/v)$ of the above sample run. Thus, unlike the general case, in order to argue that a write immediately following a fence statement is atomic, we only need to prove that its matching remote write action is left-mover. There is a dual of this result.

Lemma 5. *If in any TSO run in which s^{loc} is executed by thread t, there does not exist any read action executed by t until the occurrence of s^{rem}, then s is atomic.*

To see why this holds, observe that a local write action is always a right-mover because the changes it makes are invisible to other threads. Then, to conclude that a write statement is atomic, one has to consider the mover type of all possible local actions that can come between the local and remote write actions. A well-known way of restricting this sequence of actions is through the use of a fence, which we state next as a special instance of the previous result which is yet another way fence statements can result in SC-like behaviors.

Corollary 4. *Let $s; C;$ fence be a code block in some m_i such that C does not contain any read of shared memory (no statements of the form $r := \mathsf{mem}[e]$). Then s and all the writes in C are atomic.*

Compositionality. Library implementations can be seen as programs which are to be executed in arbitrary contexts. Unlike SC semantics where atomicity of methods carry over to arbitrary execution contexts as long as there is a separation of memory footprints, atomicity of methods under TSO semantics does not immediately translate into atomicity in other execution contexts even when the footprints are distinct. We let *non-interfering context* (for P) denote any program P' which does not access any location that P does. We will now state our main compositionality results.

Theorem 1 (Compositionality-Remote). *Let m be an atomic method in P such that all remote write actions of m are left-movers. Then, m remains atomic* *in any non-interfering context which executes a fence statement every time m completes (returns).*

Theorem 2 (Compositionality-Local). *Let m be a method in P such that all local actions of m are right-movers. Then, m remains atomic in any non-interfering context which executes a fence statement before each call to m.*

These results show that placing a fence statement relative to library calls can benefit from mover analysis. One can omit an exit fence (entry fence) to m if the conditions of Thoerem 1 (Theorem 2) hold.

Completeness. Call a TSO run *unambiguous* if there do not exist two distinct write actions updating the same location with the same value. If the definition of $\approx$ is strengthened to require that the mapping between reads and the writes from which they obtain their value (known usually as the reads-from mapping), then the requirement of unambiguity is not needed. We have the following result.

Theorem 3. *Let P be a program and s a memory update statement in P. Let r be an unambiguous TSO run of P, in the form $\alpha \cdot s^{loc} \cdot \beta \cdot s^{rem}$ where s^{loc} is executed by t. Then r has an $\approx$-equivalent run in which s is atomic iff there is a permutation of $\beta \sim_\pi \beta_1\beta_2$ such that $r \approx \alpha \cdot \beta_1 \cdot s^{loc} \cdot s^{rem} \cdot \beta_2$.*

Proof (Sketch). One direction is by definition. For the other direction, assume that such a permutation does not exist and let $\text{len}(\beta) = k$. Without loss of generality, assume that s^{loc} cannot move to the right of $\beta[1]$ and s^{rem} cannot move the left of $\beta[k]$. Otherwise, move both actions to the right and to the left until such actions which must exist by the assumption are found. Then, it must be the case that there is an increasing sequence $i_1, \dots, i_n$ of indices in $[1, k]$ such that $\beta[i_j]$ cannot move to the right of $\beta[i_{j+1}]$ for $1 < j < n$ with $i_1 = 1$ and $i_n = k$. But if such a sequence exists, s cannot be atomic by the unambiguity assumption.

4   Abstracting TSO Programs

Our approach so far allows us to at least alleviate some of the difficulties in reasoning by showing that certain write statements can be taken to be atomic. In this section, we go one step further and show that abstraction can be used to turn a program with TSO-specific runs into one that contains only SC-like runs.

Let us call two TSO-runs r and r' *computationally equal* if there are two sequences of increasing index values, $i_1 \dots i_m$ and $j_1 \dots j_m$ over the state indices that occur in r and r' such that $i_1 = j_1 = 0$, $i_m = \text{len}(r)$, $j_m = \text{len}(r')$, for all $1 \leq n \leq m$ we have $q_{i_n} = q'_{j_n}$, and all transitions from q_{i_n} to $q_{i_{n+1}}$ and from q'_{j_n} to $q'_{j_{n+1}}$ are executed by the same thread. Intuitively, computationally equal runs will result in identical execution paths, even though there may be syntactic differences between the executed statements.

```
Recv()
  Rdy:=1;  r[2]:=Buf;                   Send(d)
  if r[2]=0 then                          Buf:=d;  r[1]:=Rdy;
    r[1]:=Flag;                           while r[1]=0 {r[1]:=Rdy;}
    while r[1]=0 {r[1]:=Flag;}            Flag:=1;
    r[2]:=Buf;
```

Fig. 1. Sender/Receiver template with a triangular race.

Definition 3 (Program Abstraction). *Let P and P' be two programs. We say that P' abstracts P, if either (i) P' has a failed run (ending at an assertion violation), or (ii) P does not have a failed run and for each terminated run $r \in \mathbf{R}_{tso}(P)$, there exists a terminated run $r' \in \mathbf{R}_{tso}(P')$ computationally equal to r.*

Intuitively, P' abstracts P if P' contains an assertion violation or has more behaviors than P. This means that if P' can be proven to contain no assertion violations, then neither does P. We should note that the other direction, that when P does not contain an assertion violation neither should P', does not hold in general.

Assume that we have a program P with TSO-specific runs. We construct an abstraction P' of P such that if r is a TSO-specific run of P, then there will be a run r' of P' computationally equal to r such that r' is SC-like. As we shall see computational equality allows us to remove dependencies between memory reads and writes by abstracting one or both.

Abstraction rules. There are many ways to ensure that a syntactic manipulation of P results in another program P' abstracting the former. Here, we consider those class of rewritings which replace the read or write of a particular value with a non-deterministic value. Let $\star$ be a special notation to denote an expression that can evaluate to any integer value. Then replacing any expression with e with $\star$ is an abstraction. The possible instances are rewriting $r := \mathtt{mem}[e]$ as $r := \star$; $r := e$ as $r := \star$; and $\mathtt{mem}[e] := r$ as $\mathtt{mem}[e] := \star$. It is possible to introduce non-determinism conditionally as well, i.e. abstract only if a certain property holds (see example below).

Example - Send/Receive. Consider the code given in Fig. 1. The intended operation proceeds as follows: The sender begins by preparing the message (represented by writing d into Buf), and then spins on Rdy. After observing Rdy equal to 1 it sends the message ready signal by setting $Flag$ to 1. The receiver begins by setting Rdy (initially 0) to 1 to tell the sender that it is ready to receive a message. Before spinning on $Flag$, the receiver reads the current content of Buf (0 means message not in yet). If it observes a non-zero value denoting a valid message, it skips the entire spinning block. Otherwise, it spins on $Flag$ and after observing it to be equal to 1, it reads the message from Buf. Let us consider the set of TSO runs in which two threads t and u run Recv and Send() respectively.

This program does have a triangular race depicted by the following memory trace

$$\mathsf{W}^l_t(Rdy/1) \cdot \mathsf{R}_t(Buf/0) \cdot \mathsf{W}^l_u(Buf/d) \cdot \mathsf{W}^r_u(Buf/d) \cdot \mathsf{R}_u(Rdy/0) \cdot \mathsf{W}^r_t(Rdy/1)$$

The first three actions, the local write to Rdy and read of Buf by t followed by a write to Buf by u gives the triangular race. The remaining part of the execution shows how the race can be extended into a non SC-like run.

One might be tempted to abstract the read of Buf by t altogether. However, that would make the rest of the code behave incorrectly since a non-zero value for Buf means a valid message which need not be equal to what u is about to write, d. Let us instead consider the following abstraction for the statement r[2] := Buf:

```
if * then atomic{assume Buf = 0; r[2] := Buf;} else atomic{assume Buf ≠ 0; r[2] := *;}
```

Informally, this rewriting introduces abstraction only when $Buf \neq 0$. We claim that in the new abstract program P' the write to Rdy by Recv is atomic. Let $\boldsymbol{r}$ be a run in $\mathbf{R}_{tso}(P')$ whose memory trace is of the form

$$\alpha \cdot \mathsf{W}^l_t(Rdy/1) \cdot \gamma \cdot \mathsf{W}^r_t(Rdy/1) \cdot \beta$$

where α, τ and β are sequences of memory actions. We have to show that there exists another run $\boldsymbol{r'}$ of P' computationally equal to $\boldsymbol{r}$ in which the write to Rdy is atomic.

First, observe that γ cannot contain the write to $Flag$ by u because that action only happens when u ends its spinning by reading 1 from Rdy which can only happen in β, i.e. after the remote write action $\mathsf{W}^r_t(Rdy/1)$. This in turn means that the farthest t can go in γ is the reading of $Flag$. Any read action is a right (and left) mover with respect to another action not writing to the location read. Thus, in case γ contains read(s) of $Flag$ they can all move to right of $\mathsf{W}^r_t(Rdy/1)$.

Since a local write action is always a right mover, we are left with the read of Buf by t. If the remote write action $\mathsf{W}^r_u(Buf/d)$ is not in γ, then we are done. Assume that $\mathsf{W}^r_u(Buf/d)$ happens after some prefix γ_p of γ, i.e.

$$\alpha \cdot \mathsf{W}^l_t(Rdy/1) \cdot \gamma_p \cdot \mathsf{W}^r_u(Buf/d) \cdot \gamma_q \cdot \mathsf{W}^r_t(Rdy/1) \cdot \beta$$

If the read of Buf by t happens in γ_q, we are done. So assume that the read of Buf happens in γ_p. Since it happens before the remote write action, the state at which the abstract read statement occurs must have $Buf = 0$. According to the abstraction, this means that the **then** branch must have been taken, which sets r[2] to 0 (by reading the contents of Buf). If the abstracted statement is executed after $\mathsf{W}^r_u(Buf/d)$, then because $Buf \neq 0$ holds after the remote write, the **else** branch will be taken. That in turn implies that r[2] can be assigned any value, including 0. So, the sequence

$$\alpha \cdot \gamma'_p \cdot \mathsf{W}^r_u(Buf/d) \cdot \gamma'_q \cdot \mathsf{W}^l_t(Rdy/1) \cdot \mathsf{W}^r_t(Rdy/1) \cdot \gamma_2 \cdot \beta$$

where γ'_p does not contain any action by t is also a memory trace of a run of P' computationally equal to r. Since γ was taken to be arbitrary, we conclude that the write to Rdy by t is atomic.

Execution Context. Observe that our argument also establishes the remote write action to Buf as a left mover. However, there is a fundamental difference between the two arguments. Since we proved the atomicity of the write to Rdy by showing that all actions of t until the remote write action to Rdy occurs are right-movers, the result there being no other local actions by t until the remote write action occurs. On the other hand, because our argument for the atomicity of the write to Buf is based on showing that its remote write action is a left-mover, the result depends on the contents of the store buffer. In other words, if one wants to have atomicity of these writes in any execution context, Recv must end with a fence whereas Send must begin with a fence, in accordance with the compositionality results, Theorems 1 and 2, respectively.

5   Mechanical Verification of Write Atomicity

In this section, we present a program transformation to mechanically prove that a particular write is SC-like. Due to space constraints, we keep the description brief, only highlighting the essential aspects.

The execution of method m by some thread t is simulated by the execution of two methods $\tau_l(m)$ and $\tau_r(m)$ by threads t and t', respectively. The statements of the methods $\tau_l(m)$ and $\tau_r(m)$ are in a bijection; the former are called local, the latter are called remote. The local writes done in $\tau_l(m)$ by t are only visible to t. Initially, all the remote writes in $\tau_r(m)$ are disabled. Every time a local write is executed by t, the associated remote write in $\tau_r(m)$ is enabled. When the remote write is committed to the memory is left unspecified, capturing the asynchronous nature of buffer flushes. The local reads done in $\tau_l(m)$ either read the most recent local update to the same location if its associated remote write has not been executed yet by t'; otherwise, the value in the shared memory. A remote read does not access memory at all; it merely copies the value that was observed by its associated local read, which was registered to a dedicated auxiliary location. A local fence statement in $\tau_l(m)$ can execute only if all prior enabled remote statements in $\tau_r(m)$ are executed. We state the main technical result of this section.

Theorem 4 *[Soundness of Transformation]. Let P be a program and P^S denote its transformation. Then, for every TSO-run of P there exists a computationally equal canonical SC-run of P^S, and for every SC-run of P^S, there exists a computationally equal TSO-run of P.*

Once P^S is obtained, any SC analysis tool can be deployed on it.

Remark. An immediate concern about our construction is the increase in the number of threads (2-fold) and the number of instructions (2-fold). One might worry that this increase could slow down each round of mover type checking, which essentially is quadratic in the size of the program as every instruction has to be compared with every other instruction of the program. In order to argue that this will not be the case, we make two observations. First, since each local write is invisible to concurrent accesses, involving them in mover checks is unnecessary: they are by definition both-movers. Second, since each remote read is essentially copying the value that was read by its associated local read, they are again oblivious to interference and thus are both-movers. In other words, the mover types are only needed to be checked for local reads and remote writes, which implies that the number of mover checks to be done in the transformed program is the same as the number of mover checks to be done in the original program.

6   Conclusion

Analyses based on determining the mover types of local and remote actions may lead to less synchronization, not only because of the removal of fence statements but also because of increased confidence in the correct use of optimistic and racy reads which are very tricky to reason about. This is a line of work on which we are planning to do further research. Another question is whether one can specify sufficient conditions the satisfaction of which guarantees the mover type of a write under SC semantics carries over to TSO semantics. That is, it is interesting to determine when we can claim that a remote write is a left-mover when its corresponding statement under SC semantics is shown to be left-mover, thus lifting the results of an SC analysis to TSO.

Acknowledgment. This work is supported by EPSRC grants EP/H005633/1, EP/K008528/1 and TUBITAK grant 111E135.

References

1. Alglave, J., Kroening, D., Nimal, V., Poetzl, D.: Don't sit on the fence. In: Biere, A., Bloem, R. (eds.) CAV 2014. LNCS, vol. 8559, pp. 508–524. Springer, Heidelberg (2014)
2. Alglave, J., Kroening, D., Nimal, V., Tautschnig, M.: Software verification for weak memory via program transformation. In: Felleisen, M., Gardner, P. (eds.) ESOP 2013. LNCS, vol. 7792, pp. 512–532. Springer, Heidelberg (2013)
3. Alglave, J., Kroening, D., Tautschnig, M.: Partial orders for efficient bounded model checking of concurrent software. In: Sharygina, N., Veith, H. (eds.) CAV 2013. LNCS, vol. 8044, pp. 141–157. Springer, Heidelberg (2013)
4. Alglave, J., Maranget, L.: Stability in weak memory models. In: Gopalakrishnan, G., Qadeer, S. (eds.) CAV 2011. LNCS, vol. 6806, pp. 50–66. Springer, Heidelberg (2011)
5. Batty, M., Dodds, M., Gotsman, A.: Library abstraction for c/c++ concurrency. In: Proceedings of the 40th Annual ACM SIGPLAN-SIGACT Symposium on Principles of Programming Languages, POPL 2013, pp. 235–248. ACM (2013)

6. Batty, M., Owens, S., Sarkar, S., Sewell, P., Weber, T.: Mathematizing c++ concurrency. In: Proceedings of the 38th Annual ACM SIGPLAN-SIGACT Symposium on Principles of Programming Languages, POPL 2011, pp. 55–66. ACM (2011)

7. Boehm, H.J. and Adve, S.V.: Foundations of the c++ concurrency memory model. In: Proceedings of the ACM SIGPLAN Conference on Programming Language Design and Implementation, PLDI 2008, pp. 68–78. ACM (2008)

8. Bouajjani, A., Derevenetc, E., Meyer, R.: Checking and enforcing robustness against TSO. In: Felleisen, M., Gardner, P. (eds.) ESOP 2013. LNCS, vol. 7792, pp. 533–553. Springer, Heidelberg (2013)

9. Burckhardt, S., Alur, R., Martin, M.M.: Checkfence: Checking consistency of concurrent data types on relaxed memory models. In: Proceedings of the ACM SIGPLAN Conference on Programming Language Design and Implementation, PLDI 2007, pp. 12–21. ACM (2007)

10. Burckhardt, S., Musuvathi, M.: Effective program verification for relaxed memory models. In: Gupta, A., Malik, S. (eds.) CAV 2008. LNCS, vol. 5123, pp. 107–120. Springer, Heidelberg (2008)

11. Dan, A.M., Meshman, Y., Vechev, M., Yahav, E.: Predicate abstraction for relaxed memory models. In: Logozzo, F., Fähndrich, M. (eds.) Static Analysis. LNCS, vol. 7935, pp. 84–104. Springer, Heidelberg (2013)

12. Elmas, T., Qadeer, S., Tasiran, S.: A calculus of atomic actions. In: Proceedings of the 36th Annual ACM SIGPLAN-SIGACT Symposium on Principles of Programming Languages, POPL 2009, pp. 2–15. ACM (2009)

13. Ferreira, R., Feng, X., Shao, Z.: Parameterized memory models and concurrent separation logic. In: Gordon, A.D. (ed.) ESOP 2010. LNCS, vol. 6012, pp. 267–286. Springer, Heidelberg (2010)

14. Gotsman, A., Musuvathi, M., Yang, H.: Show no weakness: sequentially consistent specifications of TSO libraries. In: Aguilera, M.K. (ed.) DISC 2012. LNCS, vol. 7611, pp. 31–45. Springer, Heidelberg (2012)

15. Jagannathan, S., Laporte, V., Petri, G., Pichardie, D., Vitek, J.: Atomicity refinement for verified compilation. ACM Trans. Program. Lang. Syst. 36(2), 6 (2014)

16. Koskinen, E., Parkinson, M., Herlihy, M.: Coarse-grained transactions. In: Proceedings of the 37th Annual ACM SIGPLAN-SIGACT Symposium on Principles of Programming Languages, POPL 2010, pp. 19–30. ACM (2010)

17. Lipton, R.J.: Reduction: a method of proving properties of parallel programs. ACM Commun. 18(12), 717–721 (1975)

18. Mador-Haim, S., et al.: An axiomatic memory model for POWER multiprocessors. In: Madhusudan, P., Seshia, S.A. (eds.) CAV 2012. LNCS, vol. 7358, pp. 495–512. Springer, Heidelberg (2012)

19. Norris, B., Demsky, B.: CDSchecker: Checking concurrent data structures written with c/c++ atomics. In: Proceedings of the ACM SIGPLAN International Conference on Object Oriented Programming Systems Languages & Applications, OOPSLA 2013, pp. 131–150. ACM (2013)

20. Owens, S.: Reasoning about the implementation of concurrency abstractions on x86-TSO. In: D'Hondt, T. (ed.) ECOOP 2010. LNCS, vol. 6183, pp. 478–503. Springer, Heidelberg (2010)

21. Ridge, T.: A rely-guarantee proof system for x86-TSO. In: Leavens, G.T., O'Hearn, P., Rajamani, S.K. (eds.) VSTTE 2010. LNCS, vol. 6217, pp. 55–70. Springer, Heidelberg (2010)

22. Rinard, M.C., Diniz, P.C.: Commutativity analysis: A new analysis technique for parallelizing compilers. ACM Trans. Program. Lang. Syst. 19(6), 942–991 (1997)

23. Sewell, P., Sarkar, S., Owens, S., Nardelli, F.Z., Myreen, M.O.: X86-TSO: a rigorous and usable programmer's model for x86 multiprocessors. ACM Commun. **53**(7), 89–97 (2010)
24. Shasha, D., Snir, M.: Efficient and correct execution of parallel programs that share memory. ACM Trans. Program. Lang. Syst. **10**(2), 282–312 (1988)
25. Vafeiadis, V., Narayan, C.: Relaxed separation logic: A program logic for c11 concurrency. In: Proceedings of the ACM SIGPLAN International Conference on Object Oriented Programming Systems Languages & Applications, OOPSLA 2013, pp. 867–884. ACM (2013)

Android Platform Modeling and Android App Verification in the ACL2 Theorem Prover

Eric Smith and Alessandro Coglio[✉]

Kestrel Institute, Palo Alto, USA
{eric.smith,coglio}@kestrel.edu
http://www.kestrel.edu

Abstract. We present our work in using the ACL2 theorem prover to formally model the Android platform and to formally verify Android apps. Our approach allows the verification of the full functional correctness of apps as well as security properties. It also lets us detect or prove the absence of "functional malware", malicious app functionality that is triggered by complex conditions on state and that causes the app to calculate the wrong results or otherwise behave incorrectly. Our formal Android model is an executable simulator of a growing subset of the Android platform, and app proofs are done by automated symbolic execution of the app's event handlers using the formal model. By induction, we prove that an app satisfies an invariant, including the correctness properties of interest, for all possible sequences of events.

1 Introduction

Android devices [32] are vulnerable to security compromises carried out by rogue apps that may abuse the user's trust by masquerading as benign apps [12,40]. The Android security mechanisms are coarse and complex [11,34] and may be bypassed via exploitable flaws in the platform [2,24].

A more detailed characterization of an app's behavior, especially its access to user data, can enable users to make more informed decisions about trusting and installing the app. A suitable formal specification of the app can be used for this purpose, and trust can be established via a formal proof that the app's code satisfies the specification. This requires a formal model of the platform that the app runs on—both language and API.

The work described in this paper contributes to the goal of establishing trust in apps based on formal specifications and proofs. We used the ACL2 theorem prover [39] to build a formal model of a subset of the Android platform that supports non-trivial apps. We developed a proof methodology based on induction and symbolic execution of the app's event handlers, showing that each handler preserves the app's invariant, which includes all properties of interest, including functional correctness.

We applied this proof methodology to verify the full functional correctness of a slightly simplified version of a calculator app written by others. For a version of the app that contains malware, the correctness proof fails in a way that

© Springer International Publishing Switzerland 2016
A. Gurfinkel and S.A. Seshia (Eds.): VSTTE 2015, LNCS 9593, pp. 183–201, 2016.
DOI: 10.1007/978-3-319-29613-5_11

reveals the malware. In the process of verifying the app, we also uncovered a subtle functional bug that may be representative of malware that is triggered by complex conditions on an app's state and whose malicious action is the calculation of incorrect results. This "functional malware" differs from more explicit, and potentially more easily detectable, malware that, for example, sends private user data to a remote server when the device is in a certain location at a certain time. The latter kind of malware makes API calls to test the trigger conditions and perform the malicious actions, while functional malware may not make any suspicious API calls. For example, functional malware in a navigation app could deliberately lead users off course, perhaps even directing them to dangerous places.

Our approach is sound, precise, and high-assurance, in contrast to existing approaches for vetting Android apps. Static analysis is imprecise, leading to false warnings, sometimes unsound, and cannot check arbitrary functional correctness properties. Dynamic analysis cannot cover all possible cases. Manual code inspection is not high-assurance, because hidden malicious functionality can be overlooked or misunderstood. Our approach can prove virtually any true property about an app, with high assurance. Its main disadvantage is that it requires significant user effort, but we are working to improve the automation of the proof process.

Our work makes the following contributions:

– A formal model of a non-trivial subset of the Android platform.
– A formal proof methodology for Android apps.

2   Background

2.1   Android

Most Android apps are written in Java [31]. Besides using a subset of the standard Java API, these apps use the Android API, which provides access to hardware devices (camera, GPS, etc.), GUI elements (buttons, text boxes, etc.), inter-app communication (e.g., to open a given URL in a web browsing app), and so on. In addition to the Java source files, an app contains other resources, which often take the form of XML files. An app's Java source code is compiled to Java Virtual Machine (JVM) bytecode [23] using a standard Java compiler. The Android development tools are used to convert the JVM bytecode to Dalvik bytecode [32], which is assembled with the XML and other resource files (e.g., images) into an installable app package.

An Android app is structured in terms of 'activities', each of which is a single "screen" in the app's GUI. Within an activity are various 'views'—rectangular regions of the screen that represent GUI elements, such as text boxes and buttons that can be clicked. Events in Android include click events for these views. An app can register listeners for such events, either statically in its layout XML or programmatically by calling `setOnClickListener()`. When these events occur, the Android GUI thread invokes the appropriate methods of the registered listeners.

An app's XML 'manifest' indicates, among other things, the initial activity to be created when the app starts.

Android also includes lifecycle events (*Create, Start, Resume, Restart, Pause, Stop,* and *Destroy*) that can be dispatched to the app. The sequencing of these events must be consistent with the activity lifecycle state machine [31] (a typical flow is: *Create, Start, Resume, Pause, Stop, Destroy*) but can otherwise occur at any time. For example, a *Pause* event may occur when another app opens in front of the current app. Apps typically implement handlers to respond to these events (e.g., to save data when the app is paused) by overriding methods of the `Activity` class, such as `onPause()`.

Various entities belonging to the app are identified using numeric resource IDs. These resource IDs are defined in special classes, namely the `R` class ('resource' class) and its inner classes, generated by the Android development tools. For example, an XML layout entity `<Button android:id="@+id/btnSeven" ...>` will cause the `R$id` class to contain a final static field called `btnSeven` whose `ConstantValue` attribute is some large, unpredictable number, e.g., 2131034114. In Java source code, the button object can be obtained by the method call `findViewById(R.id.btnSeven)`, but in the bytecode only the numeric ID is present.

Android includes a permission mechanism to limit apps' access to hardware and other resources. For example, an app must possess the `INTERNET` permission to open network sockets and the `CALL_PHONE` permission to initiate phone calls. An app declares, in its XML manifest, the set of permissions that it requests. When an app is about to be installed, the requested permissions are shown to the user, who decides whether to proceed with the installation, and thus grant the app all the requested permissions. This permission mechanism is coarse-grained: for instance, the `INTERNET` permission gives an app carte blanche to connect to any host at any time to send any data.

Malware. Several kinds of malware affect Android devices [12,40]. Tools like [16] can be effective at detecting malware that exfiltrates private user data by (necessarily) making suspicious API calls. The mere presence of certain API calls may be suspicious, e.g., an app that opens a network connection, when the app's purported functionality does not involve the network. The presence of an API call may be legitimate, but the information that flows to the API calls may be suspicious, e.g., an app reads a user's contacts and sends them over the network, when the app's purported functionality does not include that.

A more stealthy kind of "functional malware" may not exfiltrate private user data, and instead intentionally calculate incorrect results. The severity of this kind of malware depends on how much the user relies on the app calculating correct results: it may range from an annoyance to loss of life, e.g., if a military navigation app sends a squad off-course to a dangerous place. Functional malware may be triggered under complex conditions on an app's state variables, eluding detection via code inspection. Functional malware may involve API calls, but not necessarily suspicious ones; or it may not involve any API calls.

Unlike many other approaches, our work addresses functional malware. Of course, it also addresses inadvertent errors. The difference between functional malware and an unintentional bug is one of developer's intent; but the impact may be similar. Our app verification approach establishes functional correctness, ruling out both intentional and unintentional bugs.

2.2   ACL2

The ACL2 theorem prover [39] consists of a first-order specification language based on side-effect-free Common Lisp and automated proof methods for reasoning about programs and models written in the language. Two strengths of ACL2 are its sophisticated term rewriter and its heuristic application of induction [4]. ACL2 supports reasoning about programs written in languages other than its native Common Lisp dialect via embeddings that capture the languages' semantics in terms of ACL2's native language. Below we describe how we use this approach to reason about JVM bytecode representing Android apps.

3   Platform Modeling

Since our motivation for modeling the Android platform is app verification, our formal model describes not the internal structure and layers of the platform stack, but the top-level interface that the platform provides to apps. This interface consists of the language that apps are written in and the API calls exchanged between apps and platform, including callbacks.

3.1   Formal JVM Bytecode Model

To reason about an Android app, we intercept its JVM bytecode during compilation (before Dalvik bytecode is generated). To assign semantics to this bytecode, we defined in ACL2 a formal model that is an executable interpreter of the Java Virtual Machine [38]. Our model is similar to the M5 model developed by J Moore and others [29], but covers more features (e.g., exceptions, string interning, and class initialization). Theorems about JVM bytecode programs are expressed using this formal model; we prove that when the program of interest is executed on the model, starting from a state where certain properties hold, then certain other properties always hold on the resulting state. This follows the style pioneered in [27].

While we do not consider our JVM model to be a novel contribution of this paper, we summarize its behavior here for concreteness. The state of the JVM in our model includes the Java heap, static area (where static fields are stored), and, for each thread, a call stack that includes invocation frames for each method that the thread is currently executing. Also included are auxiliary data structures for synchronization and locking, string interning, etc.

Each JVM instruction is modeled by specifying the effect on the JVM state when that instruction is executed. For example, the iadd instruction for integer addition is modeled as follows:

```
(defun execute-IADD (th s)
  (modify th s
          :pc (+ 1 (pc (top-frame th s)))
          :stack (push (bvplus 32
                               (top (pop (stack (top-frame th s))))
                               (top (stack (top-frame th s))))
                       (pop (pop (stack (top-frame th s))))))))
```

The function `execute-IADD` modifies the data structures of thread `th` in the JVM state `s`. In particular, it pops two operands off of the operand stack in the top invocation frame of the call stack, adds them, and pushes the sum back onto the operand stack. It then increments the program counter `:pc` by 1, which is the length of the `iadd` instruction.

To run an entire program, we repeatedly step the machine state by fetching and dispatching on the next instruction. We use ACL2's `defpun` utility to soundly introduce the JVM interpreter as a partial function [25].

A crucial feature of our JVM model is that, in addition to running bytecode programs on concrete inputs, it can be used for symbolic execution of bytecode programs on arbitrary inputs. A typical theorem says, in essence, "When we run the JVM model on this bytecode program, for any input satisfying this predicate, the resulting state has the following properties." The symbolic execution is performed using the ACL2 rewriter to repeatedly step and simplify the state, symbolically executing one instruction at a time and building up a symbolic representation of the current state in terms of the symbolic inputs. This technique is standard in the ACL2 community. In this way, our formal JVM model captures the semantics of the JVM bytecode language and allows us to reason about the code that constitutes Android apps.

3.2   Formal Android Model

We extended the formal JVM model described above to a formal model of the Android platform, capable of executing and reasoning about simple Android apps. A state in the Android model contains a JVM state and several additional Android-specific state components. More precisely, our model of the Android state contains:

- A JVM state, as discussed above. This contains the persistent data used by the app, including its heap and static fields.
- The app's activity stack, including the current activity on top of the stack, and any activities that are currently paused, below the top activity.
- The set of currently allowed events (e.g., button clicks) for which the app has registered event handlers.
- A parsed representation of the app's manifest—see Sect. 2.
- The app's layout information, parsed from the app's XML layout files and indexed by the layouts' numeric IDs. This includes information about the views (e.g., buttons) in the app's GUI and their associated event handlers (e.g., `onClick` listeners) and is used by our model of the `setContentView()` API method when it constructs the GUI for an activity.

- A map from the addresses of `View` objects to their listeners, used to dispatch control when handling events. A listener is a pair of a method (often, but not always, the `onClick()` method of some class) and an object on which to invoke the method (often this is an `Activity` object or an instance of an anonymous class whose sole purpose is to define the listener). This map is updated by our model of the `setOnClickListener()` API method.
- A map from symbolic string names of views, used in the layout XML, to the corresponding numeric resource IDs. This is used to translate events from user-meaningful form to internal form. We build this map by inspecting the names and values of the static fields of the `R$Id` resource class generated when the app is built.
- A map from resource IDs to the addresses of their corresponding `View` objects. This is used to determine the actual objects on which to dispatch events (e.g., click events) and by our model of the `findViewById()` API method.
- The API call history, a ghost variable that lets us reason about the API calls that the app has (and, critically, has not) made, including a record of the event whose handler made each API call.
- The event history, a ghost variable that lets us talk about the sequence of events given to the app so far. If we are verifying that the app implements an abstract state machine, we can abstract this event history and feed it to the abstract state machine. The resulting abstract state should then be the abstraction of the machine's current concrete state. Proving that this property is preserved by all event handlers in the app is the core step of our app proof methodology described below.
- The event currently being handled, if any, so that we can record in the API history which event was being handled when the API call was made. API calls may be allowed for some events but not others. For example, a sound recorder app may be allowed to start recording only when the user presses the *Record* button.

Event Handling. Our Android model supports running an app on a sequence of input events, by executing their event handlers in order. This can be done on a concrete sequence of events, to test an app. More importantly, it can be used for proof. We prove that, for any sequence of events, running the app's handlers for those events preserves the app's invariant. At this level, events are represented in terms that are meaningful to the user. For example, (`:resume`) represents the event that resumes the current activity, and (`:click "myButton"`) represents a click of the button whose name in the layout is `myButton`. In order to actually handle these events, our model must determine the objects on which the handler methods should be invoked, so it first converts the events into an internal form. For lifecycle events, this adds to the event the heap address of the topmost activity object on the activity stack, giving something like (`:resume 12345`). Click events are internalized by mapping the symbolic name of the button to a numeric resource ID and then to the actual address of the `View` object with that ID, giving something like (`:click 6789`). Currently our model only handles lifecycle events and click events, but adding support for other events should be straightforward.

Once the event has been elaborated to internal form, we dispatch it to the appropriate handler by executing the code for the handler using the underlying JVM model. For a lifecycle event, we execute an `invokevirtual` instruction for the appropriate handler method (e.g., `onResume()`) on the given `Activity` object, which causes the app's `onResume()` handler method to run. Such methods almost always begin by calling through to the corresponding method of the parent class, e.g., `super.onResume()`. This causes code from the Android API implementation to run, e.g., `android.app.Activity.onResume()`. Our model includes special modeling for these lifecycle API calls. For example, the model for `onResume()` causes the `onClick` listeners in the resuming activity to again be added to the set of allowed events. To handle a click event, assuming it is already in internal form, we look up the `onClick` listener for the given `View` object and call the indicated method. In our model, handlers execute to completion and cannot be interrupted. This corresponds to Android's use of an app's main 'UI thread' to execute its handlers. Future work would include adding support for background services, which an app can use to offload expensive computation from its UI thread.

The sequential processing of events in our model corresponds to the way in which the Android platform internally enqueues events and delivers them to an app's unique UI thread. By proving properties over all possible event sequences, we ensure that the properties hold no matter how the Android platform enqueues and delivers the events.

Events that are not currently allowed by the app (according to the set of allowed events in the Android state) are ignored, e.g., a click on a view that has no registered `onClick` listeners, or an illegal lifecycle event, such as stopping an activity that has not been started. Every event is also recorded in the event history, so that the invariant can refer to the state that the app should be in, given the events seen so far.

3.3 Formal API Model

A major challenge in reasoning about Android apps is to properly model calls to API methods. We are following a "demand-driven" approach in which we add models of API methods as we encounter calls to them in apps that we want to verify. Some methods such as `sendTextMessage()` do not really need to be modeled because they affect only the external world, not the state of the app itself: we simply record them in the API history, so that we can express properties such as "the app has not sent any text messages", and continue with execution. When the API call does affect the app's state, if possible we simply execute on our model the actual code of the API from the Android implementation. API calls treated this way include many calls in `java.lang` (e.g., dealing with `Strings` and `Enums`) and setters and getters such as `Activity.setTitle()` and `View.isClickable()`. There are situations where simply executing the API call does not work, either because the code is unavailable (e.g., native methods) or too complicated, or because it affects parts of the Android state that we model. To model such methods, we define executable ACL2 functions and include them in our Android model. Methods that are modeled in this way include `setOnClickListener()`, `findViewById()`, `setContentView()`, and the activity lifecycle event handlers `onStart()`, `onResume()`, etc.

Our model of running an app begins by building an initial Android state for the app (where many components, such as the API history, are initially empty) and then calling the app's `onCreate()` method. Further events are then handled in order.

4   App Verification

Our platform model provides a formal semantics for non-trivial Android apps. This allows us to formally prove that apps satisfy their functional specifications, which implies the absence of the kind of functional malware discussed in Sect. 1.

Our methodology is based on formulating an invariant for the app: a predicate over states of the Android model that is preserved as the app runs. The invariant characterizes correct behavior, often using an abstraction to a high-level state machine, and also makes many Android-specific assertions, such as specifying the set of currently active event listeners. Each event is proved to preserve the invariant, using the ACL2 rewriter to perform symbolic execution, as described below. Failed proofs may require the invariant to be strengthened. Once an inductively-strong invariant is obtained, an induction over event sequences establishes that the invariant holds for all possible event sequences. This section discusses the app verification process in more detail, using the running example of verifying a calculator app.

4.1   Calculator App

The Red Team of the DARPA APAC Program [9] developed several apps, including a calculator that applies the four arithmetic operations to floating-point numbers. Since our JVM bytecode model does not include floating-point numbers yet, we modified the app to operate on integers instead, using Java's normal modular arithmetic. We also slightly simplified the GUI of the app to not use features that are currently not covered by our model. The malware in the app replaces the running result with a random number under certain conditions described later, but we simplified it to return a fixed result of 88888888 instead, because we do not yet model random numbers. These simplifications do not fundamentally change the structure of the app.

4.2   Representation

Our Android model includes a parser, written in ACL2, that turns an app's JVM bytecode class files and XML files into an S-expression-based ACL2 representation usable by our platform model.

A parsed app, with the platform underneath, forms a state machine. The initial state S_0 is defined by our model of app initialization discussed above. Each transition is triggered by a platform-initiated event (e.g., pause app, resume app) or a user-initiated event (e.g., click a button). The deterministic transition function T maps an input event E and a state S to the next state $T(E, S)$; it is lifted to sequences of events by defining $T^*((E_1, \ldots, E_n), S) = T(E_n, \ldots T(E_1, S) \ldots)$, and $T^*(\epsilon, S) = S$, where ϵ is the empty sequence. Our platform model currently supports a single app (state machine) at a time, but can be extended to support multiple apps.

For the calculator app, the state machine has an input event for each calculator button (0 1 2 3 4 5 6 7 8 9 + - * / = C) and each app lifecycle event. The state includes a `TextView` GUI object whose content is the string shown on the calculator display. The main correctness theorem for the app says that the contents of the display are always correct, given the sequence of input events supplied to the app so far. We defined an output function O that maps a state S to this display string $O(S)$. Different output functions could be defined for different apps, each extracting from the state the app-specific observables of interest.

4.3   Specification

The execution of the parsed app on the platform model corresponds to a low-level state machine whose states are states of our Android model, as described above, and whose transitions are expressed in terms of the execution of JVM bytecode and API calls. Often a functional specification for an app is naturally expressed as a higher-level state machine, whose states and transitions are defined in user-oriented terms rather than code-oriented terms. The correctness of the code with respect to the specification can then be expressed as a simulation [28] of the high-level machine by the low-level machine.

A state machine specification for the calculator app is sketched in Fig. 1. Each state has a name (in bold, e.g., `value`) and one or more state variables (in italics, e.g., *val*); the underlined state variable is the one shown on the calculator display. In each state, *val* is the latest result, which is 0 when the calculator starts or when C (clear) is entered. In `value-op` and `value-op-value`, *op* is the latest operator entered. In `value-op-value`, entering = or an operator *op'* combines *val2* with *val* by applying *op*, completing the pending operation and replacing the latest result; if *op'* was entered, it becomes the latest operator. Figure 1 does not show the expressions assigned to state variables when transitions are taken, e.g., a *digit* transition from `value-op-value` to `value-op-value` assigns $10 \times val2 + digit$ to *val2*. Exploiting that 0 is identity for addition, entering a *digit* in value sets *val* to 0, *op* to +, and *val2* to *digit*, as if there were a pending $0 + \ldots$ operation.

We formalized this state machine specification in ACL2. The formalization includes a constant s_0 for the initial state, a deterministic transition function t that maps an input event e and a state s to the next state $t(e, s)$ (and is lifted to t^* over sequences of events, analogous to T^* above), and an output function o that maps a state s to the content of the calculator display $o(s)$.

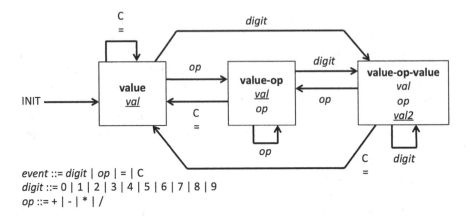

event ::= digit | op | = | C
digit ::= 0 | 1 | 2 | 3 | 4 | 5 | 6 | 7 | 8 | 9
op ::= + | - | * | /

Fig. 1. A state machine specification for the calculator app

4.4   Invariants and Proofs

Often the simulation relation between a low-level and a high-level state machine is defined as an abstraction function [18] from the low-level inputs and states to the high-level inputs and states. For the calculator app, the abstraction function α maps each calculator button press event to the corresponding input in Fig. 1 and each app lifecycle event to no input in Fig. 1; it also maps each app/platform state to a state in Fig. 1.

In our Android platform model, the app/platform state S includes the history of input events. Thus, given an abstraction function to a high-level state machine specification, the correctness of the app with respect to the specification can be expressed as a predicate over the low-level app/platform states. Intuitively, the app's invariant says that the app is in fact in the state that it should be in, given the sequence of inputs seen so far. If $H(S)$ is the history of input events in S, the predicate is $\Omega(S) \equiv [O(S) = o(t^*(\alpha^*(H(S)), s_0))]$, i.e., the observable outputs that result from executing the app's code on the inputs $H(S)$, which take the initial state S_0 to S, are the same that result from running the high-level state machine on the corresponding abstract inputs $\alpha^*(H(S))$, where α^* is the homomorphic lifting of α from events to event sequences. If Ω includes all the states S reachable from S_0, i.e., if $\Omega(T^*((E_1, \ldots, E_n), S_0))$ holds for every event sequence $E_1, \ldots, E_n$, then the app's code is observationally equivalent to the specification, i.e., it yields the same outputs for the same inputs. For the calculator app, the code is observationally equivalent to Fig. 1. $\Omega(T^*((E_1, \ldots, E_n), S_0))$ is provable by induction if Ω is an invariant, i.e., if Ω holds on the initial state (base case: $\Omega(S_0)$) and is preserved by each transition (induction step: $\Omega(S) \implies \Omega(T(E, S))$). Since Ω alone does not provide a sufficiently strong induction hypothesis, the following invariants are defined, and proved together:

1. A stronger correctness predicate that involves not only outputs (the calculator display) but also states: $\Sigma(S) \equiv [\alpha(S) = t^*(\alpha^*(H(S)), s_0) \wedge O(S) = o(\alpha(S))]$,

from which the weaker $\Omega(S)$ is easily proved. While α, t, and S_0 are specific to the app under verification, Σ has the same form for every app whose specification is a state machine with an abstraction function, e.g., the calculator app.

2. Code-level predicates on the app's state, e.g., that a Java `int` field is never negative or is always within a certain range. Formulating these predicates requires an understanding of the app's code, but failed proof attempts in ACL2 often suggest them.

3. Platform-level structural predicates about the Java heap containing the objects that form the app under verification, the Android GUI objects being consistent with the XML files, Java fields having values of the right types, and so on. These constraints are largely boilerplate and we believe that they could be automatically generated at the same time as the app is parsed into its ACL2 representation. For the calculator, we manually defined several predicates of this kind, because their automatic generation is not implemented yet.

Once a sufficiently strong invariant has been defined, proving its establishment in the initial state and preservation by each transition can be carried out by symbolic execution using the ACL2 rewriter. To prove preservation, we start with an arbitrary Android state assumed to satisfy the invariant. We then show that the execution of an arbitrary event results in a state that still satisfies the invariant. The proof naturally splits into cases for each possible allowed event (disallowed events have no effect on the state), and we usually prove each event separately. Some application-specific rewrite rules are often needed (e.g., rules about bit-vector math for the calculator app), and the proofs also use our growing library of rewrite rules about the Android model itself. Otherwise, proofs for simple apps are largely automatic; for the calculator app, the proof corresponding to each button click event is a single line of ACL2 code that invokes our tactic called `def-event-proof`. This tactic unfolds the application of the invariant to the initial state (to expose necessary assumptions for symbolic execution), performs the symbolic execution, often resulting in several cases, and finally, in each case, unfolds the invariant applied to the final state and simplifies the result. In successful proofs, everything simplifies to 'true'.

A key intermediate formula that arises in the proof of the preservation of the invariant is $\alpha(T(E,S)) = t(\alpha(E), \alpha(S))$, i.e., each low-level transition has a corresponding high-level transition—a typical commuting diagram in simulation. If an app's code has no loops (as is the case for the calculator app), ACL2 can automatically prove the invariant's establishment and preservation, provided that an appropriate set of rewrite rules is enabled. The absence of loops is not so uncommon in simple Android apps, where the platform already provides a GUI loop that reads inputs and invokes app code to process them. Verifying apps whose event handlers contain loops is future work and will likely involve formulating and proving appropriate loop invariants; Σ and the other invariants discussed above apply to the platform GUI loop.

We found it convenient to verify the calculator app in two stages. We defined an intermediate state machine whose structure closely resembles the Java code, but without involving any Java or Android concepts. Its states are records whose components correspond to the app's Java fields, and its transitions are defined in terms of record component updates that correspond to the Java code. This intermediate state machine is an abstraction of the code in the ACL2 logic, which in particular does not involve the platform-level structural invariants discussed above. It may be possible to obtain this intermediate machine automatically, using the techniques in [38]. We prove that the app's code simulates the intermediate machine and that the intermediate machine simulates the high-level machine. The two theorems are composed to obtain a proof of correctness of the calculator app with respect to Fig. 1.

4.5   Malware Discovery

The calculator app keeps a count of the operations performed since the last = was entered (or since the app started), e.g., after entering ... = 1 + 2 * 3 the count is 2. The malware (in our simplified version of) the app replaces the running result with 88888888 when the count reaches 3. This is functional malware, which does not involve API calls.

We attempted to prove that the calculator app with malware satisfies the specification in Fig. 1. As it should, the verification fails. The output from the failed ACL2 proof exposes the malware: a proof subgoal that cannot proved is that when the operation count is 3, the correct running result is 88888888. In general, failed proof subgoals can expose the conditions that trigger an app's malware and the malicious computations that violate the functional specification.

This is a very simple example of functional malware, which is also fairly easy to detect by the user. However, it is suggestive of more serious, and hard to detect, kinds of functional malware. An example is a military navigation app whose intentional miscalculations send a squad off-course to a dangerous place.

4.6   Functional Bugs

After manually removing the malware from the calculator app, we found two functional bugs in the app that prevented a successful proof. The bugs are also present in the original, unsimplified version.

The operation count is stored in a Java int, which wraps around and becomes negative if 2^{31} operations are entered without entering =. Since the condition under which the display is updated includes that the count is larger than 1, the display stops updating as the count becomes negative (until it wraps around again to become positive). Since it is impractical to enter 2^{31} operations, this bug has arguably only theoretical significance (some may argue that it is in fact not a bug). Nonetheless, we fixed this bug in the app code.

The other bug may occur in practice: under certain easily achievable conditions, the display is not updated to show the running result. For example, starting the calculator and entering - 1 2 3 4 5 + shows 12345 instead of −12345 on the display (the + should show the partial result 0 − 12345, where 0 is the initial display). The details of this bug are unimportant, but are caused by what we regard as an unnecessarily complicated implementation of the calculator: this bug eluded our manual code inspection. While this bug was not malware planted by the Red Team, and is not earth-shattering in its significance, it may be representative of functional malware where a cleverly crafted, non-straightforward implementation may sometimes produce an incorrect result under conditions that cannot be easily detected by manual inspection. After fixing this last bug, we proved the correctness of the app with respect to Fig. 1.

5   Related Work

In [26], JML [20] is used to specify contracts for API and application methods, and the KeY theorem prover [21], which is based on dynamic logic [17], is used to verify that the Java code of those methods satisfies the contracts. Our formal model of the Android API is more comprehensive, e.g., we model callbacks, which are not modeled in [26]. The app specifications in [26] consist of contracts for various app methods, which are implicitly informally "composed" into an overarching correctness argument for the apps. In contrast, our app verification is carried out with respect to an explicit overarching app specification expressed in user-oriented terms (not code-oriented terms like contracts). The translator from Java/JML to KeY in [26] embodies the dynamic logic semantics of Java and JML and is thus a critical component of that approach; in our approach, all the semantics is explicated in ACL2.

In [19], a pencil-and-paper concrete and symbolic operational semantics for Dalvik and for a few Android API methods is defined, and used as the foundation to implement a symbolic executor of Android apps. The symbolic executor is connected to an SMT solver. The tool is shown to infer the conditions under which an example app performs certain privileged actions. Our approach also uses symbolic execution, but our semantics is mechanized inside a theorem prover, and we use ACL2's rewriter for symbolic execution. It is not clear whether their approach can verify the full functional correctness of apps, due to the use of an SMT solver rather than a more general (but likely less automatic) theorem prover such as ACL2.

In [33], a pencil-and-paper operational semantics for a few Dalvik instructions and a few Android API methods is defined, and a progress property is proved. The paper mentions work in progress on a symbolic executor, but no app verification results are reported. Our Android model is mechanized inside a theorem prover and covers more features of the Android platform.

Other formal models of the Android platform [1,5,13,36] are more abstract than ours, focused on security aspects and properties. These formal models are in a sense complementary to ours: it should be possible to formalize abstraction mappings from our model to those models, ensuring that the security properties of the more abstract models apply to the more concrete model.

Static analysis of app code to help detect malware (e.g., [7,14,16]) is complementary to our approach. It is more automated (e.g., no functional specification is needed) but less precise; it cannot prove deep properties like functional correctness.

In [6], post-conditions of API method calls are calculated from pre-conditions via an algorithm that processes propositional formulas. It may be possible to use our API model and the ACL2 theorem prover for that purpose, which may lead to higher precision in the malware detection tool described in that paper.

Proposals to improve the Android security mechanisms (e.g., [10,30,37]) or to add on-device virtualization (e.g., [22]) require extensions to the platform, which the developers of all the fragmented versions of Android would have to agree on. If implemented, these extensions may prevent certain classes of malware, but not the kind of functional malware that our approach addresses.

Collecting data at run time and analyzing it to detect malware patterns (e.g., [35]) is likely to be more automatic than our approach but may allow malware to execute before it is detected. It also may raise privacy concerns if the analysis is performed off-device.

Dynamic analysis in off-device sandboxes prior to deployment (e.g., [3]) has similar coverage limitations as conventional testing. In addition, some malware may detect when it is being run in an emulator and behave differently than when it is run on a device.

Automatically transforming app code to enforce security policies (e.g., [41]) may affect performance and potentially functionality and may not be agreeable to app developers. This approach may thwart certain classes of malware, but not the kind of functional malware that our approach addresses.

6   Takeaways

App Verification Methodology. Many aspects of the app verification work described in Sect. 4 are not specific to the calculator app. We expect that the same proof methodology can apply to a large class of apps:

- Automatically parse the app's code and XML files into a deeply embedded representation inside the theorem prover, obtaining a low-level state machine based on the formal semantics of the JVM and of the Android platform, as in Sect. 4.2.
- Formalize the app's specification as a high-level state machine, expressed in user-oriented terms (not in internal Android-oriented terms), as in Sect. 4.3.
- Define an abstraction function from the low-level state machine to the high-level state machine, as in Sect. 4.4.
- Formulate a sufficiently strong state invariant on the low-level state machine (like Σ in Sect. 4.4) that implies the desired relation between the high-level state machine and the low-level state machine (like Ω in Sect. 4.4). The invariant includes not only simulation conditions, but also code-level invariants and platform-level invariants, as explained in Sect. 4.4.
- Use symbolic execution to prove that the low-level state machine's invariant is established by initialization and preserved by each event.
- If convenient, formalize intermediate state machines (between the low-level one and the high-level one), staging the abstraction functions accordingly. Prove simulations of each machine by the one immediately below it, and finally

compose the simulation theorems into one overarching simulation of the high-level state machine by the low-level state machine. As mentioned in Sect. 4.4, for the calculator app we used an intermediate state machine.

State Invariants vs. Trace Invariants. By keeping suitable history (e.g., the sequence of events processed so far) in our model of the Android state, we are able to express properties of interest (such as Σ and Ω in Sect. 4.4) as state invariants instead of more complex trace invariants, which involve multiple successive states of execution.

Iterative Invariant Strengthening. It may be difficult to formulate a sufficiently strong invariant in one attempt. The first attempt typically results in an invariant that is too weak. However, the failed proof output from ACL2 often readily suggests how to strengthen the invariant. The failed proof output consists of one or more proof subgoals, each consisting of a number of hypotheses and a conclusion. When these hypotheses express some impossible condition (e.g., that an integer variable is outside it possible range of values), the invariant must be strengthened to exclude that impossible condition (e.g., the range of the variable must be part of the invariant). Several iterations may be needed before reaching a sufficiently strong invariant.

Bugs Uncovered by Failed Proof Attempts. Bugs in the app (i.e., the fact that the app does not satisfy the specification) are often exposed by failed proof attempts. In some cases, the hypotheses of a failed proof subgoal, when they do not correspond to an impossible situation (i.e., the failed proof is not due to the invariant being too weak), reveal corner cases in which the invariant is broken. This may indicate either a bug in the app or perhaps a need to reformulate the invariant.

An ACL2 Trick. There are cases in which failed ACL2 proof subgoals do not explicitly expose the problem, because the ACL2 rewriter rewrites an untrue conclusion to 'false' and replaces it with the negation of one hypothesis—the untrue conclusion has disappeared from the proof subgoal. This happens, for instance, when attempting to prove that some term x equals a certain constant c, when instead the term equals some other constant c': The goal $x = c$ is rewritten to 'false' and it disappears. To debug this, we can introduce an uninterpreted nullary function f and attempt to prove $x = f()$. The new proof attempt will of course fail, but the rewriter will rewrite x to the correct constant c', displaying the failed proof subgoal $c' = f()$. Then we can revise our original proof attempt to prove $x = c'$ instead.

Android Platform Modeling. The Android documentation informally describes the interaction of apps with the Android platform, without explicitly describing most of the internal state of the platform, aside from app lifecycle states and similar aspects. Formalizing the Android platform involves creating an explicit model of the internal Android state. In order to do that, we tried to imagine how the implementation could support the behaviors described in the documentation (e.g., maintain a mapping from resource IDs to references to View objects), and defined our state (and transition) model accordingly.

Android API Modeling. The large size of the Android API makes its formal modeling challenging. We believe that the best approach to address this challenge is to model the API in a demand-driven fashion, i.e., formalize the API classes and methods as they are needed to verify apps. API methods written entirely in Java need not be explicitly modeled; instead, their code can be symbolically executed along with the app code. However, it may be beneficial to explicitly model API methods that have complex code that may complicate symbolic execution. It should be also noted that, as suggested in [6], typical apps use a relatively small "popular" subset of the Android API: thus, it is not necessary to model most of the Android API in order to verify interesting apps.

7 Conclusion and Future Work

We have described our ongoing work on formally modeling the Android platform and verifying Android apps. Compared to existing research, our Android model has the highest coverage of Android features, and our Android app verification goes deeper to include proofs of full functional correctness. A major motivation for this work is to ensure the absence of functional malware in apps, which other detection approaches to do not address. Our approach can be used to prove deep properties of apps with high assurance.

The proof methodology described in this paper, based on state machines and simulations, can verify a large class of app properties. But the ACL2 logic and our Android model can express other kinds of assertions over the deeply embedded apps. Examples are program-level properties such as the fact that certain API calls are made only under certain conditions and with certain data, which enables much finer distinctions than coarse Android permissions such as INTERNET. Other examples are hyperproperties (i.e., predicates over multiple executions) [8], including security policies like non-interference [15], which could express the non-leakage of private user data to network sockets, text messages, and other destinations. To verify these kind of properties, extensions to our proof methodology may be needed, e.g., invariants over multiple states from different execution traces.

We are extending our formal model to cover more Android features and are tackling the verification of larger and more complex apps. We would also like to extend our approach to support reasoning about multiple apps, including their communication via Android's 'intent' mechanism.

Another direction for future research is the modeling and proof of non-functional aspects of apps, e.g., to reason about resource usage or covert channels.

Acknowledgments. This material is based on research sponsored by DARPA under agreement number FA8750-12-X-0110. The U.S. Government is authorized to reproduce and distribute reprints for Governmental purposes notwithstanding any copyright notation thereon.

We would also like to thank Garrin Kimmell, James McDonald, and Allen Goldberg for their helpful reviews of this paper.

References

1. Armando, A., Costa, G., Merlo, A.: Formal modeling and reasoning about the Android security framework. In: Palamidessi, C., Ryan, M.D. (eds.) TGC 2012. LNCS, vol. 8191, pp. 64–81. Springer, Heidelberg (2013)
2. Armando, A., Merlo, A., Migliardi, M., Verderame, L.: Would you mind forking this process? A denial of service attack on Android (and some countermeasures). In: Gritzalis, D., Furnell, S., Theoharidou, M. (eds.) SEC 2012. IFIP AICT, vol. 376, pp. 13–24. Springer, Heidelberg (2012)
3. Bläsing, T., Batyuk, L., Schmidt, A.-D., Camtepe, S.A., Albayrak, S.: An Android application sandbox system for suspicious software detection. In: Proceedings of 5th International Conference on Malicious and Unwanted Software (Malware) (2010)
4. Boyer, R.S., Moore, J.S.: A Computational Logic. Academic Press, New York (1979)
5. Chaudhuri, A.: Language-based security on Android. In: Proceedings of the ACM SIGPLAN Fourth Workshop on Programming Languages and Analysis for Security (PLAS) (2009)
6. Chen, K.Z., Johnson, N., D'Silva, V., Dai, S., MacNamara, K., Magrino, T., Wu, E., Rinard, M., Song, D.: Contextual policy enforcement in Android applications with permission event graphs. In: Proceedings of the 20th Annual Network and Distributed System Security Symposium (NDSS) (2013)
7. Chin, E., Felt, A.P., Greenwood, K., Wagner, D.: Analyzing inter-application communication in Android. In: Proceedings of the 9th International Conference on Mobile Systems, Applications, and Services (MobiSys) (2011)
8. Clarkson, M., Schneider, F.: Hyperproperties. J. Comput. Secur. **18**(6), 1157–1210 (2010)
9. DARPA Information Innovation Office. Automated program analysis for cybersecurity (APAC) program. http://www.darpa.mil/program/automated-program-analysis-for-cybersecurity
10. Enck, W., Gilbert, P., Han, S., Tendulkar, V., Chun, B.-G., Cox, L.P., Jung, J., McDaniel, P., Sheth, A.N., TaintDroid, : An information-flow tracking system for realtime privacy monitoring on smartphones. ACM Trans. Comput. Syst. (TOCS) **32**(2), 5:1–5:29 (2014)
11. Enck, W., Ongtang, M., McDaniel, P.: Understanding Android security. IEEE Secur. Priv. Mag. **7**(1), 50–57 (2009)
12. Felt, A.P., Finifter, M., Chin, E., Hanna, S., Wagner, D.: A survey of mobile malware in the wild. In: Proceedings of the ACM CCS Workshop on Security and Privacy in Smartphones and Mobile Devices (2011)
13. Fragkaki, E., Bauer, L., Jia, L., Swasey, D.: Modeling and enhancing Android's permission system. In: Foresti, S., Yung, M., Martinelli, F. (eds.) ESORICS 2012. LNCS, vol. 7459, pp. 1–18. Springer, Heidelberg (2012)

14. Fuchs, A., Chaudhuri, A., Foster, J.: SCanDroid: automated security certication of Android applications. Technical report CS-TR-4991, Department of Computer Science, University of Maryland, College Park (2009)
15. Goguen, J., Meseguer, J.: Security policies and security models. In: Proceedings of the IEEE Symposium on Security and Privacy, pp. 11–20 (1982)
16. Gordon, M.I., Kim, D., Perkins, J., Gilham, L., Nguyen, N., Rinard, M.: Information-flow analysis of Android applications in DroidSafe. In: Proceedings of the 21st Annual Network and Distributed System Security Symposium (NDSS) (2014)
17. Harel, D., Kozen, D., Tiuryn, J.: Dynamic Logic. MIT Press, Cambridge (2000)
18. Hoare, C.A.R.: Proof of correctness of data representations. Acta Informatica **1**(4), 271–281 (1972)
19. Jeon, J., Micinski, K., Foster, J.: SymDroid: symbolic execution for Dalvik byte-code. Technical report CS-TR-5022, University of Maryland, College Park (2012)
20. The Java Modeling Language (JML). http://jmlspecs.org
21. The KeY project. http://www.key-project.org
22. Lange, M., Liebergeld, S., Lackorzynski, A., Warg, A., Peter, M.: L4Android: a generic operating system framework for secure smartphones. In: Proceedings of the 1st ACM Workshop on Security and Privacy in Smartphones and Mobile Devices (SPSM) (2011)
23. Lindholm, T., Yellin, F., Bracha, G., Buckley, A.: The Java Virtual Machine Specification - Java SE 8 Edition, March 2014. http://docs.oracle.com/javase/specs/jvms/se8/html
24. Lineberry, A., Richardson, D.L., Wyatt, T.: These aren't the permissions you're looking for. In: DEFCON 18 (2010)
25. Manolios, P., Moore, J.S.: Partial functions in ACL2. J. Autom. Reasoning **31**, 107–127 (2003)
26. Haghighi Mobarhan, M.A.: Formal specification of selected Android core applications and library functions. Master's thesis, Chalmers University of Technology, University of Gothenburg (2011)
27. McCarthy, J.: A formal description of a subset of Algol. Technical report Stanford Artificial Intelligence Project Memo No. 24, Stanford University (1964)
28. Milner, R.: An algebraic definition of simulation between programs. Technical report CS-205, Stanford University (1971)
29. Moore, J.: Proving Theorems about Java and the JVM with ACL2. http://www.cs.utexas.edu/users/moore/publications/marktoberdorf-02/index.html
30. Nauman, M., Khan, S., Zhang, X.: Apex: extending Android permission model and enforcement with user-defined runtime constraints. In: Proceedings of the 5th ACM Symposium on Information, Computer and Communications Security (ASIACCS) (2010)
31. Open Handset Alliance. Android Development Resources. http://developer.android.com
32. Open Handset Alliance. Android Open Source Project. http://source.android.com
33. Payet, E., Spoto, F.: An operational semantics for Android activities. In: Proceedings of the ACM SIGPLAN Workshop on Partial Evaluation and Program Manipulation (PEPM) (2014)
34. Shabtai, A., Fledel, Y., Kanonov, U., Elovici, Y., Dolev, S., Glezer, C.: Google Android: A comprehensive security assessment. IEEE Secur. Priv. Mag. **8**(2), 35–44 (2010)

35. Shamili, A.S., Bauckhage, C., Alpcan, T.: Malware detection on mobile devices using distributed machine learning. In: Proceedings of the 20th International Conference on Pattern Recognition (ICPR) (2011)
36. Shin, W., Kiyomoto, S., Fukushima, K., Tanaka, T.: A formal model to analyze the permission authorization and enforcement in the Android framework. In: Proceedings of the IEEE Second International Conference on Social Computing (SOCIAL-COM) (2010)
37. Smalley, S., Craig, R.: Security enhanced (SE) Android: bringing flexible MAC to Android. In: Proceedings of the 20th Annual Network and Distributed System Security Symposium (NDSS) (2013)
38. Smith, E.W.: Axe: an Automated Formal Equivalence Checking Tool for Programs. Ph.D. dissertation, Stanford University (2011)
39. University of Texas at Austin. The ACL2 theorem prover. http://www.cs.utexas.edu/moore/acl2
40. Vidas, T., Votipka, D., Christin, N.: All your droid are belong to us: a survey of current Android attacks. In: Proceedings of the 5th USENIX Workshop on Offensive Technologies (WOOT) (2011)
41. Rubin, X., Saïdi, H., Anderson, R.: Aurasium: practical policy enforcement for Android applications. In: Proceedings of the USENIX Security Symposium (2012)

AUSPICE: Automatic Safety Property Verification for Unmodified Executables

Jiaqi Tan[⊠], Hui Jun Tay, Rajeev Gandhi, and Priya Narasimhan

Department of Electrical and Computer Engineering,
Carnegie Mellon University, Pittsburgh, USA
tanjiaqi@cmu.edu, htay@andrew.cmu.edu, rgandhi@ece.cmu.edu,
priya@cs.cmu.edu

Abstract. Verification of machine-code programs using program logic has focused on functional correctness, and proofs have required manually-provided program specifications. Fortunately, the verification of shallow safety properties such as memory isolation and control-flow safety can be easier to automate, but past techniques for automatically verifying machine-code safety have required post-compilation transformations, which can change program behavior. In this work, we automatically verify safety properties for unmodified machine-code programs without requiring user-supplied specifications. Our novel logic framework, AUSPICE, for automatic safety property verification for unmodified executables, extends an existing trustworthy Hoare logic for local reasoning, and provides a novel proof tactic for selective composition. We demonstrate our automated proof technique on synthetic and realistic programs. Our verification completes in 6 h for a realistic 533-instruction string search algorithm, demonstrating the feasibility of our approach.

1 Introduction

Interactive theorem proving using logic is a promising technique for reasoning about executable (i.e., machine-code) programs, as it provides a succinct specification of the program. However, formally reasoning about machine-code is challenging as accounting for low-level details and writing proofs interactively can be tedious. Logics have been developed to formally reason about the low-level state (e.g., registers, main memory) in machine-code programs: Myreen et al. developed a Hoare logic for realistically modeled machine-code [16]. These logics are designed to verify the correctness of programs, and hence must capture the complete execution state of the program, which requires manually supplied specifications e.g., loop invariants, and function pre-/post-conditions. Hence, techniques for reasoning about program correctness ease the job of the proof author [17], but do not fully automate proof generation. Fortunately, verifying shallow safety properties can be easier, as we are only concerned with the parts of program state which affect our desired safety properties. Thus, there are more opportunities for proof automation. Zhao et al. [27] proposed a program logic for automatically verifying safety properties in executables, but programs must be compiled with a modified

ⓒ Springer International Publishing Switzerland 2016
A. Gurfinkel and S.A. Seshia (Eds.): VSTTE 2015, LNCS 9593, pp. 202–222, 2016.
DOI: 10.1007/978-3-319-29613-5_12

compiler and safety checks must be added post-compilation [27], thus developers cannot observe how the safety checks added to their programs may change them.

In this paper, we present a novel logic framework, AUSPICE, for automatically verifying safety properties for **unmodified** machine-code programs: programs generated by an unmodified compiler, without any post-compilation transformations (e.g., binary rewriting). Thus, any safety checks must be added as source-code statements. This enables developers to gain assurance of their program's behavior and safety from observing the added safety checks. Our contributions are: (i) a novel logic framework, AUSPICE, for automatically verifying safety properties in *unmodified* machine-code programs, (ii) a logic, $\mathcal{L}_{\mathcal{LR}}$, which enables *local reasoning* to ensure that safety properties are asserted and checked for every instruction in a machine-code program, (iii) a proof tactic for *selective composition* which enables the automatic verification of safety properties without manual inputs, and (iv) an empirical evaluation of AUSPICE on verifying real-world machine-code. *To the best of our knowledge, AUSPICE is the first logic framework which enables the fully automated proving of safety properties for unmodified ARM machine-code programs,* avoiding the post-compilation transformations required by ARMor [27]. We currently target ARM machine-code programs, although our technique can be applied to other architectures.

Intuition. Our safety property verification uses Hoare logic to reason about machine-code. Hoare logic was designed to reason about program correctness, hence, typical Hoare logic proofs must reason about the "global" effects of programs, i.e., capture all possible values of program state. Our first intuition is that our safety properties at each instruction are affected only by the program state immediately before the instruction runs. This enables us to consider only a subset of program state and perform "local" reasoning (Sect. 3), and avoid requiring manually supplied specifications. Second, previous efforts to automate safety property verification [27] relied on binary rewriting to insert safety checks. In unmodified machine-code, safety checks must be implemented entirely in source-code. Our second intuition is that, when verifying safety properties for unmodified machine-code, safety checks inserted in a program's source-code can span a larger part of a program than our "local" scope of reasoning described above. Hence, we develop a novel proof tactic, *selective composition* (Sect. 4), which uses the Hoare logic Compose rule (Sect. 2.4) to help us reason about safety properties using additional contextual information not available in purely local reasoning.

1.1 Problem Statement

Goals. The main objective of our logic framework is to automatically prove safety properties for machine-code programs which have been compiled using an unmodified compiler, with no post-compilation modifications (e.g., binary rewriting). The goals of our logic framework are: (i) to use an independently developed, trustworthy logic so that our approach is trustworthy; (ii) to fully automate our proof by not requiring manual inputs from the user, and (iii) to formalize the notion of safety for the execution of a machine-code program.

Non-goals. We do not intend to prove the correctness of machine-code programs, and we are not concerned with the security and privacy of applications implemented by the machine-code.

Scope. We choose to verify safety properties for the machine-code of programs rather than their source-code so that (i) we do not need to trust the compiler used, thus minimizing our Trusted Computing Base (TCB), and (ii) our verification does not need access to the source-code of the program. We require no modifications to the compiler used to generate the executables which we verify. Our logic framework currently targets ARM machine-code programs, although our technique can be applied to machine-code for other architectures by (i) parameterizing the Hoare logic [16] with a different instruction semantics, and (ii) defining execution safety for the target architecture. We verify safety properties for user programs running on a commodity operating system (currently Linux).

Assumptions. Our logic framework uses the trustworthy formalization of the ARM Instruction Set Architecture (ISA) developed by Myreen et al. [15] at Cambridge University (the "Cambridge ARM model"). Thus, our verification inherits the assumptions and limitations of this model. We assume that the behavior of the program being verified is not affected by exceptions, interrupts, and page table operations, as these are not modeled in the model. We are also unable to verify safety properties in the presence of system calls, as the model does not capture the effects of specific system calls on user programs. We are also unable to verify programs with concurrent behavior, nor unstructured control-flow jumps (e.g., `longjmp` and switch statements). We assume that the compiler and program obey the ARM-THUMB Procedure Call Standard (ATPCS) [1], which specifies the behavior for function calls/returns, and that the OS correctly isolates concurrently executing user programs. We also assume that the target program being verified was compiled with a well-known, unmodified compiler with well-known function prologues and epilogues, and that the machine-code contains function boundaries. We also require programs to be statically compiled so that all code to be executed is present, and that programs are not recursive.

2 Background

2.1 ARM Architecture

First, we review aspects of the ARM architecture pertinent to defining execution safety for ARM machine-code programs. ARM is a RISC, load/store architecture, and data instructions operate only on register contents but not memory [2]. There are 6 processor modes, and we focus on the user mode, which an operating system (OS) runs applications in. The remaining modes handle various types of exceptions, including system calls. Each ARM processor mode has a different set of visible registers, and we focus on only the registers visible in user mode: registers `r0` through `r15`, and the status register (CPSR). We also consider the ATPCS [1], which specifies conventions for procedure calls and returns. By the convention in the ATPCS, registers `r13`, `r14`, `r15` store the stack pointer (SP), link register (LR) for return addresses and program counter (PC). We highlight these registers for their impact on control-flow safety. The state of an ARM processor comprises the registers r0 to r15, the processor status register CPSR, and the processor's main memory (modeled as an array of 2^{32} byte-addressed bytes).

2.2   Safety Properties for ARM Machine-Code Programs

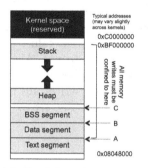

(a) Stack-based Memory safety: Linux Process Memory Layout

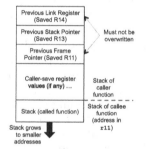

(b) Stack-based Control-flow safety: Function Activation Record

Fig. 1. Safety properties

Next, we discuss the safety properties we wish to prove for ARM machine-code programs. At a high-level, we wish to prove that the execution of a machine-code program is isolated from any harmful effects of potentially malicious user input. Specifically, we wish to prove that the control-flow of a machine-code program cannot be hijacked and changed at runtime due to user input, and that new behaviors cannot be introduced through code injection or modification. We do this by proving that (i) machine-code loaded to memory cannot be overwritten; that (ii) function-return addresses saved to the program's stack cannot be changed; and that (iii) only machine-code initially loaded to memory is executed. Concretely, at the machine-code level, we prove two safety policies, *memory isolation*, and *control-flow isolation*, which together provide the machine-code safety properties sufficient to show that our desired high-level safety property holds. This is similar to Control-Flow Integrity [3], except that we disallow the use of arbitrary function pointers on a program's heap. We instantiate these safety properties in the context of user programs running in an OS (currently Linux), as our goal is to provide isolation for user programs running in an OS.

Memory Isolation. The goal of our memory safety policy, *memory isolation*, is to prevent a program from modifying its own instructions to prevent the introduction of new behaviors through self-modification. In a multiprogramming OS such as Linux, each user program runs as a separate process with its own virtual memory with a common layout. In processors with 32-bits of addressable memory, each process has a 4 GB memory space, with the upper 1 GB reserved for the OS. Figure 1(a) illustrates this layout. Our memory safety policy requires that all memory writes be restricted to the area between the start of the process's stack space (marked 0xBF000000) and the start of the text segment of the code.

Control-Flow Isolation. The goal of our control-flow safety policy, *control-flow isolation*, is to ensure that there are no unexpected control-flow transfers, that only instructions in the text section of the program are executed. We also require that there can be no control-flow hijacks via modified function-return addresses. Our memory safety policy partially ensures control-flow isolation by preventing the modification of the text section. Our control-flow isolation is also enforced by protecting the return addresses for function calls saved on the program stack. First, we consider the ATPCS [1] convention. Registers r11 and r13 store the frame pointer (stack base address) and stack pointer (stack top address) respectively, while r14 stores the return address of the current function. When a function call is made, the caller function first saves its current values of r11, r13, and r14 on the stack, before loading the return address to r14. Also, the ATPCS specifies that the stack grows downwards to lower addresses. Thus, to prevent control-flow hijacks, we must ensure that all memory writes are to addresses smaller than the current function's frame pointer (r11) (Fig. 1(b)).

2.3   Hoare Logic for ARM Machine-Code Programs

We use the HOL4 theorem prover [20], and the Hoare logic [16] for ARM machine-code programs [15] developed at Cambridge, to prove safety theorems. The Cambridge ARM model has been extensively tested and validated [9], providing us with a strong, trustworthy foundation for our logic. The Cambridge ARM model uses Hoare triple theorems and separation logic [19] to describe the behavior of each instruction, and the model captures realistic details of ARM instructions, which we illustrate briefly. The model decompiles each ARM instruction to a Hoare triple theorem of the form (p) c (q), where p and q are predicates describing the state of the processor before (pre-state) and after (post-state) executing code c respectively[1]. Then, the theorem (p) c (q) informally means that for a processor in a state satisfying p before running c, after running c, the processor will have state satisfying q. The predicates p and q are pre- and post-state assertions about the values of machine resources e.g., registers, status flags and the program counter. They can also contain pure boolean assertions which describe relationships among the values of machine resources which are true before or after an instruction executes. The theorem for the ARM instruction 0xE5832000 (mnemonic "str r2 [r3]") is:

$$\vdash \text{SPEC ARM\_MODEL } (\text{aR } 3w \ r3 * \text{aR } 2w \ r2 * \text{aPC } p * \text{aMEMORY } df \ f$$
$$* \text{cond}((r3 \ \&\& \ 3w = 0w) \wedge (r3 \in df))) \ \{(p, 0xE5832000w)\}$$
$$(\text{aR } 3w \ r3 * \text{aR } 2w \ r2 * \text{aPC } (p{+}4w) * \text{aMEMORY } df \ ((r3 = {+}r2) \ f))$$

SPEC indicates that the theorem is a Hoare triple, while ARM_MODEL is the ARM-specific instruction semantics [15]. aR 2w and aR 3w are expressions which assert that a given register stores the specified value, where 2w and 3w indicate the register number whose value is being asserted, and the suffix w indicates the register number is a fixed-width word. Then, the pre-state shows that the registers r2

---

[1] In Hoare logic, p, q are named pre-, post-condition, but we use the terms pre-, post-state as we call the boolean conditions imposed by a branch the pre-condition.

and r3 contain the (symbolic) values $r2$ and $r3$ respectively, the main memory contains the map f with domain df, and the program counter has some address p before running the instruction. After running the instruction, the values of registers r2, r3 remain unchanged, and the program counter advances to $p+4$. Also, =+ is the map-update operator, hence r3 =+ r2 indicates that the memory has been updated to store the value that was in register r2 at the address given by the value that was in register r3. The expression $\mathsf{cond}((r3 \ \&\& \ 3w = 0w) \wedge (r3 \in df))$ is an assertion which specifies our memory alignment requirement for writes to the address $r3$, and that $r3$ is in the domain of the memory map f. $*$ is the separating conjunction [19] which asserts all other resources are unchanged.

2.4   Composition Rule in Hoare Logic

$$\frac{SPEC \ x \ p \ c_1 \ q \quad SPEC \ x \ q \ c_2 \ r}{SPEC \ x \ p \ (c_1; c_2) \ r} \ \text{COMPOSE} \qquad \frac{SPEC \ x \ p \ c \ q}{SPEC \ x \ (p * r) \ c \ (q * r)} \ \text{FRAME}$$

The Compose rule of Hoare logic [11] is shown above, which extends single instruction Hoare triple theorems to describe multiple instructions. One critical detail of this rule is that to apply the Compose rule to compose two Hoare triple theorems, the pre-state of the second theorem must be equal to the post-state of the first theorem. Conceptually, when instruction i_1 executes, followed by instruction i_2, as i_2 is executing immediately after i_1, so the processor state just before i_2 executes is exactly the processor state after i_1 executes.

Pre-composition Tactic. A typical proof tactic for composing Hoare triple theorems for sequential instructions, i_1, i_2, with i_1 running immediately before i_2, into a single Hoare triple theorem, is given by the following steps: (i) Using the Frame rule (shown above), add machine state assertions in i_1, but not in i_2, to i_2's theorem; (ii) Using the Frame rule, add machine state assertions in i_2, but not in i_1, to i_1's theorem; (iii) Instantiate free variables in i_2 with the post-state machine resource values from i_1. We call these steps the pre-composition tactic. This is similar to the "shift" operation described by Myreen et al. [15]. After carrying out the above theorem manipulation steps, the manipulated theorems i_1' and i_2' for both instructions will now have the post-state of i_1' matching the pre-state of i_2', allowing us to directly apply the Compose rule in Hoare logic.

For instance, consider the two instructions, i_1 ("mov r3,r4"), followed by i_2 ("sub r2, r3, #16"). We illustrate the use of the Compose rule to obtain a theorem describing the behavior of a program (or its fragment), $i_1 i_2$. The Hoare triple theorems for each of the two instructions are shown respectively:

$\vdash$ SPEC ARM_MODEL (aR 3w $r3$ $*$ aR 4w $r4$ $*$ aPC p) $\{(p, \mathit{0xE1A03004w})\}$
   (aR 3w $r4$ $*$ aR 4w $r4$ $*$ aPC $(p+4w)$)

$\vdash$ SPEC ARM_MODEL (aR 2w $r2$ $*$ aR 3w $r3$ $*$ aPC p) $\{(p, \mathit{0xE2432010w})\}$
   (aR 2w $(r3 - 16w)$ $*$ aR 3w $r3$ $*$ aPC $(p+4w)$)

Thus, in composing the two theorems i_1, i_2 in our above example, our pre-composition tactic will carry out the following steps on the theorems i_1, i_2: (i) Use the Frame rule to add aR 2w $r2$ to i_1 to get i_1'; (ii) Use the Frame rule to add aR 4w $r4$ to i_2 to get i_2'; (iii) Instantiate the value of p to $p + 4w$, and $r3$ to $r4$ in i_2' to get i_2''; (iv) Apply Compose rule to theorems i_1', i_2'' to obtain:

$$\vdash \text{SPEC ARM\_MODEL (aR 3w } r3 \ * \ \text{aR 4w } r4 \ * \ \text{aPC } p \ * \ \text{aR 2w } r2)$$

$$\{(p, 0xE1A03004w); (p + 4w, 0xE2432010w)\}$$

$$(\text{aR 2w } (r4 - 16w) \ * \ \text{aR 3w } r4 \ * \ \text{aPC } (p{+}8w) \ * \ \text{aR 4w } r4)$$

The pre-composition tactic prepares two suitable Hoare triples for reasoning about the effects of code on the same pre-state (i.e. pre-state of the first Hoare triple) by placing them in the same context (i.e. describing the effects of the code in both triples in terms of the pre-state variables of the first Hoare triple).

3 Design: The $\mathcal{L}_{LR}$ Program Logic

Next, we describe the design of our logic framework for automatically verifying safety properties, and discuss the rationale behind our design decisions. Our logic framework needs to fulfill three tasks: (1) Specify safety assertions for each instruction. A safety assertion of an instruction specifies the conditions which must be true before the instruction is executed for our safety properties to hold. (2) Ensure that the Hoare triple theorems for every instruction are encoded with their safety assertions. (3) Define, formally, the requirements for a program to possess our desired safety properties.

$$\frac{\text{SPEC } x \ (\text{cond}(ms \wedge cfi_1 \wedge cfi_2) * p) \ \{(offset, ins)\} \ q}{\text{MEMCFISAFE } x \ ((\text{MCSAt } offset \ ms \ cfi_1 \ cfi_2) * p) \ \{(offset, ins)\} \ q} \ \text{MEM\_CFI\_SAFE}$$

$$\frac{\text{MEMCFISAFE } x \ p \ c_1 \ q \quad \text{MEMCFISAFE } x \ q \ c_2 \ r}{\text{MEMCFISAFE } x \ p \ (c_1; c_2) \ r} \ \text{MEM\_CFI\_SAFE\_COMPOSE}$$

$$\frac{\text{MEMCFISAFE } x \ p \ c \ q}{\text{MEMCFISAFE } x \ (p * r) \ c \ (q * r)} \ \text{MEMCFISAFE\_FRAME}$$

Fig. 2. Logic rules for $\mathcal{L}_{LR}$. ms, cfi_1, cfi_2, cfi_3 are safety assertions for memory and control-flow isolation respectively. MCSAt is a syntactic label to group safety assertions.

3.1 Individual Instructions: Safety Assertion Specification

Figure 2 shows the MEM_CFI_SAFE rule for augmenting the Hoare triple theorem of a single instruction with its safety assertion. This rule overcomes the challenge of reasoning about safety properties at every instruction using Hoare logic. We add our safety assertions as a pure boolean condition to the pre-state of an instruction's Hoare triple. Then, when the Compose rule (Sect. 2.4) is applied to compose theorems of multiple instructions, the pre-states of successor instructions (q in the Compose rule) will be hidden, thus hiding our augmented safety assertions. Also, safety assertions which hold can be simplified to true and eliminated from the Hoare triple. Thus, for a Hoare triple describing a sequence of instructions, we cannot tell if the theorem contains safety assertions for every instruction.

The MEM_CFI_SAFE rule overcomes this challenge by ensuring that the Hoare triple for every instruction has been augmented with its safety assertions. This rule has two features. First, MEM_CFI_SAFE can be instantiated only from single instruction Hoare SPEC theorems, because code c in the SPEC theorem in the rule antecedent admits only a single instruction with the machine word ins located at address offset. Also, the second rule which generates safe MEMCFISAFE theorems, MEM_CFI_SAFE_COMPOSE, does not admit Hoare triple SPEC theorems, and only allows the composition of MEMCFISAFE theorems. Second, the MEM_CFI_SAFE rule can be instantiated only when the pre-state is augmented with our safety assertion, the pure boolean conjunction, $ms \land cfi_1 \land cfi_2$, in its pre-state. Thus, the MEMCFISAFE relation indicates the resulting Hoare triple has been augmented with safety assertions for every instruction described. MCSAt is a syntactic relation which associates our safety assertion, $ms \land cfi_1 \land cfi_2$, with the address offset which the assertion applies to. We also add the safety assertions ms, cfi_1, cfi_2 to the hypotheses of the theorem, to indicate that they are undischarged.

Safe Instruction Semantics are Sound. Our safe instruction semantics, in the form of MEMCFISAFE theorems, are a special form of Hoare triple theorems. They are augmented to ensure that every instruction described in an MEMCFISAFE theorem has an associated safety assertion, added to it as a pure boolean condition in the pre-state of the instruction's theorem. We proved the following theorem: $\vdash \forall x\ p\ c\ q\ \cdot\ \text{MEMCFISAFE}\ x\ p\ c\ q\ \Rightarrow\ \text{SPEC}\ x\ p\ c\ q$. Informally, our safety-augmented Hoare triple theorems retain a direct correspondence to the Hoare triple theorems proven by the Cambridge ARM model. Hence, our safe instruction semantics inherits the soundness of the Cambridge ARM model.

3.2   Sequential Code Blocks

Next, we describe how we obtain safety-augmented Hoare triple theorems for basic blocks of sequential code (safe basic block theorems). A basic block is a sequence of instructions which execute sequentially, with a single entry and single exit instruction. The two rules (Fig. 2) we need for building safe basic block theorems are MEM_CFI_SAFE_COMPOSE, and MEMCFISAFE_FRAME (proved using the Frame rule in separation logic). These two rules allow us to inductively build up a safe basic block theorem from safety theorems for individual instructions. The process of building up a safety theorem for a basic block of sequential code is the same as that of composing Hoare triple theorems (Sect. 2.4), except that only safety-augmented Hoare triple theorems can be composed. This process is repeated recursively for every instruction in a basic block to obtain a single safe theorem for the basic block. Our safe basic block theorems have the same semantics as Cambridge ARM Hoare triples, as proved in Sect. 3.1.

$\vdash \forall addr, NODES, FUNCS, CFG_{pred}, CFG_{succ}, ICFG_{callpred}, ICFG_{callsucc},$
$\quad ICFG_{retpred}, ICFG_{retsucc}, assns_{entry}, postcond_{exit}, prestate, poststate \cdot$
$\quad \text{FUN\_SAFE}(addr, NODES, FUNCS, CFG_{pred}, CFG_{succ}, ICFG_{callpred}, ICFG_{callsucc},$
$\quad\quad\quad ICFG_{retpred}, ICFG_{retsucc}, assns_{entry}, postcond_{exit}, prestate, poststate) \Leftrightarrow$

$(\quad (\forall node \cdot node \in NODES \Rightarrow (\min(node, addr) = addr))$
$\quad \wedge (\forall min \cdot min \in NODES \Rightarrow (CFG_{pred}(min) = \emptyset \wedge ICFG_{callpred}(min) = \emptyset \wedge ICFG_{retpred}(min) = \emptyset)$
$\quad \Rightarrow (\forall node \cdot (node \in NODES \Rightarrow node \neq min) \Rightarrow (\min(node, min) = min))$
$\quad\quad \Rightarrow \exists pd_1, x, c_1, p_1, q_1 \cdot \text{HOARE\_WITH\_ASSERT}(pd_1, assns_{entry}, min, node, x, c_1, p_1, q_1) \wedge$
$\quad\quad (prestate = \text{aPC } min * p_1))$
$\quad \wedge (\forall out \cdot out \in NODES \Rightarrow (CFG_{succ}(out) = \emptyset)$
$\quad\quad \Rightarrow (\forall funcnode \cdot (funcnode \in FUNCS \Rightarrow out \notin ICFG_{callsucc}(funcnode)))$
$\quad\quad \Rightarrow \exists pd_1, assn_1, node, x, c_1, p_1, q_1 \cdot \text{HOARE\_WITH\_ASSERT}(pd_1, assn_1, out, node, x, c_1, p_1, q_1) \wedge$
$\quad\quad (poststate = q_1) \wedge (pd_1 \Rightarrow postcond_{exit}))$
$\quad \wedge (\forall node, pred \cdot node \in NODES \Rightarrow pred \in CFG_{pred}(node) \Rightarrow \exists pd_1, assn_1, x, c_1, p, q, pd_2,$
$\quad\quad assn_2, c_2, r, node' \cdot \text{HOARE\_WITH\_ASSERT}(pd_1, assn_1, pred, node, x, c_1, p, q) \wedge$
$\quad\quad \text{HOARE\_WITH\_ASSERT}(pd_2, assn_2, node, node', x, c_2, q, r) \wedge (pd_1 \Rightarrow assn_2))$
$\quad \wedge (\forall node, succ \cdot node \in ICFG_{callsucc}(succ) \Rightarrow succ \in ICFG_{callpred}(node) \Rightarrow$
$\quad\quad \exists pd_1, assn_1, x, c_1, p, q, nodes, funcs, cfg_1, cfg_2, cfg_3, cfg_4, cfg_5, cfg_6, assn_2, pd_2, r \cdot$
$\quad\quad \text{HOARE\_WITH\_ASSERT}(pd_1, assn_1, node, succ, x, c_1, p, q) \wedge$
$\quad\quad \text{FUN\_SAFE}(succ, nodes, funcs, cfg_1, cfg_2, cfg_3, cfg_4, cfg_5, cfg_6, assn_2, pd_2, q, r) \wedge (pd_1 \Rightarrow assn_2))$
$\quad \wedge (\forall node, pred \cdot node \in ICFG_{retsucc}(pred) \Rightarrow pred \in ICFG_{retpred}(node) \Rightarrow$
$\quad\quad \exists pd_1, assn_1, x, c_2, p, q, pd_2, assn_2, r, node', nodes, funcs, cfg_1, cfg_2, cfg_3, cfg_4, cfg_5, cfg_6 \cdot$
$\quad\quad \text{FUN\_SAFE}(pred, nodes, funcs, cfg_1, cfg_2, cfg_3, cfg_4, cfg_5, cfg_6, assn_1, pd_1, p, q) \wedge$
$\quad\quad \text{HOARE\_WITH\_ASSERT}(pd_2, assn_2, node, node', x, c_2, q, r) \wedge (pd_1 \Rightarrow assn_2)) \quad)$

Fig. 3. FSI rule: judgment for interprocedural function safety

3.3 Function Judgment for Local Reasoning

Global vs. Local Reasoning. In a typical correctness proof for a program using Hoare logic, we would repeatedly apply the Compose rule to the Hoare triple for every instruction in the program to obtain a single Hoare triple describing the entire program. This is a "global reasoning" process which identifies the final values of all registers, main memory, etc. at the end of the program's execution. In the presence of loops and function calls, loop invariants and pre- and post-conditions for functions will need to be manually provided.

For safety assertions to hold in a program, we only need to ensure that the safety assertions for each instruction hold locally at that instruction. For the safety assertions at instruction i_2 to hold, we consider every instruction i_1 that can execute immediately before i_2. The machine-resource values in the post-state of each i_1 must satisfy the safety assertions at i_2. This is analogous to the pre-composition process (Sect. 2.4). As long as the machine-resource values in the post-states of predecessor instructions i_1 enable the safety assertion at i_2 to be true, the safety assertion holds. Also, any pure boolean condition from the post-state of predecessor instructions i_1 will also apply to the pre-state of instruction i_2. Hence, safety properties hold on a per-instruction basis. To check if a safety assertion holds for an instruction, we only need to perform "local reasoning" by considering the post-state and boolean conditions of all predecessor instructions.

Safe Function Judgment. We define the FUN_SAFE rule (Fig. 3), which encodes what it means for a function to be safe. This rule encodes our "local reasoning" process for verifying that safety assertions hold. Thus, proving that the machine-code of a given function is safe involves proving that the FUN_SAFE theorem holds for the function. First, we rearrange MEMCFISAFE theorems to form HOARE_WITH_ASSERT theorems, which make explicit the hypotheses (i.e., undischarged safety assertions) of the theorems, and rearrange machine resource expressions into tuples for pattern-matching.

$$\vdash \text{HOARE\_WITH\_ASSERT}(pd, assn, pc_{pre}, pc_{post}, x, c, p, q) \Leftrightarrow$$

$$(assn \Rightarrow (\text{MEMCFISAFE } x \text{ (aPC } pc_{pre} \text{ } * \text{ } p \text{ } * \text{ } \textbf{precond } pd) \text{ } c \text{ (aPC } pc_{post} \text{ } * \text{ } q)))$$

A function is comprised of basic blocks of instructions in the function. In a function's intra-procedural control-flow graph (CFG), nodes are basic blocks of the function's instructions, while edges are control transfers within the function. In a function's inter-procedural CFG, the nodes are (i) basic blocks which call other functions, (ii) basic blocks which are return-sites from callee functions, and (iii) callee functions, while edges are function calls or returns. To formally specify the requirements for a function to be safe, we consider the safety assertions which must be discharged at each edge in both the intra- and inter-procedural CFGs. We walk through each of the 6 conjunct clauses in the FSI rule in Fig. 3.

Arguments to the FUN_SAFE Relation. The FUN_SAFE relation is parameterized by the function address $addr$, a set of addresses of basic blocks in the function $NODES$, a set of addresses of callee functions $FUNCS$, and 6 maps CFG and $ICFG$ specifying the predecessors and successors of edges in the function's intra- and inter-procedural CFGs. FUN_SAFE also records, for a function, the safety assertions $assns_{entry}$, the conditions which hold at its exit $postcond_{exit}$, and the machine resource pre-state $prestate$ and post-state $poststate$.

Function Entry and Exit Specifications. The first clause states that the address of the function is the lowest basic block address for the function. The second clause states that the safety assertions $assns_{entry}$ and pre-state $prestate$ of the function are specified by the entry basic-block of the function. The third clause states that the function's guaranteed exit condition $postcond_{exit}$ and post-state $poststate$ are specified by the exit basic-block of the function.

Intra-procedural Safety Requirements. The fourth clause specifies that for each intra-procedural CFG edge, the safety assertions of the instruction at the destination of each edge must be discharged by the post-condition of the instruction at the source of the edge, i.e., $(pd_1 \Rightarrow assn_2)$. Also, in the spirit of the Hoare Compose rule, we require that the post-state of the predecessor instruction q, is equal to the pre-state of the successor instruction.

Inter-procedural Safety Requirements. The fifth and sixth clauses specify the requirements for inter-procedural CFG edges. The fifth clause specifies that for call edges, the safety assertions of the called function must be discharged by the post-condition of the calling basic block $(pd_1 \Rightarrow assn_2)$. The sixth clause specifies that for return edges, the safety assertions of the basic block which is the return site for the function must be discharged by the post-condition of the returning function ($pd_1 \Rightarrow assn_2$). In both clauses, we require that the post-state of the predecessor node must equal the pre-state of the successor node.

Compositional Reasoning for Functions. Although the FSI rule appears to be recursively defined without a base case, this rule actually collapses to include only the first four clauses for functions which do not call any other functions. This implies that our safety property proving requires the CFG of the program to have no cycles, i.e. we are unable to analyze recursive programs.

4   Implementation: Proofs Using $\mathcal{L}_{LR}$

We describe the implementation of our automatic safety property verification. Our framework consists of 128 lines of HOL4 definitions and 11.8 KLOC of proof scripts in ML. Algorithm 1 summarizes the overall workflow of the AUSPICE safety property proof process. First, AUSPICE computes basic blocks and extracts function boundaries from the machine-code of the program (Line 14). Next, AUSPICE obtains the Hoare triple theorems from the Cambridge ARM model for each machine-code instruction (Line 15), adds safety assertions to the Hoare triple theorem for each instruction (Sect. 4.1), and composes the individual instructions' theorems into a single Safe Basic Block theorem for each basic block (Line 16). AUSPICE's proof process takes place on a per-function basis beginning from the entry-function. For each function, all callee functions called by that function are analyzed before the function itself is analyzed (Line 3). Next, AUSPICE applies the Selective Composition tactic (Sect. 4.2) to the safe basic block theorems to propagate branch conditions and function prologue information to the appropriate theorems for the function (Lines 6 and 7). The main process for

---

Algorithm 1. Overall AUSPICE Workflow

```
 1: function SAFEFUNCTIONANALYSIS(function_name, bb_safe_thms list)
 2:     cfg ← Compute Control-Flow Graph for function_name
 3:     for all callee functions, callee do
 4:         SAFEFUNCTIONANALYSIS(callee, bb_safe_thms)
 5:     end for
 6:     bb_safe_thms ← SC-FWDPROPAGATE-BRANCHCONDS(bb_safe_thms, cfg)
 7:     bb_safe_thms ← SC-FWDPROPAGATE-FUNCPROLOGUE(bb_safe_thms, cfg)
 8:     assertion_info ← SAFETYASSERTIONANALYSIS(bb_safe_thms, cfg)
 9:     bb_safe_thms ← AUGMENTTHEOREMS(bb_safe_thms, assertion_info)
10:     safety_theorem ← FSI_RULE(bb_safe_thms, cfg)
11:     return safety_theorem
12: end function
13: function AUSPICE((addr, instr) list)                    ▷ List of machine-code instructions
14:     (bb list) ← Compute basic blocks in program
15:     (bb_instr_thms list) ← Obtain Hoare triple theorem for each instr in each bb
16:     (bb_safe_instr_thms list) ← map (λx.ADDSAFETYASSERTIONS(x)) bb_instr_thms
17:     bb_safe_thms ← map (λx.COMPOSESAFEINSTRS(x)) bb_safe_instr_thms
18:     return SAFEFUNCTIONANALYSIS(main, bb_safe_thms)
19: end function
```

discharging safety proof obligations is the `SafetyAssertionAnalysis` function (Line 8), which implements the proof search process using abstract interpretation (Sect. 4.3). Then, the results of the assertion analysis are applied to each of the basic blocks' theorems, and the `FSI_rule` function (Line 10) generates the `FUN_SAFE` safety theorem for the target function being proved to be safe.

4.1   Automatic Safety Property Specification

To illustrate the safety assertions we augment instructions with, consider the instruction word `0xE5832000` (`str r2 [r3]`) located at address `0x81E0`. We first obtain the following Hoare logic theorem from the decompiler:

$$\vdash \text{SPEC ARM\_MODEL (aR 3w } r3 * \text{aR 2w } r2 * \text{aPC } (\mathit{0x81E0}) * \text{aMEMORY } df \; f$$
$$* \text{cond}((r3 \;\&\&\; 3w = 0w) \wedge (r3 \in df))) \{(\mathit{0x81E0}, \mathit{0xE5832000w})\}$$
$$(\text{aR 3w } r3 * \text{aR 2w } r2 * \text{aPC } (\mathit{0x81E4}) * \text{aMEMORY } df \; ((r3 = +r2) \; f))$$

Suppose the `text` section of this program lies in the range $[0x80B4, 0x85F4]$. This instruction writes to the byte locations $r3, r3 + 1, r3 + 2, r3 + 3$. Thus, we set the first conjunct in the safety assertion ms to $\{r3 + 3; r3 + 2; r3 + 1; r3\} \subseteq \{addr \mid \text{0x85F8} \leq addr \wedge addr \leq \text{0xBF000000}\}$ which asserts that the memory locations written to are in our allowed safe region. Then, the first control-flow safety conjunct, cfi_1 is set to $\exists pc.pc = \text{0x81E4} \wedge pc \in \{addr \mid \text{0x80B4} \leq addr \wedge addr \leq \text{0x85F4}\}$, which asserts that the address of the next instruction to be executed lies in the `text` section of the binary. Next, the second control-flow safety conjunct, cfi_2 is set to $\{r3 + 3; r3 + 2; r3 + 1; r3\} \subseteq \{addr \mid addr < \text{r11}\}$, which asserts that the memory locations written to cannot overwrite the saved link register (`lr`, stored in register `r11`) value on the stack.

4.2   Selective Composition Proof Tactic

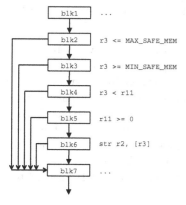

Fig. 4. Possible structure for program with safe `str r2 [r3]`.

Next, we discuss the steps for automatically proving that safety properties hold using $\mathcal{L}_{LR}$. After augmenting single instruction theorems with safety assertions (Sect. 3.1) and obtaining safe basic block theorems (Sect. 3.2), we need to prove that the antecedents in the FSI rule (Fig. 3) hold. Each of the top-level conjuncts of FSI requires either a `HOARE_WITH_ASSERT` theorem for safe basic blocks or a `FUN_SAFE` theorem for safe functions. We also need to prove that the pre-condition pd_1 of each predecessor CFG node discharges the safety assertion $assn_2$ in the successor CFG node.

From Sect. 4.1, we can see that the safety assertion at each instruction contains three conjuncts: one for memory-isolation and two for

---

Algorithm 2. Selective Composition: Branch-condition Forward Propagation

---

1: **function** SC-FWDPROPAGATE-BRANCHCONDS(bb_safe_thms **list**)
2:     $info$ **map** $\leftarrow \emptyset$ ▷ Conditions to propagate to each CFG node
3:     **procedure** PROPAGATEONESTEP($info$ **map**, $last\_info$ **map**, cfg)
4:         **for all** $node \in cfg$ **do**
5:             $curr\_node\_preds \leftarrow$ FINDPREDS($cfg, node$)
6:             $pred\_preconds \leftarrow (map\ (\lambda x.$GETTHMPRECONDS($x$))\ $curr\_node\_preds$)
7:             $last\_info\_preconds \leftarrow (map\ (\lambda x.last\_info[x])\ curr\_node\_preds$)
8:             **if** $length(curr\_node\_preds) == 1$ **then**
9:                 $info[node] = pred\_preconds \bigcup last\_info\_preconds$
10:            **end if**
11:        **end for**
12:    **end procedure**
13:    **repeat**
14:        $last\_info \leftarrow info$
15:        $info \leftarrow$ PROPAGATEONESTEP($info$, $last\_info$, cfg)
16:    **until** $last\_info == info$
17:    **return** $info$
18: **end function**

---

control-flow isolation. In a safe program, for the theorem of a given instruction i_2, its predecessor (safe basic block or function) theorem i_1 should have a pre-condition which implies the safety assertion of i_2. Observe that the safety assertion for each instruction has three conjuncts, and each of the range conjuncts (ms and cfi_1 in Sect. 4.1) is specified by two conjuncts: one each for the lower and upper bounds of the valid memory locations written to. Thus, the safety assertion at each instruction comprises multiple conjuncts. However, in a machine-code program, each basic block can only carry out one of the "elementary" arithmetic comparison operations (one of $<, >, \leq, \geq$, etc.), because each $cmp*$ instruction is a branch and will mark the end of the basic block it belongs to. Hence, information from multiple predecessor basic blocks are required to discharge the safety assertion at each instruction.

Forward Propagation of Branch Conditions. In Sect. 3.3, we noted that we must use a *local reasoning* process to ensure our proof process is automatic, because global reasoning would require manually-specified information. However, our safety assertions contain multiple conjuncts, whereas each basic block in machine-code can provide only one conjunct in its pre-condition. To enable our proof process to use pre-conditions from predecessors which are more than one edge away from a given basic block in the program CFG, we selectively "propagate" the pre-conditions of basic blocks forward. We call this process "selective composition", where we apply the pre-composition tactic (Sect. 2.4) forward to successor theorems under certain conditions.

To illustrate the process of selective composition, consider, for example, the store instruction `str r2 [r3]`. Figure 4 shows the CFG of the possible structure of the basic blocks in a program with safety checks to ensure that the store instruction is safe. Then, we need the pre-conditions from basic blocks $blk_2, blk_3, blk_4, blk_5$ to be available at blk_5 to discharge the safety assertion at blk_6. At each of the nodes $blk_2, blk_3, blk_4, blk_5$, there are two Hoare triple theorems: one where each blk_i executes blk_{i+1} next (for $i \in \{2,3,4,5\}$), and one where the safety check fails, and each blk_i goes on to execute blk_7. However, we do not compose $blk_2, blk_3, blk_4, blk_5$ to form a single Hoare triple theorem, because the resulting block of code will have multiple exits, which is not captured by our safe basic block theorem (the MEM_CFI_SAFE_COMPOSE rule), which only admits single-exit blocks. Instead, we iteratively apply the pre-composition tactic (Sect. 2.4) for basic blocks $blk_2, blk_3, blk_4, blk_5$. This lets us place the analysis of the machine-code in blocks $blk_2, blk_3, blk_4, blk_5, blk_6$ in the context of the pre-state values of machine resources in blk_2. This then allows us to discharge the safety assertion at blk_6 with the combined pre-conditions of $blk_2, blk_3, blk_4, blk_5$ at blk_5. We call this process "selective composition" because we carry out the pre-composition process without applying the composition rule. Note that this selective composition process succeeds only when the target basic block which the pre-conditions are being propagated forward to have only one predecessor basic block. Only then is the pre-condition from the predecessor block blk_i the only pre-condition that will apply at the successor block blk_{i+1}.

Algorithm 2 describes the Selective Composition tactic for the forward propagation of branch-conditions in pseudocode. The tactic uses a fixed-point intraprocedural static-analysis over the Hoare triple theorems of a function. The static-analysis identifies branch-conditions to propagate forward from each theorem to its successor theorems (Lines 3 to 16; FindPreds returns the predecessors for a given node in the CFG of the function, while GetThmPreconds returns the pre-conditions for a given Hoare triple theorem). The analysis also ensures that branch-conditions are propagated forward only when the target node has only one predecessor in the CFG (Line 8). The analysis returns the branch-conditions to add to each node's theorem in the program's CFG (Line 17).

Local Use of Global Information. Next, we describe the second instance of *selective composition*. Recall that for control-flow isolation, we require that the address of each instruction executed must be within the text section of the program. The address of the next instruction to be executed can be statically determined at every point of the program except where a function returns to its caller. Consider a typical machine-code instruction for returning from a function call pop {pc}. Control is being returned from the function by restoring the saved link register value from the stack to the program counter. The instruction will be specified by the Hoare triple theorem:

$\vdash$ SPEC ARM_MODEL (aPC p * aR 13w $r13$ * aMEMORY $df\ f$ * cond$((($f $r13$) && $3w = 0w) \wedge$

$(($f $r13) \in df))) \{(p, 0xE8BD8000w)\}$ (aPC (f $r13$) * aR 13w $(r13{+}4w)$ * aMEMORY $df\ f$)

Here, aMEMORY df f is an assertion that the main memory is the map f which when applied to an address $addr$, returns the word stored at $addr$, and df is a set specifying the address domain of f. Thus, in the post-state of this instruction, we can see that the next instruction to be executed is at address $f\ r13$. However, the memory map f does not contain any information that enables us to determine the value of $f\ r13$. The return address for a (non-leaf) function is saved to the stack in the function prologue before any instructions in the function. An example of such an instruction is push {lr}, with the following Hoare triple:

⊢ SPEC ARM_MODEL (aR 14w $r14$ * aR 13w $r13$ * aPC p * aMEMORY df f

    cond(((f $(r13 - 4w)$) && $3w = 0w$) ∧ ((f $(r13 - 4w)$) ∈ df))) {$(p, 0xE92D4000w)$}

    (aR 14w $r14$ * aR 13w $(r13 - 4w)$ * aPC $(p+4w)$ * aMEMORY df (($r13 - 4w = +r14$) f))

The memory in the post-state of the function is ((r13 - 4w =+ r14) f), which contains the value of the link register, r14, at the top of the stack, at the address r13 - 4. Hence, the information we need to discharge the control-flow safety assertion at the function exit is the memory expression at the post-state of the function prologue, and the new value of register r13. After substituting the post-state memory and register r13 values of the function prologue into the return instruction, the program counter in the return instruction post-state will contain ((r13 - 4w =+ r14) f) (r13 - 4w) which simplifies to r14, and the safety assertion simplifies to r14 ∈ {addr | 0x85F8 ≤ addr ∧ addr ≤ 0x85F4}, which can be discharged by any caller of the function, which supplies a concrete value of r14. As long as the prologue precedes every instruction in the function, and the function does not alter the callee-saved registers until its epilogue, this substitution is valid. Again, we can use the pre-composition tactic to substitute the value of the memory (and registers) at the post-state of the function prologue into every subsequent basic block in the function. Unlike the forward-propagation of branch-conditions, a fixed-point analysis is not required, and we directly substitute the information from the function prologue in every subsequent basic block in the function.

4.3   Automatic Discharge of Proof Obligations

There are two ways to discharge the safety assertions of a theorem. First, for a given safety theorem, the pure boolean conditions of the pre-state of the theorem preceding it may imply the safety assertion holds for the current theorem. Second, if the former does not hold, then the safety assertion is added to the hypotheses of the preceding instruction, and the Frame rule is used to add the undischarged assertion to the theorems of the preceding instructions. We use abstract interpretation [7] to identify safety assertions which cannot be discharged. At each instruction, our analysis records the safety assertions which need to be framed to the safe instruction theorem for that instruction.

We use a flow-sensitive backwards fixed-point analysis. Our analysis proceeds across all nodes in the CFG of a function in reverse topological order in each iteration. Each CFG node is a basic block in the function, and each node is associated with a safe basic-block theorem (Sect. 3.2). At each node, the analysis checks that for each predecessor node, the instruction theorem for that node has pure boolean conditions which can discharge the safety assertions at the current node's theorem. For safety assertions which the predecessor node's theorem cannot discharge, our analysis adds the assertion to the predecessor node's theorem, propagating the assertion backwards up the CFG. Our analysis

Algorithm 3. Safety Assertion Analysis

```
 1: function SAFETYASSERTIONANALYSIS(bb_safe_thms map, cfg)
 2:     info map ← ∅
 3:     procedure ASSERTIONANALYSISSTEP(info map, last_info map, cfg)
 4:         for all node ∈ cfg do
 5:             for all pred ∈ FINDPREDS(cfg, node) do
 6:                 pred_preconds ← GETTHMPRECONDS(pred) ⋃ last_info[pred]
 7:                 node_asserts ← GETTHMASSERTS(node) ⋃ last_info[node]
 8:                 for all assert ∈ node_asserts do
 9:                     if PROVE(pred_preconds, assert) == False then
10:                         info.term[pred] ← info.term[pred] ⋃ assert
11:                         a_path ← FINDASSERTPATH(last_info.path[node], assert)
12:                         info.path[pred] ← info.path[pred] ⋃ a_path
13:                         ABORTIFASSERTPATHISCYCLE(a_path)
14:                     end if
15:                 end for
16:             end for
17:         end for
18:     end procedure
19:     repeat
20:         last_info ← info; info ← ASSERTIONANALYSISSTEP(info, last_info, cfg)
21:     until last_info == info
22:     return info
23: end function
```

is also inter-procedural, and context-sensitive. Each function is summarized at its call-site by a FUN_SAFE theorem for that particular call-site.

In the general case, this analysis may not terminate. If there are safety assertions being propagated which have values that change with a loop, the analysis will not terminate: the free variable instantiation at loop boundaries will generate new safety assertions to be framed whenever the assertion is propagated across the back-edge of the loop. We prevent the assertion analysis from running forever by (i) recording the propagation path of safety assertions, and (ii) aborting the analysis if a cycle is detected on this path. Then, we inform the user that we are unable to prove our safety properties for the program.

Algorithm 3 describes our static-analysis algorithm. GetThmPreconds (Line 6) and GetThmAsserts (Line 7) return the pure boolean conditions in the pre-state and the safety assertion at a node's theorem respectively. PROVE tries to discharge the given safety assertion, assert, using the given conditions pred_preconds from the predecessor theorem, and returns true if it can discharge the safety assertion, and false otherwise (Line 9). If the safety assertion cannot be discharged, it is added to the analysis information for the node's predecessor node (Line 10), so that it will be framed to the predecessor node's theorem after the analysis. The analysis information also records the path along which each assertion is propagated in info.path (Line 12). Then, the analysis checks if there is a cycle along the propagation path of the assertion (Line 13) in the function AbortIfAssertPathIsCycle, and terminates the AUSPICE proof process if a cycle is found. This is because if a cycle is found along which the pre-composition tactic causes the safety assertion term to change with each iteration, the analysis is likely to not terminate as it will keep adding new safety assertion terms to the analysis information on each successive iteration of the analysis.

5   Discussion

Soundness of Proof Rules. AUSPICE's proof rules for single instruction (Sect. 3.1) and basic block (Sect. 3.2) safety are sound, because we derive our MEM_CFI_SAFE, MEM_CFI_SAFE_COMPOSE, and MEMCFISAFE_FRAME proof rules from the Hoare triples for machine-code programs in the Cambridge model, which Myreen et al. have shown to be sound [16]. Also, using the HOL4 proof assistant to define our proof rules further ensures they are sound. In addition, we proved (Sect. 3.1) that safe single instruction and basic block theorems in AUSPICE derived from our proof rules have the same instruction semantics as the ARM machine-code semantics defined by the trustworthy, validated Cambridge ARM model [9,15].

Correctness of Safety Rule. Next, we give a brief, informal argument of the correctness of our proof rule for safe programs. The FUN_SAFE theorem (Fig. 3) can be proven for a program if and only if safety assertions are specified for every instruction, and if these safety assertions hold before that instruction begins executing (except for the first instruction, which relies on the OS to correctly initialize the processor state for the program). We argue this by Structural Induction on the Control-Flow Graph (CFG) of a program. Each node in our CFG of a function in a program is either a single-entry, single-exit basic block with sequentially executing code, or a (callee) function called by the function.

Base Case. The MEM_CFI_SAFE rule (Sect. 3.1) ensures every instruction's theorem contains our safety assertions (Sect. 2.2). The MEM_CFI_SAFE_COMPOSE rule ensures every basic block's theorem is built up only from single-instruction theorems with added safety assertions. The requirement that post-states of predecessor theorems and pre-states of successor theorems must be equal in MEM_CFI_SAFE_COMPOSE ensures every basic block's theorem accumulates the safety assertions for every composed safe instruction theorem. Then, for a program with only a single instruction or basic-block, if the OS correctly initializes the processor state, the safety assertions will hold for the single instruction or single basic block.

Inductive Case. We take the CFG of a function, G, and partition its vertices into a single vertex, g, and all other vertices, G'. By the Inductive Hypothesis, the FUN_SAFE theorem holds for G'. Then, consider the edges E connecting G' to g. In the absence of function pointers and unstructured jumps (longjmp), the edges E are either (i) intra-procedural control-flow transfers between basic blocks in the function, (ii) function calls from a basic block in the function to a callee function, or (iii) function returns from a callee function to a basic block in the function. Then, for FUN_SAFE to be true, the fourth to sixth conjunct clauses of the FUN_SAFE rule must be true, so the pre-conditions of the theorems of all predecessor vertices to g in the CFG discharge the safety assertions at g, making the safety assertions at g hold, for any type of possible control-flow transfer to g. Thus, our FUN_SAFE rule ensures that we have captured all the possible control-flow transfers in a machine-code program. For FUN_SAFE to be correct, we require correct CFG predecessor and successor maps, which are straightforward to compute without function pointers and unstructured jumps.

Limitations. Our machine-code safety properties (Sect. 2.2) have been formulated to ensure they can be automatically proven to hold in machine-code programs. These properties are sufficient, but not strictly necessary to meet our high-level goal of preventing the control-flow of a machine-code program from being hijacked due to user input. The strictness of our safety properties helps automate the verification process. Our requirement that machine-code instructions do not alter memory addresses greater than the current function's frame pointer address also prevents functions from modifying any variables passed by reference from the stacks of caller functions. Instead, functions passing data by reference must store this data either on the program's heap, or use memory allocated in the program's data section. We believe this is a small inconvenience to enable the fully automated verification of safety properties.

6 Evaluation

We aim to show that we can verify real-world programs, and we pick programs with constructs which are challenging to verify. We also measure our runtime to show the feasibility of our verification. Our test programs were compiled using an unmodified gcc toolchain for the ARMv7 architecture with -O0 optimization. Figure 5 summarizes our test programs. sort implements Bubble Sort, which has a doubly-nested loop, and also contains 2 other functions to exercise our inter-procedural analysis. memcpy is an implementation of the C library function which we developed, and shows we can verify a real-world function. stringsearch is an application in the MiBench commercially-representative embedded benchmark [10], and it implements the Boyer-Moore string search algorithm, and demonstrates our verification on real-world programs.

Test Program	Instructions	Functions	Description
memcpy	116	2	Real-world memcpy
sort	337	5	Nested loops, function calls/returns
stringsearch	530	5	Boyer-Moore string search (MiBench [10])

Fig. 5. Test programs, their sizes, and the purpose of each test.

Figure 6 shows the time taken to verify the safety of each of our test programs. We carried out the verification on an 2.6 GHz Core i7 system. The majority of

	Cambridge ARM Decompiler	Safe Basic Blocks	Abstract Interpretation	Safe Function	Total Proof Time
`memcpy`	1.3 mins	2.7 mins	5.7 mins	6.7 mins	16.4 mins
`sort`	2.5 mins	11.2 mins	36 mins	73 mins	122.7 mins
`stringsearch`	2.8 mins	15.3 mins	327.6 mins	17.8 mins	363.5 mins

Fig. 6. Verification runtime.

the verification time is spent in the abstract interpretation (Sect. 4.3) and the proof of the safe function theorem (Sect. 3.3). We believe these are feasible times for verifying safety properties, as programs only need to be verified once on installation.

7 Related Work

Many techniques have been developed for verifying machine-code programs using logic. Certified assembly programming uses a Hoare logic with separation logic to build certified libraries [18,26], but specifications must be manually annotated in programs, and verification is interactive. Tan and Appel [21] developed a program logic for multi-entry, multi-exit machine-code fragments to reason about unstructured control-flows in executables in Foundational Proof Carrying Code (FPCC). They require a special compiler to generate machine-code annotated with types [13], while we verify unmodified executables compiled using an off-the-shelf compiler. iTalX [22] infers types for x86 assembly programs, reducing the amount of type annotations required from a modified compiler. Executables have also been verified without using a program logic, although concise theorems cannot be proven. Bedrock [6] provides "mostly-automated" verification for generic program properties, and provides memory safety as a side-effect, for programs written using its idealized machine language, from which concrete architectures can be targeted. Xu et al. [25] verify safety properties for machine-code using static-analysis. RevGen [5] decompiles machine-code to the intermediate representation of the LLVM compiler framework, enabling other analyses to be reused, whereas we use a validated model of ARM machine-code. Thakur et al. [23] perform model-checking on machine-code without requiring a precomputed, fixed, inter-procedural CFG. Sequoll [4] also performs model-checking on machine-code programs, and like our work, uses the Cambridge ARM model [15], but it uses temporal logic to reason about worst-case execution time (WCET) in the NuSMV model-checker, whereas our approach uses Hoare logic. XFI [8] and ARMor [27], are software fault isolation (SFI) [24] implementations which ensure and verify that (x86 and ARM, respectively) executables possess memory and control-flow safety properties. XFI requires modules being verified to be annotated with hints. PittSFIeld [12] verifies that its SFI safety rewriting for x86 binaries is correct, as opposed to verifying that the executables it produces are safe. RockSalt [14] also provides verified SFI by providing a verified checker which checks that programs are isolated, whereas our work produces a safety proof for each program. ARMor [27] is closest to our work. They require machine-code to be compiled with a modified compiler, after which the program must undergo binary rewriting to insert safety checks. In contrast, we can prove safety properties automatically for unmodified executables using our logic framework and *selective composition* proof tactic.

8   Conclusion and Future Work

We have presented a novel logic framework, AUSPICE, for automatically verifying safety properties in unmodified ARM machine-code programs. Our framework consists of a program logic, $\mathcal{L}_{LR}$, which uses a subset of a trustworthy Hoare logic for ARM executables [15,16], and extends it for *local reasoning*, and the *selective composition* proof tactic, which fully automates the verification of safety properties. We demonstrated the feasibility of our fully automated safety property verification on one synthetic and two real-world (including a real-world benchmark [10]) examples. In future, we intend to validate our approach on more programs, and expand our verification to programs with system calls.

Acknowledgment. We thank Lu Zhao for his help with ARMor [27], Magnus Myreen for his help with the Cambridge ARM model [15,16], and Xinyu Zhuang for his feedback.

References

1. The ARM-THUMB Procedure Call Standard (2000). http://infocenter.arm.com/help/topic/com.arm.doc.espc0002/ATPCS.pdf
2. ARM Architecture Reference Manual, ARMv7-A and ARMv7-R edition (2014)
3. Abadi, M., Budiu, M., Erlingsson, U., Ligatti, J.: Control-flow Integrity. In: ACM CCS (2005)
4. Blackham, B., Heiser, G.: Sequel: a framework for model checking binaries. In: IEEE RTAS (2013)
5. Chipounov, V., Candea, G.: Enabling sophisticated analyses of x86 binaries with RevGen. In: HotDep (2011)
6. Chlipala, A.: Mostly-automated verification of low-level programs in computational separation logic. In: PLDI (2011)
7. Cousot, P., Cousot, R.: Abstract interpretation: a unified lattice model for static analysis of programs by construction or approximation of fixpoints. In: POPL (1977)
8. Erlingsson, U., Abadi, M., Vrable, M., Budiu, M., Necula, G.: XFI: software guards for system address spaces. In: OSDI (2006)
9. Fox, A.: Formal specification and verification of ARM6. In: Basin, D., Wolff, B. (eds.) TPHOLs 2003. LNCS, vol. 2758, pp. 25–40. Springer, Heidelberg (2003)
10. Guthaus, M.R., Ringenberg, J.S., Ernst, D., Austin, T.M., Mudge, T., Brown, R.B.: Mibench: a free, commercially representative embedded benchmark suite. In: IEEE WWC Workshop (2001)
11. Hoare, C.A.R.: An axiomatic basis for computer programming. Commun. ACM **12**(10), 576–580 (1969)

12. McCamant, S., Morrisett, G.: Evaluating SFI for a CISC architecture. In: USENIX Security (2006)
13. Morrisett, G., Crary, K., Glew, N., Grossman, D., Samuels, R., Smith, F., Walker, D., Weirich, S., Zdancewic, S.: TALx86: a realistic typed assembly language. In: Workshop on Compiler Support for System Software (WCSSS) (1999)
14. Morrisett, G., Tan, G., Tassarotti, J., Tristan, J., Gan, E.: RockSalt: better, faster, stronger SFI for the x86. In: PLDI (2012)
15. Myreen, M.O., Fox, A.C.J., Gordon, M.J.C.: Hoare logic for ARM machine code. In: Arbab, F., Sirjani, M. (eds.) FSEN 2007. LNCS, vol. 4767, pp. 272–286. Springer, Heidelberg (2007)
16. Myreen, M.O., Gordon, M.J.C.: Hoare logic for realistically modelled machine code. In: Grumberg, O., Huth, M. (eds.) TACAS 2007. LNCS, vol. 4424, pp. 568–582. Springer, Heidelberg (2007)
17. Myreen, M., Gordon, M., Slind, K.: Machine-code verification for multiple architectures: an application of decompilation into logic. In: FMCAD (2008)
18. Ni, Z., Shao, Z.: Certified assembly programming with embedded code pointers. In: POPL (2006)
19. Reynolds, J.: Separation logic: a logic for shared mutable data structures. In: IEEE LICS (2002)
20. Slind, K., Norrish, M.: A brief overview of HOL4. In: Mohamed, O.A., Muñoz, C., Tahar, S. (eds.) TPHOLs 2008. LNCS, vol. 5170, pp. 28–32. Springer, Heidelberg (2008)
21. Tan, G., Appel, A.W.: A compositional logic for control flow. In: Emerson, E.A., Namjoshi, K.S. (eds.) VMCAI 2006. LNCS, vol. 3855, pp. 80–94. Springer, Heidelberg (2006)
22. Tate, R., Chen, J., Hawblitzel, C.: Inferable object-oriented typed assembly language. In: PLDI (2010)
23. Thakur, A., Lim, J., Lal, A., Burton, A., Driscoll, E., Elder, M., Andersen, T., Reps, T.: Directed proof generation for machine code. In: Touili, T., Cook, B., Jackson, P. (eds.) CAV 2010. LNCS, vol. 6174, pp. 288–305. Springer, Heidelberg (2010)
24. Wahbe, R., Lucco, S., Anderson, T., Graham, S.: Efficient software-based fault isolation. In: SOSP (1993)
25. Xu, Z., Miller, B., Reps, T.: Safety checking of machine code. In: PLDI (2000)
26. Yu, D., Hamid, N.A., Shao, Z.: Building certified libraries for PCC: dynamic storage allocation. In: Degano, P. (ed.) ESOP 2003. LNCS, vol. 2618, pp. 363–379. Springer, Heidelberg (2003)
27. Zhao, L., Li, G., Sutter, B.D., Regehr, J.: ARMor: fully verified software fault isolation. In: EMSOFT (2011)

Author Index

Printed in the United States
By Bookmasters